Human Dignity and International Law

Human Dignity and International Law

Edited by

Andrea Gattini, Rosana Garciandia and Philippa Webb

BRILL
NIJHOFF

LEIDEN | BOSTON

Cover illustration: "Intonaco di antiche stanze, 1993–1994" ("Plaster in Ancient Rooms"). Artist: Mr. Giorgio Celiberti (1929-), Italy.

The Library of Congress Cataloging-in-Publication Data is available online at http://catalog.loc.gov
LC record available at http://lccn.loc.gov/2020919698

Typeface for the Latin, Greek, and Cyrillic scripts: "Brill". See and download: brill.com/brill-typeface.

ISBN 978-90-04-43564-3 (hardback)
ISBN 978-90-04-43565-0 (e-book)

This book is printed on acid-free paper and produced in a sustainable manner.

Contents

Notes on Contributors

Niki Aloupi
is Professor at University Paris II Panthéon-Assas and Judge Advocate at the National Court for Asylum in France (CNDA).

Téa Braun
is the executive director of the Human Dignity Trust, a London-based organisation that uses the law to defend the human rights of LGBT people globally. Since 2012, Téa has been involved in supporting court cases in all regions of the world that seek to decriminalise LGBT people and challenge other discriminatory actions against them, including several landmark cases that are pushing the boundaries of international and constitutional law. She has overseen ground-breaking global research on the extent to which discriminatory sexual offences laws continue to foment stigma, discrimination and violence against LGBT people, women, children and persons with disabilities, including *Good Practice in Human Rights Compliant Sexual Offences Laws in the Commonwealth*(2019). Téa is a member of the Law Society of British Columbia, Canada (non-practising) and her expertise is in international human rights law and comparative constitutional law, with a particular focus on women's human rights and LGBT human rights. In addition to several years in private legal practice in Canada, she has also previously held inter-governmental appointments as Gender Equality Advisor to the Secretariat of the Pacific Community and Human Rights Advisor to the Commonwealth Secretariat. She has advised multiple governments, civil society organisations and litigants across Africa, Asia, the Pacific and the Caribbean.

Pasquale De Sena
is Full Professor of International Law and International Human Rights Law at the Faculty of Law, Catholic University, Milan (2011-); P.H.D. International Law, University of Florence (1991); visiting Professor at Université de Strasbourg (2007), Université Paris I, Panthéon Sorbonne (2010), Université Paris II, Panthéon Assas (IHEI; 2012); visiting scholar at the Max Planck Institute for Comparative Public Law and Public International Law (Heidelberg 1995) and Guest Researcher the Max Planck Institute for International, European and Regulatory Procedural Law (Luxembourg 2015); associate fellow of the "Centre d'études des normes juridiques" (Paris, EHESS: 2010–2016). Lectures at the International Institute of Human Rights "René Cassin" (2007, 2008, 2010) and The Hague Academy of International Law (2016; special

course on 'Dignité humaine et droit international'). Co-founder and general editor of the legal journal *Diritti umani e diritto internazionale* (2007-). Permanent member of the Inter-Ministerial Committee for Human Rights of the Italian Government (2013-). He has published 2 authored books, coedited 2 collective books and written about 70 articles and book chapters on Public International Law.

Octávio Luiz Motta Ferraz
is a Reader in Transnational Law at King's College London, where he also co-directs the Transnational Law Institute and is an affiliate of the Brazil Institute. He is the author of *Health as a Human Right. The Politics and Judicialization of Health in Brazil* (Cambridge University Press 2020) and has an extensive list of other publications in the fields of human rights, health and development. He has been a consultant for the World Bank and the Open Society and a senior research officer to the UN Special Rapporteur on the Right to Health.

Micaela Frulli
is Full Professor of International Law at the University of Florence. She was Marie Curie Fellow at the European University Institute (2010) and coordinated several research projects. Her research interests include international criminal law, the law of immunities, the law of international organizations. Amongst her publications: *The duty of care of International Organizations towards their Civilian Personnel*, (co-editor with Andrea de Guttry and Edoardo Greppi, Asser Press, 2018); *War Crimes and the Conduct of Hostilities. Challenges to Investigation and Adjudication* (co-editor with *Judge* F.Pocar and M. Pedrazzi, Elgar, 2013). She is member of the Editorial Board of QIL *Questions of international* and member of the *International Law Association* (ILA) study group on the role of individual in international law.

Rosana Garciandia
is a Research Associate and Visiting Lecturer in Public International Law at King's College London. Her research focuses on the international law of state responsibility and the response of international law to contemporary forms of slavery and human trafficking. In March 2020, she was selected to present her work on State Responsibility for Modern Slavery with Professor Philippa Webb at the British Institute of International and Comparative Law's International Comparative Law Quarterly (ICLQ) 2020 Annual Lecture. She is also a Fellow of the Macrocrimes Center of the University of Ferrara and, as a consultant at the United Nations University Center for Policy Research, she has worked with the UN Special Rapporteur on Contemporary Forms of Slavery, Urmila

Bhoola. She has extensive experience working at international organisations in the areas of EU Law (European Law Institute), human rights (EU Agency for Fundamental Rights) and international anti-corruption law (United Nations Office on Drugs and Crime).

Andrea Gattini
is Professor of International Law at the Law School of the University of Padua. He is an associated member of the International Law Association, *Institut des Hautes études internationales* (Paris) and of several other international academic institutions. Formerly, he was External Scientific Fellow at Max Planck Institute Luxembourg for Procedural Law (Department of International Law and Dispute Resolution). He served as counsel of the Federal Republic of Germany before the International Court of Justice (2008–2012).

Francesca Ippolito
is currently Associate Professor of International Law at the University of Cagliari, Italy. She has been selected for the Research Center of the Hague Academy of International Law on International Migrations in 2010 (directors G. Goodwin-Gill and P. Weckel) and has been Visiting Fellow at the School of Law of the University of Glasgow, Galway, the University of Sevilla and Valencia as well as Visiting Professor at the University Montesquieu-Bordeaux IV and University of Grenoble-Alpes. She regularly participates in national and international research projects and has written on international migration law, child law, international human rights and EU institutional issues. Her most recent books include (with G. Borzoni and F. Casolari), *Bilateral Relations in the Mediterranean. Prospects for migration issues*, Edward Elgar Publishing, 2020 (with M.E. Bartoloni, M. Condinanzi), *The proliferation of integration principles in EU law: towards a more policy consistency?* Routledge, 2018 (with G. Biagioni), *Migrant children: challenges for international law*, Napoli, Editorale Scientifica Italian (ESI), 2016(with S. Iglesias Sanchéz), *The protection of vulnerable groups. The European Human Rights Framework*, Oxford (Hart Publishing), 2015 (with S. Trevisanut), *Migration in the Mediterranean: Mechanisms of international cooperation*, Cambridge (Cambridge University Press), 2015 (with A. Abass), *Regional approaches to asylum seekers protection: an international law perspective*, London (Ashgate), 2014.

Stefan Kirchner
is Associate Professor of Arctic Law at the Arctic Centre of the University of Lapland and docent of Fundamental and Human Rights at the same university. He has taught courses on human rights and international law in Finland,

Italy, Germany, Ukraine, Lithuania and Greenland and has worked as a lawyer in private and government practice in his native country, Germany.

Timo Koivurova
is a research professor and director of the Arctic Centre (University of Lapland, Finland). He is also a docent at the universities of Turku and Eastern Finland (international law).

Robert Kolb
is Professeur de droit international public à l'université de Genève.

Alessandra Pietrobon
is full Professor of International Law and Humanitarian and Disarmament Law at the University of Padova. She published several articles on the subject in international top journals and recently wrote the first comprehensive book on interstate arbitration.

Giorgio Sacerdoti
is emeritus professor of international law at Bocconi University Milan, specializing on international trade, investments, arbitration, anti-corruption. From 2001–2009 he was a member of the Appellate Body of the WTO. He is president of the Italian Jewish Contemporary Documentation Centre – CDEC and a member of the Italian Advisory Commission on Religious Liberty.

Matteo Sarzo
holds a PhD in International Law from the University of Padova (Italy) and Paris I – Panthéon Sorbonne. He has published several articles in the field of public international law, focusing on immunities, international adjudication, human rights and international investment law. He is the author of a recent book dealing with the role performed by international courts in shaping the direct effect of international rules to be applied in the domestic legal orders.

Christian Tomuschat
is professor em., Faculty of Law, Humboldt University Berlin. Dr. juris h.c. (Zürich and Tartu). Former member, UN Human Rights Committee (1977–1986), former member and chairperson, International Law Commission (1985–1996). Judge at the Administrative Tribunals of the Inter-American Development Bank and the African Development Bank. Coordinator of the Commission for Historical Clarification, Guatemala (1997–1999). President of the

OSCE Court of Conciliation and Arbitration (2013–2019). Called for lecturing at the Hague Academy of International Law (1993 and 1999). Recent publications: Enforcement of International Law, Heidelberg Journal of International Law 2019; Flexibility in International Dispute Settlement. Conciliation Revisited, ed. together with Marcelo Kohen, 2020.

Tullio Treves
is Emeritus professor of the State University of Milan. Former Judge of the International Tribunal for the Law of the Sea. Member of the *Institut de droit international* and of the Curatorium of the Hague Academy of international Law. Arbitrator and advocate in international disputes. Senior Public International Law Consultant, Curtis, Mallet-Prevost, Colt & Mosle LLP. Most recent main publication: "The Expansion of International Law.- General Course on Public International Law (2015)", Collected Courses of the Hague Academy of International Law, vol. 398.

Christian Walter
is Chair of Public International Law and Public Law at Ludwig-Maximilians-Universität München. His publications include *Institutionalised International Law* (Hart 2015, with Matthias Ruffert).

Philippa Webb
is Professor of Public International Law at King's College London. She previously worked at the International Court of Justice, the International Criminal Court and United Nations Headquarters. She serves on the editorial boards of the *Leiden Journal of International Law*, the *British Yearbook of International Law* and the *Journal of International Criminal Justice*. She is a member of the governing board of the European Society of International Law. Her publications include *Oppenheim's International Law: The United Nations* (OUP, 2017) (with Dame Rosalyn Higgins GBE QC, Dapo Akande, Sandesh Sivakumaran, and James Sloan), which was awarded the ASIL Certificate of Merit 2019 for High Technical Craftmanship and Utility to Practitioners and Scholars.

CHAPTER 1

Setting the Scene: 100 Years of Human Dignity

Andrea Gattini

This book follows a conference which I organized in November 2018 at the Law School of the University of Padua on the 80-year anniversary of the enactment in Italy of the Racial laws which excluded Jewish citizens from any kind of participation in public life in Italy.

I felt a special motivation to organise the conference. One of the most reputed Italian international lawyers of the first half of twentieth century was Enrico Catellani, who had lived and worked in Padua all his life. Although he was already retired in 1938, he was not spared the indignity of marginalisation, isolation and finally persecution for being a Jew. The exact circumstances of his death are shrouded in some mystery. What we do know is that on 7 January 1945 during some days of fury and devastation unleashed by fascists in Padua as an act of reprisal for the killing of some of their comrades, some unidentified people broke into Catellani's house and savagely beat the elderly professor and his wife. Mr Catellani was left suffering in the house, while Mrs Catellani was brought to the hospital where she died shortly afterwards of her injuries.

As a young scholar, I did not know anything about Catellani. No commemorative plaque in the University remembered him, or other professors who had been expelled from the Padua University in 1938. The first time I heard the name of Catellani was from the international law professor with whom I was working as an assistant at the Law School in Padua in the 1980s. After a copious dinner with foreign visiting professors, he sometimes indulged in telling the story of Catellani's death, which in his narrative ran as follows: Catellani was an extremely fearful old man and during the last years of the war he had hidden in his house and taught his wife, who was not Jew, to say to all the neighbours that her husband was travelling abroad. In January 1945, it was icy in Padua and unfortunately poor Mrs Catellani slipped on the pavement and was brought to hospital. She strictly kept to Professor Catellani's instructions and did not say anything about the whereabouts of her husband, who died of starvation at home waiting for her return. I remember that my professor always ended his tale with a sonorous laugh, genuinely surprised and slightly annoyed by the embarrassed reaction of his guests. I did not find the story funny either, and did not hide my displeasure, but my youth, education and, most of all, the strict

 | DOI:10.1163/9789004435650_002

feudalistic habit of Italian university life at that time made any open rebellion unthinkable.

An occasion to openly manifest my disagreement with racially tainted abusive speech, if not outright hate speech, came some decades later. On the 150th anniversary of the establishment of the Italian State in 2011, the Principal of the University of Padua organized a commemorative event in the Aula Magna to which all professors and hundreds of students participated with the highest local authorities. The tone of the ceremony was solemn and joyous at the same time, and the speakers emphasized the civic virtues of a mature democracy. Then the President of the Veneto Region, a major exponent of the Lega Nord Party, took the floor and started to rave about the historical mistake which had been done in 1861 when the North of Italy was unified with the South. He quoted an alleged statement by a Piedmontese politician and writer of that time, D'Azeglio, according to whom the unification of the Northern Italians with the Southern Italians would have had the same effect as to lie in bed with a leper. I was shocked by the meanness and violence of his speech and my first instinct was to stand up and leave the room. I looked around, nobody among my colleagues had stood up. But neither did I.

Of course one could downplay these two anecdotes as deplorable expressions of bad taste, or lack of sensitivity or even civility.[1] One could even question the point of recalling them in the opening pages of a volume dedicated to the concept of human dignity in international law. But the question inescapably arises: how far can freedom of thought and expression go before turning to denigration, to hate speech, to exclusion, to discrimination and eventually to persecution? Is the threshold reached when a derogatory discourse becomes an institutionalised one? What the two anecdotes in their pettiness reveal is the same mindset that is at the root of all evil: the lack of empathy, the lack of respect, which grows like a poisoning weed into the refusal of the other, the denial of his or her intrinsic dignity as a human being.

The success of the 2018 Conference in Padua convinced me to share the outcome with a larger scientific community. I was very happy to find the support and commitment of two of the participants, Philippa Webb and Rosana Garciandia, who soon joined me in this endeavour.

The three of us agreed that the concept of human dignity must be handled with care, unless we risk trivialising it. As is well known, the concept of human dignity is at the core of an ongoing debate on its philosophical underpinnings,

1 The same President of the Region distinguished himself nine years later, when at the height of the Coronavirus infection in Veneto in March 2020 he yelled at a public meeting: "We all saw the Chinese eating rats".

legal implications, and theoretical and practical impact.[2] On the one hand, it is clear that the classical Kantian definition of human dignity, according to which the human being is an end in his/herself and may never be considered as a means, focused as it was on the rational autonomy of the individual,[3] is now in need of some reconsideration to better fit contemporary social and cultural norms, such as the dignity of children, of persons with disabilities, of women, of those fleeing armed conflict, and finally of all creatures.[4] On the other hand, the concept of human dignity as the normative foundation of all human rights has been increasingly challenged from both legal and philosophical perspectives.[5] While it is clear that the concept cannot be reduced to a "placeholder" or a "conversation stopper", it is true that, at least from a positivist legal perspective, one cannot simply dispose of human dignity as an extra-legal concept, and at the same time consider it as the foundation of the whole system of human rights law.[6]

Our starting point in this book is the acknowledgment that the concept of human dignity entered the official language of international law just after the Second World War. Article 1 of the Universal Declaration of Human Rights adopted by the General Assembly of the United Nations on 10 December 1948 reads: "All human beings are born free and equal in dignity and rights. They are

2 See among others Christopher McCrudden (ed.), *Understanding Human Dignity, Proceedings of the British Academy* (OUP 2013); Marcus Dūwell et al. (eds.), *The Cambridge Handbook of Human Dignity. Interdisciplinary Perspectives* (CUP 2014); more recently Stephen Riley, *Human Dignity and Law. Legal and Philosophical Investigations* (Routledge 2018). For a brief but exhaustive overview see Philipp Gisbertz, 'Overcoming Doctrinal School Thought: A Unifying Approach to Human Dignity', (2018) 31 *Ratio Juris* 196.

3 See Immanuel Kant, *Grundlegung der Metaphysik der Sitten* (Hartknoch Riga 1785), *p. 66–67:* 'Handle so, daß du die Menschheit sowohl in deiner Person, als auch in der Person eines jeden anderen jederzeit zugleich als Zweck, niemals bloß als Mittel brauchest.'

4 See T. Hill, 'Kantian perspectives on the rational basis of human dignity', in Marcus Düwell et al. (eds.), *The Cambridge Handbook of Human Dignity,* cit., 215, at 218.

5 For some pointed critical voices see Costas Douzinas, *Human Rights and Empire: The Political Philosophy of Cosmopolitanism* (Routledge 2007) (human dignity as an "empty signifier"); Michael Rosen, 'Dignity: The Case Against', in Christopher McCrudden (ed.), *Understanding Human Dignity,* cit., 143 (human dignity as "conceptually muddy"); Govert Den Hartogh, 'Is human dignity the ground of human rights?', in Marcus Düwell et al. (eds.), *The Cambridge Handbook of Human Dignity,* cit., 200 et seq. (human dignity as a "buck-passing" concept).

6 See Stephen Riley, 'Human Dignity as a *Sui Generis* Principle' (2019) 32 *Ratio Juris* 439, at 452, who comes to the conclusion that human dignity is a *sui generis,* unifying principle of law dictated by practical reason in order to give expression to the simultaneously moral, political and legal commitment to the central status of individuals. For a recent study on the complex relation between the concept of human dignity as a "program" and human rights as positive law see Pablo Gilabert, *Human Dignity and Human Rights* (OUP 2019).

endowed with reason and conscience and should act towards one another in a spirit of brotherhood". Needless to say that the appearance of the concept in that precise historical moment was not merely fortuitous. Despite all the political, philosophical, religious and ethical differences among the nine members of the Drafting Committee, they all shared the common belief that, after the appalling crimes of the Nazi regime, there was a need to affirm the principle that the dignity of all human beings is the foundation of all rights and the basis for international peaceful coexistence.

The awareness of the importance of the concept of human dignity for all and each political community is nowhere better illustrated than in Article 1 of the *Grundgesetz,* the German Basic Law of 1949, which in just four words set in stone validates and underpins the whole fabric of the new German constitutional order: "Die Menschenwürde ist unantastbar" - human dignity is untouchable. Leaving aside the unending German constitutional debate on the positivist scope and range of Article 1 of the *Grundgesetz,*[7] what is relevant for our purposes is that, far from being just historical forerunners, the UN Declaration and the *Grundgesetz* are a glowing testimony to a new foundation of international and national social contracts.[8]

7 The debate in the Federal Republic started from the very beginning with the well-known view of Theodor Heuss, one of the fathers of the Grundgesetz and later Federal President, according to whom the concept of human dignity was a "nicht interpretierte These", i.e. a not interpretable postulate. *Grosso modo,* German authors follow two trends: a reductionist one, which tends to limit the scope of the concept to exceptional situations, in order to avoid its trivialization or use in particularly debated or conflict situations (see i.a. Hasso Hoffmann, 'Die versprochene Menschenwürde' (1993) 118 *Archiv des öffentlichen Rechts* 353; Horst Dreier, 'Human Dignity in German Law', in Marcus Düwell et al. (eds.), *The Cambridge Handbook of Human* Dignity, cit., 375) and a foundationalist one, which tends to encourage the radiating effect of the concept in all branches of the German legal system (see i.a. Jochen von Bernstorff, 'Der Streit um die Menschenwürde im Grund- und Menschenrechtsschutz' (2013) 19 *Juristenzeitung* 905; Matthias Mahlmann, *Elemente einer ethischen Grundrechtstheorie* (Nomos 2008), 248 et seq). Even if a comparative study of human dignity in different legal systems may be of great theoretical interest and sheds light on the practical relevance of the concept in different contexts (see Catherine Dupré, *The Age of Dignity. Human Rights and Constitutionalism in Europe*, Hart 2015), one cannot but agree with Riley that, in the light of the cosmopolitan concern expressed in the very concept of human dignity, "there is no sense in talking about the isolation of human dignity to one legal system" (see Stephen Riley, 'Human Dignity as a *Sui Generis* Principle', cit., at 446).

8 Recently some authors have tried to reduce the significance of the Nazi past and in particular of the Holocaust as the trigger of Article 1 of the UN Universal Declaration of Human Rights and of the German constitutional debate which lead to Article 1 Grundgesetz, see i.a. Samuel Moyn, *The Last Utopia: Human Rights in History* (Harvard University Press 2010) 7, for whom the whole international institutional human rights movement is anyway "closely linked to an epoch-making reinvention of conservatism" (so in 'Personalism, community, and the origins of human rights', in Stanley, Hoffmann, Moyn (ed.), *Human Rights*

Divergent views on the genealogy, ontology, epistemology or legitimacy of the concept of human dignity should not deter us from using it as a legal tool, provided that a workable definition of its scope is given. One of the scholars who has dedicated much of their intellectual efforts to this topic, Christopher McCrudden, has observed that "a principled interpretation of a grand principle often seems to call for agreement on what the effect of applying the principle is, whilst nevertheless disagreeing on what a theoretical basis for the principle may be".[9] Therefore, as far as legal literature is concerned, there seems to be broad agreement that the concept of human dignity conveys at least four aspects: the prohibition of inhumane treatment; the possibility for individual choice and the conditions for self-fulfillment; the protection of group identity and culture; and finally the creation of the necessary conditions for the satisfaction of essential needs.[10]

While in the present book we have tried to cover as many aspects of the concept as possible, we have chosen a slightly different perspective and focused on the rights of minorities and particularly vulnerable groups. Another methodological choice we made was to look at the contribution that international law and international lawyers may have in the definition and protection of human dignity. Studying the life and the work of Catellani, I soon realized that he had always stayed within the mainstream of enlightened liberalism of the end of the nineteenth century and early twentieth century, being moderately colonialist at the time of the first Italian colonial adventures, moderately interventionist in the First World War, and moderately conservative in domestic political life at the time of the insurgence of fascism. After the First World War he had been nominated as a life senator in Italian Parliament, and in the meantime he had become protestant and later received a doctoral degree *honoris causae* in Oxford in 1931. In short, when he retired from Padua University in the middle of the 1930s, he could look back with some satisfaction at a successful and fulfilled professional life. And yet, at the end of his life, the whole horror

in the Twentieth Century (CUP 2011) 85, 87). See *contra* and more convincingly Matthias Mahlmann, 'The Good Sense of Dignity: Six Antidotes to Dignity Fatigue in Ethics and Law', in Christopher McCrudden (eds.), *Understanding Human Dignity*, cit., 593, 601. The felicitous concept of "affirmative genealogy" has been coined with the goal of keeping alive the memory of the affirmation of the concept and of promoting its ever-developing actualization, see Hans Joas, *The Sacredness of the Person. A New Genealogy of Human Rights* (Georgetown Univ. Press 2013) (original, *Die Sakralität der Person. Eine neue Genealogie der Menschenrechte* (Suhrkamp 2011)).

9 Christopher McCrudden, 'Human Dignity and Judicial Interpretation of Human Rights' (2008) 19 *European Journal of International Law* 655, 697. Similarly, Oscar Schachter, 'Human Dignity as a Normative Concept' (1983) 77 *American Journal International Law* 848, 849.

10 Ibid, at 686 et seq. Not dissimilarly, but from a more philosphical perspective see Matthias Mahlmann, 'Six Antidotes to Dignity Fatigue', cit., 600: "autonomous subjectivity, basic respect, non-instrumentalization, non-objectification, and non-reification".

of fascism, which he had never really opposed and whose excess he had always thought to escape thanks to his privileged position, overcame and annihilated him. I wonder whether in the terrible hour of his agony he saw all his life pass by and asked himself what had gone wrong and when and why.

It is a commonplace to observe that the movement for the international protection of human rights arose from the ashes of the Second World War and found its first expression in the Preamble of the Charter of the United Nations.[11] What we have said about the Universal Declaration of 1948 or the German *Grundgesetz* of 1949 could be read in this light too. However, this narrative is not completely true. It is one thing to officially accept a concept in an international institutionalised discourse; it is a completely different thing for the concept to appear and be discussed in the political and social arena. One should never forget that the first mention of human dignity in a legal text and in its modern sense predates the Universal Declaration of Human Rights by a whole century: the French decree of 1848 abolishing slavery in the French empire.[12] Furthermore, by focusing exclusively on the legal texts issued after the Second World War, we risk erasing from memory the lively discussion on the foundation of human rights, which had taken place in the 1920s and 1930s, and which involved not only philosophers and theologians but also international lawyers.[13]

Hence, we come back to the idea of the Conference and of the present book. How did international lawyers contribute, if at all, to the debate on the international protection of human rights in the 1930s, at a time when fascist regimes took hold of half of Europe, equaling and soon surpassing the Soviet dictatorship in disregard and violation of human dignity? How do international lawyers react now, at a time in which the appalling ghosts of a past which we had thought was forever buried are resurging in Europe and elsewhere?[14]

Was the catastrophe of the Second World War necessary to raise the awareness among international lawyers of the need for an international agenda of human rights based on the concept of human dignity? Is this concept still indispensable today? These are the two fundamental questions that this book addresses, and

11 UN Charter Preamble, 2nd para.: "(We the peoples of the United nations determined) to reaffirm faith in fundamental human rights, in the dignity and worth of the human person, in the equal rights of men and women and of nations large and small".

12 See Rebecca Scott, 'Dignité/Dignidade: Organizing against Threats to Dignity in Societies after Slavery', in Christophers McCrudden (ed.), *Understanding Human Dignity*, cit., at 61 et seq.

13 See John W. Burgers, 'The Road to San Francisco: The Revival of the Human Rights Idea in the Twentieth Century' (1992) 14 *Human Rights Quarterly* 447; Lynn Hunt, *Inventing Human Rights*, (Norton & Co. 2007).

14 For a timely and unfortunately still quite isolated study see the 2018 issue of the *Netherlands Law Review* on "Populism and International Law", edited by Janne Nijman and Wouter Werner.

which its editors hope it will usefully contribute to answering. Of course, the two questions are linked in many ways. As Primo Levi, a great Italian writer and survivor of a Nazi extermination camp, drily wrote in the conclusion of his last essay: "It happened once, hence it can happen again: this is the core of what I have to say".[15]

Inspired by the Conference held in Padua, that awareness explains the structure of the book, which studies the contribution of a selected number of international lawyers in the 1930s and presents reflections on how the international lawyers of our time may contribute to defining and protecting human dignity. The first part of the book is dedicated to a historical overview of the debate in the 1930s. We have focused on extremely influential authors, whose names readily come to mind such as Kelsen, Lauterpacht, and Politis. A special tribute is dedicated to two Italian Jewish international lawyers, Sereni and Vitta, who unlike the elderly Catellani, as young scholars were fortunate enough to escape from Fascist Italy and after the War contributed in a substantial way to restoring the international reputation of Italian public and private international law, respectively.

The issues covered in the second part of the book do not, and cannot, purport to be exhaustive. Human dignity can be a two-edged sword, capable of both liberal and conservative readings. A liberal reading pushes for the protection and extension of the sphere of individual choices and liberties (such as those concerning LGBTQ persons) and makes place for a new generation of rights (such as the right to live in a healthy environment or to be free from poverty). On the contrary a conservative reading emphasises the limits of legitimate choices (such as those concerning the commercialisation and commodification of the human body, or the protection of human embryos) and the setting of limits on the development of science (such as through the prohibition on human reproductive cloning).[16]

The present book relies on the concept of human dignity in the liberal sense, or more precisely as a tool for the reaffirmation and further empowerment of human rights. There are two main reasons for this choice. The first is that the conservative reading, in pursuing the goal of restricting individual choices or testing the limits to science, is very much influenced, and possibly inescapably so, by the

15 Primo Levi, *I sommersi e I salvati*, (Einaudi 1986), 164: "E' avvenuto, quindi può accadere di nuovo: questo è il nocciolo di quanto abbiamo da dire".

16 See for instance Roger Brownsword, 'Human dignity from a legal perspective', in Marcus Düwell et al. (eds.), *The Cambridge Handbook of Human Dignity*, cit., 1, 9 et seq., and with a specific focus on bioethics see Derick Beyleveld, Roger Brownsword (eds.) *Human Dignity in Bioethics and Biolaw* (OUP 2001). For a strong criticism of the conservative reading see Stéphanie Hennette-Vauchez, 'When Ambivalent Principles Prevail: Leads for Explaining Western Legal Orders' Infatuation with the Human Dignity Principle', (2007) 10 *Legal Ethics*, 193, who sees in the principle's "quite sudden and global apotheosis" an attempt to reinvigorate jus-naturalist approaches of law (at 195). The author rightly highlights the double edge dimension of the concept, which can be declined not only in terms of rights but also in

religious beliefs of its proponents to a much major degree than by their sociological or philosophical outlooks. This implies treading into a debate, which would stray us far away from the original thrust of the Conference. The second reason is that, when reflecting on the present standing of the liberal concept of human dignity, we came to realize how much in need it is of a renewed effort to reaffirm and to strengthen its effectiveness.

The issues range from those in which the concept of human dignity has been long established (including the prohibition on slavery, religious freedom, social and labour rights), to those for which the concept of human dignity may still be subject to some debate (such as the human dignity of indigenous peoples as a distinctive collective), to other less studied issues concerning particularly vulnerable persons or groups, such as those exposed to the risk of discrimination and denial of rights like undocumented migrants in general or, taking a more specific focus, migrant female domestic workers.

The issues chosen, despite their diversity, all share the common aspect of their topicality, which is further proof of the irreplaceability of the concept of human dignity in our age. It is not any longer time to stand up and walk out, but to stand up and speak loud and clear.[17]

---

terms of duties towards the community, and traces back this possible double understanding to German legal philosophy as epitomized in Kant's moral laws (at 197). The interpretation of the human dignity principle as a matter of public order or public policy is evident not only in the famous "dwarf-throwing" case before the French Conseil d' Etat (C.E. 27 October 1995, *Ville d' Aix en Provence et Commune de Morsang sur Orge*), but also in the ECJ's jurisprudence (ECJ C-36/02, *Omega Spielhallen v. Oberbuergermeisterin der Bundesstadt Bonn, ECJ 2004-I,* 9641), final ruling at 9655: 'Community law does not preclude an economic activity consisting of the commercial exploitation of games simulating acts of homicide from being made subject to a national prohibition measure adopted on grounds of protecting public policy by reason of the fact that that activity is an affront to human dignity'.

17 This book is just a little contribution to answer Philipp Alston call, P. Alston, 'The Populist Challenge to Human Rights', 9 *Journal of Human Rights Practice 2017*, 1, at 14: 'The point is simply that we cannot wait, we need to start acting; we need to do whatever we can to strengthen respect for international human rights. We need to commit to the principles in our own lives, in our own areas. We are going to need to operate in a much more creative fashion both internationally and locally [...] The response is really up to us'.

In the last phase of reading the proofs of the book, the appalling images and news of the assassination through suffocation of George Floyd by a police officer in Minnesota on 25 May 2020 shocked the world. Reports then came out regarding similar crimes in the recent past and also following Mr Floyd's death. One could not have imagined that in 2020 such hideous racially motivated crimes could be committed by public officials in the United States. The upsurge of racially motivated crimes against Black people is extremely disturbing. We apologize for not having included in this book a chapter on the serious threat to human dignity posed by the discrimination, hostility and violence that confront Black communities, not only in the United States and not only by public authorities. Now more than ever "Black lives matter".

CHAPTER 2

Italian International Lawyers Facing Racial Laws: the Fate of Angelo Piero Sereni and Edoardo Vitta

Tullio Treves

1 Introduction

The attitude of the small world of Italian international lawyers vis-a-vis the fascist regime was one of acquiescence and in some cases of active collaboration. However, the best international lawyers, by education and culture alien to fascism, found refuge in selecting for their studies subjects concerning the general theory of public and private international law. These subjects were far from politics and allowed them to stay away from commenting and taking a stand on the questionable foreign policy and illegal acts of the regime, from the occupation of Corfu to the war in Ethiopia, not to speak of the aggression to France (a "stab in the back") and the disastrous involvement of Italy in the Balkans. As shown very well in essays by Giulio Bartolini, only second-rate scholars wrote enthusiastically along the lines of the Regime.[1]

Jewish international lawyers were not many, although some of them, as Giulio Diena and Enrico Catellani, had left a mark before fascism. My focus in this chapter will be on two Italian Jewish international law scholars who, in key moments of their academic careers, were struck by the racial laws of 1938, and who were excluded from teaching and participating in competitive examinations ("concorsi") for becoming professors: Angelo Piero Sereni[2] and Edoardo Vitta.[3]

I had the venture of knowing both of them personally. I met Sereni at the University of Bologna in 1965, when I had just obtained my law degree and was making the first steps of my academic career as "assistente volontario" to

1 G. Bartolini, 'The Impact of Fascism on the Italian Doctrine of International Law' (2012) 14 *Journal of the History of International Law* 237; 'Le leggi razziali e la dottrina italiana di diritto internazionale', in G. Resta, V. Zeno Zencovich, *Leggi razziali: passato e presente,* (Roma 3 Press 2015), 55.

2 A short biography by P. Mengozzi can be found in Birocchi, Cortese, Mattone, Miletti (a cura di) *Dizionario Biografico dei giuristi italiani (XII-XX secolo)*, (Il Mulino 2013), 1851.

3 A short biography by F. Mosconi can be found in *Dizionario Biografico dei giuristi italiani (XII-XX secolo)*, Ibid, 2057.

© KONINKLIJKE BRILL NV, LEIDEN, 2021 | DOI:10.1163/9789004435650_003

Professor Mario Giuliano. The occasion was a lecture by Professor Ignaz Seidl-Hohenfeldern, whom Sereni had invited to Bologna. A short chat with Professor Sereni immediately made me aware of his friendly and open attitude to a then very young scholar and to students.

I met Edoardo Vitta many times, in particular in the seventies, during the years in which his tenure at the Faculty of Law of the University of Torino coincided with mine at the Faculty of Political Sciences of the same University. We discussed many subjects of common interest – he was then finishing his monumental Treatise on Private International Law and I was at the time mostly interested in this branch of International Law. I could often enjoy his generous hospitality in his house on the banks of the River Po. I later had the privilege of visiting him in his beautiful residence at San Casciano Val di Pesa.

2 The Early Stages of Their Academic Careers

The age difference between Sereni and Vitta was not great: just five years, as Sereni was born in 1908 and Vitta in 1913. But those five years marked a difference between the two precocious international law scholars struck by fascist discrimination and persecution in 1938. In that very year, Sereni became full professor at the University of Ferrara at the age of 30, after having written well recognized monographs on public and private international law subjects. His academic career in Italy was crushed at its culminating moment, having won the « concorso » and obtained a chair. In 1938, Edoardo Vitta was only 25. He was a promising assistant professor at the University of Florence and was aspiring to follow the steps of his illustrious father Professor Cino Vitta, a famous administrative law scholar twice called to teach at the Hague Academy of International Law. Edoardo Vitta's career in Italy was nipped in the bud.

Neither Sereni nor Vitta had ever taken positions against the Fascist Regime. Both had even signed articles defending the fascist aggression of Ethiopia. It was immediately clear to them that the only reason for their situation was that they were Jews and that Italy was engulfed in the anti-semitic vortex started by Nazi Germany. Italy was no longer the country were their fathers and grandfathers had lived peacefully.

I have no documents concerning whether Sereni and Vitta received manifestations of friendship or solidarity from their international law colleagues. I doubt they did and certainly such manifestations, if there were any, were not public. I remember that my father, who was in a similar situation and was excluded from participating to a « concorso » for a professorship by the racial

Laws of 1938,[4] remembered that since the passing of the racial laws, certain colleagues would cross the street when they saw him walking on the sidewalk, in order to avoid any contact. It is very likely that Sereni and Vitta had similar experiences.

3 Leaving Italy: a Difficult Decision

The decision of both scholars was to leave Italy. Not an easy choice having family, and family history, in Italy. Sereni left for the United States. He settled in New York in the numerous Italian Jewish exile community. He found a teaching position at Columbia University. He was helped in this by a recommendation of Hersch Lauterpacht, then Professor at Cambridge University, who appreciated Sereni's book on Agency in International Law.[5] Although aware of Sereni's articles in support of the Ethiopian fascist war, Lauterpacht agreed to recommend him. He explained in a letter to Winfried Jenks: "I am very willing to forgive him that. I would be very unhappy if, placed as I am by accident in a secure and pleasant post, I were to refuse to help an unfortunate man because he was a patriot or an opportunist". In New York, Sereni also started to work as a lawyer, founding with an American colleague a small law firm that, under different names, has grown and still exists.

Sereni continued to write on international law in American scholarly journals and published in 1943 *The Italian Conception of International Law.* This book had the political aim to show to the English-speaking world the contribution to international law made by Italian scholars throughout the centuries. In examining briefly the position of Italian scholars towards Fascism, Sereni states that "Italian scholars have made no attempt to please fascism" and that the choice of abstract theoretical themes justified the view that "the Italian school impliedly condemned Fascist practices".[6] This view, unfortunately only partially based on facts, shows the political aim of contributing to highlighting the continuity of the Italian doctrine's achievements and to consider Fascism as a parenthesis. Sereni's generosity is evident, considering his personal history, including in particular, that his chair at the University of Ferrara had been

4 See the well documented book by C. Nitsch, *Renato Treves esule in Argentina: Sociologia, Filosofia Sociale, Storia,* (Accademia delle Scienze di Torino, 2014)serie V, vol. 38, Fasc. 2.

5 See H. Lauterpacht's letter in E. Lauterpacht, *The Life of Hersch Lauterpacht,* (Cambridge University Press 2010), 287, and the discussion about its dating in Bartolini, "Le leggi razziali" quoted above, footnote 44.

6 A.P. Sereni, *The Italian Conception of International Law,* (The Lawbook Exchange 1943), 275.

occupied by Lea Meriggi, the most militantly Fascist of Italian international law scholars.

Vitta migrated to Palestine, attached as he was to Jewish values, probably influenced by his brother in law, the Zionist and militant anti-fascist Sion Segre. In Palestine, he could continue his scholarly endeavours lecturing at various Universities and managing to publish in 1940, in French, in the prestigious Dutch collection *Bibliotheca Visseriana,* his first book: *La validité des traités internationaux*.[7] With the establishment of the State of Israel in 1948, having been appointed Scientific Secretary of the Constitutional Committee of the Provisional Council of State, "he contributed (as he tersely states in his biographical note in the *Recueil des Cours*) to the preparation of the first organic laws of the State … also taking part in the preparation of a new civil code". This latter experience and his attentive examination of the functioning of a plurality of personal statutes in Israel were the basis of his pioneering studies on this subject.

4 Returning to Their Academic Home: Challenge and Recognition

After the fall of Fascism and the establishment of democracy in Italy, both scholars decided to return to Italy. It was not an easy decision as both had made important contributions to the scientific environment of the countries to which they had migrated. It was not an easy return either. The academic community was trying to restore its democratic tone. Professors wanted to forget about Fascism and about the servitude they had been submitted to during the Regime. The return of banned Jewish scholars in their midst was for many an unwelcome reminder.

Sereni was reinstated in his position of Professore straordinario at the University of Ferrara in 1945 and, in 1948, retroactive to 1939, he was recognized as Professore ordinario, the position he had been denied by the racial laws. He then moved in 1958 to the University of Bologna, were he taught up to his untimely death in 1966. During this period, he published his comprehensive multi-volume treatise on public international law. He never reached what would have been the natural culminating position of his career, the University of Rome.

When he returned to Italy in 1953, Vitta was forty. He had a substantial production in public and private international law but no position in the Italian

7 E. Vitta, *La Validité des Traités Internationaux* (Brill 1940).

University. He was given the provisional non-tenured position of "professore incaricato" of international law at the University of Bologna, which he held up to 1958. But there was no place for him in the "concorsi" for chairs of international law. He was an outsider, not affiliated with any of the dominant "schools" of international law. It was only in 1959 that, with the support of Giorgio Balladore Pallieri, he won a "concorso" in "Institutions of Public Law", a discipline then considered as less prestigious than its components, Constitutional law, Administrative Law and, for some, International Law. He taught this subject at the University of Cagliari, remaining, for more than a decade, geographically and *ratione materiae* somehow isolated from the community of international lawyers. He could go back to continental Italy only when in 1971 the University where his father had taught, the University of Torino, entrusted him with a chair, not in the international law field, however, but in the minor although promising subject of Regional Law. It was only a few years later, when he had completed his monumental and unique *Treatise of private international law*,[8] that the Turin Faculty moved him to a new chair of Private International Law. Almost forty years after 1938, Edoardo Vitta was back in the fold of International Law! In 1979 he moved to the University where he had studied, the University of Florence where, after a short period teaching constitutional law, he held until his death in 1988 the chair of private international law. The publication in 1972–75 of his treatise won him finally broad respect in Italy and consolidated his already high standing abroad. In fact, he was the protagonist of the reform of Italian private international law and gave the general course of private international law at the Hague Academy in 1979.

5 Concluding Remarks

Neither Sereni nor Vitta wrote on the impact of the racial laws on their life and career. They did not talk about it either. Perhaps they considered themselves more fortunate than other Jewish colleagues that perished in the concentration camps or encountered great difficulties in their exile. They preferred to teach a lesson in scientific probity and lack of animosity with the formidable scientific endeavours they accomplished after their return to Italy.

The task of my generation, who had the privilege of coexisting with these masters in the free atmosphere of democratic Italy, was to learn from them not only international law but also the lesson of scientific dedication and of

8 E. Vitta, Diritto internazionale privato (3 vols., Turin, 1972–1975).

internationalist outlook their lives taught, and to transmit such lesson to the new generations.

In the difficult times we are entering, characterized by collective loss of historical memory and by the return in public discourse of intolerant and nationalistic attitudes we hoped were buried, knowledge by the new generations of the events started in 1938 and reflection on them is necessary and urgent.

CHAPTER 3

Hersch Lauterpacht and Human Dignity

Robert Kolb

1 Introduction

In this very short contribution we shall be looking at the way ideas linked to "human rights" evolved in the thinking of one of the greatest international lawyers of the 20th century, Sir Hersch Lauterpacht.[1] The point is not to enter into a detailed analysis, for which much space would be needed, but just to make some inroads into the matter by painting a landscape from an eagle's (rather than a simple bird's) height perspective.

Born of 16th of August 1897 in Zolkiew (Poland), H. Lauterpacht studied law in Vienna, Berlin and London. He became doctor of law in Vienna in 1922 and later again doctor of law in London in 1927. In his both doctoral works he took opposite positions on the issue of private law analogies, largely denying them in 1922 (in the positivistic Viennese environment)[2] and largely admitting them in 1927 (when he could more freely express his own matured thinking).[3] Having become Lecturer at the London School of Economics, he was eventually appointed professor of law in Cambridge in 1938. Member of the International Law Commission since 1948, and judge at the International Court of Justice since 1954, he finally died on 8th May 1960, following a surgical intervention.

The greatest concern in his writings on international law is the strengthening of the international legal order against anarchical sovereignty, and in particular the attempt to fight against unilateralism in the application of the law by ensuring authoritative rulings on issues of law and on disputes through

1 On the biography of Sir Hersch Lauterpacht, see mainly, for a very short presentation R. Kolb, *Les cours généraux de droit international public de l'Académie de la Haye* (Bruylant 2003), 178. For a fuller account, cf. M. Koskenniemi, *The Gentle Civiliser of Nations* (Cambridge University Press 2001), 353 ff; E. Lauterpacht, *The Life of Sir Hersch Lauterpacht* (Cambridge University Press 2010); P. Sands, *East West Street* (W&N 2016), 57 ff.

2 H. Lauterpacht, *Das völkerrechtliche Mandat in der Satzung des Völkerbundes*, Ph.D. Vienna, 1922, Chapter IV.

3 H. Lauterpacht, *Private Law Sources and Analogies of International Law* (The Lawbook Exchange 1927).

 | DOI:10.1163/9789004435650_004

the intervention of international arbitrators and judges.[4] The human rights thinking of Sir Hersch is divided into two phases. The first one is foreshadowing the emergence of such rights; the second is placed amidst their birth and affirmation and makes an important contribution thereto. Even the term 'human rights' instead of 'rights of man' seems to owe some part of paternity to Sir Hersch. Due to the subject matter of the conference giving rise to this paper, it may perhaps be recalled that Sir Hersch suffered in his young years from anti-Semitic feelings, all the more since he was then actively involved in the Zionistic movement. Let us now move to the two phases in his human rights thinking.

II Phase I (1922–1943): *Humanité diffuse*

In this first phase, Hersch Lauterpacht did not directly touch on 'human rights' issues, which were at that time not part of positive international law. But in the context of his doctrine of international law he often touched on issues having some degree of link with conceptions of human dignity. Three such building blocks of human rights *avant la lettre* can be mentioned. *First*, there is the question of the subjects of international law, i.e. its legal persons. Hersch Lauterpacht insisted on the point that not only States have rights and duties under international law but also individuals.[5] He stresses in particular their capacity for undertaking themselves international legal action in order to protect their rights, and buttresses this position by a series of precedents such as the abortive Statute of an International Prize Court (1907), the Center-American Court of Justice (1908), the PCIJ's precedent on the *Competence of the Courts of Danzig* (1928) or the procedure at the mixed arbitral tribunals or some other arbitrations, as the one concerning the *Lena Goldfields* case. He also mentions in the same chapter the fundamental rights of individuals under special régimes of international law,[6] e.g. the minimum standard of treatment of aliens (which he considers as giving rights not only to States under diplomatic protection, but also directly to individuals), or the treaties relating to minorities, mandates, stateless persons

4 H. Lauterpacht, *The Function of Law in the International Community* (Oxford University Press 1933).

5 H. Lauterpacht, 'Règles générales du droit de la paix' (1937) 62(4) *RCADI* 217 ff.

6 Ibid., 228 ff.

or refugees. He here comes closest to the enunciation of a branch of international law related to human rights.[7]

Second, there is the issue of the relations of municipal and international law. As is known, Hersch Lauterpacht was a staunch defender of the strongest possible monism.[8] International law and municipal law are not neatly separated. In particular, their subjects are not by essence different, since the individual is a subject of municipal as well as of international law. This unity-driven conception as to the legal orders allows Hersch Lauterpacht to place the individual at the core of all legal systems. By professing a monism with priority of international law – that is, in case of conflict of norms the international legal position will prevail over the municipal legal position – he also strengthened the protections the individual could derive from international law.

Third, there are a series of utterances all over the life of Hersch Lauterpacht which are indirectly relevant to the place and protection of the individual against arbitrary power. Here are some examples. A uniform practice cannot create customary law or law in general if it is contrary to the general conceptions of law, in particular the general principles of law of civilized peoples. And Hersch Lauterpacht coins here the salient phrase: 'commune crimen non facit jus'.[9] Or: gravely immoral treaties cannot be binding (e.g. treaties oppressing the individual). However, this early expression of *jus cogens* must be put, for Hersch Lauterpacht, under the sway of the judgment of an impartial tribunal.[10] There should be no unilateral invocation of a pretended immorality in order to cast away unwelcome treaty obligations. Here comes back Hersch Lauterpacht's main obsession: no unilateral repudiation of *pacta sunt servanda* by each State at will and whim; rather, impartial adjudication instead. Still, a punitive action against a State is possible; sovereignty is no obstacle to it. Thus, punitive damages can be awarded.[11] Finally, the practice of States could growingly withhold recognition from a dictatorial government.[12] As can be seen, all these positions have as a common core that they attempt to 'civilize' the legal process and to ensure that it will remain rooted in human values. A natural law conception shines through them.

---

7 The concept of human rights was not unknown at that time, and some international lawyers promoted it: cf. A. Mandelstam, 'La protection internationale des droits de l'homme' (1913) 38(4) *RCADI* 125 ff.

8 Ibid. (footnote 5) 129 ff.

9 Ibid., 159.

10 Ibid., 306 ff.

11 Ibid., 350–1.

12 H. Lauterpacht, *Recognition in International Law* (Cambridge University Press 1947), 115 ff.

III Phase II (1943–1960): *Humanité cristallisée*

1943 is the year in which Hersch Lauterpacht published his first article devoted directly to human rights in international law.[13] This is the time of international criminal law and international human rights law, to which Hersch Lauterpacht contributed directly. It has to be borne in mind that a significant part of Hersch Lauterpacht's family was wiped out in the holocaust. His engagement in the human rights movement was a natural outflow of his doctrinal positions before the war but also of the dramatic experiences during the conflict. In 1946, Hersch Lauterpacht became member of the UK War Crimes Executive. He then went to Nuremberg as legal assistant to the UK Chief Prosecutor, Sir Hartley Shawcross. At the same time, he contributed in various writings to nascent human rights law. In the context of universal human rights under the UN system, Hersch Lauterpacht had three main concerns. He pursued them with inflexible insistence and unfailing attention.

a) *Legal Obligations*. First, Hersch Lauterpacht emphasized the existence of true international legal obligations in the context of human rights.[14] That was not obvious in 1947, at the time of his seminal course at the Hague Academy. The UN Charter contained some principally vague allusions to human rights, in the Preamble (§§ 2 and 4), Article 1 § 3 (with a non-discrimination provision), Article 13, § 1, letter b (*idem*) as well as Articles 55–56. The Universal Declaration of Human Rights (1948), for its part, was "merely" a recommendation of the UN General Assembly and as such deprived of binding legal value. Thus, were human rights in 1947/1948 only non-legal postulates for political and normative 'promotion' but not for legal protection? Hersch Lauterpacht took a clear position: there is, as a matter of international law, an obligation to respect and observe human rights.[15] The absence of a precise definition

13 H. Lauterpacht, 'The Law of Nations, the Law of Nature and the Rights of Man' (1943) 29 *Grotius Society* 1 ff. The other human rights publications of HL are the following: 'The International Protection of Human Rights' (1947) 70(1) *RCADI* 5 ff (also the first course at the Hague Academy published in English); 'Human Rights, the Charter of the UN, and the International Bill of the Rights of Man', *Report of the Forty-Third Conference of the ILA* (ILA 1948), 80 ff; 'The Universal Declaration of Human Rights' (1948) 25 *BYIL* 354 ff; 'The Proposed European Convention of Human Rights' (1949) 35 *Grotius Society* 25 ff; and lastly his major work, summing up his positions: *International Law and Human Rights*, (Frederick A. Praeger 1950).

14 See e.g. H. Lauterpacht, 'The International Protection of Human Rights' (1947) 70(1) *RCADI* 15 ff.

15 Ibid., 15–6.

of human rights adversely affects the legal character of the rights but does not destroy it.[16] In other words, human rights are still nascent and a work in progress; but their core is already fully-fledged a matter of international law.

b) *Domestic Jurisdiction*. Second, the issue was whether the concept of domestic jurisdiction as enshrined in Article 2, § 7, of the UN Charter renders nugatory the human rights protection. Can a State raise the shield of its internal matters in order to resist any international legal protection of human rights?[17] Such a defense would mean that the UN machinery and international law in general could not pursue matters of human rights on their agenda as against a State which has not consented to their competence. In this context, Hersch Lauterpacht develops his famous theory on intervention in internal affairs. Such an intervention supposes a 'dictatorial interference', i.e. a compulsion; the issuing of a recommendation on human rights matters cannot be put in that category. Hence, there is no intervention in internal affairs by the discussion of human rights matters and the adoption of recommendations. Moreover, he adds, matters of 'international concern', in particular matters regulated by a treaty such as the UN Charter, are not 'essentially' within the domestic jurisdiction of a State. Thus, once again, human rights matters do not fall under the concept of domestic jurisdiction. They can be fully dealt with at the stage of international organization and through international law.

c) *International Machinery*. Hersch Lauterpacht comes back to his favorite theme. The implementation of human rights cannot be simply left to single States (his pre-war optimism had further been tainted by the events in World War II). He emphasizes that there is nothing in the UN Charter to prevent the Human Rights Commission (under ECOSOC) to investigate a complaint and utter a recommendation on human rights issues.[18] Enforcement of human rights remains essential: there must not be merely paper declarations, but effective protection.[19] It is important that mere verbal incantation be avoided, since it would be open to the charge of insincerity and evasion, thus fooling the nascent human rights movement at its roots.[20]

16 Ibid., 17.
17 Ibid., 17 ff.
18 Ibid., 56 ff, 59.
19 Ibid., 101.
20 Ibid., 103.

Hersch Lauterpacht finally insists also on the main framework conditions for a long-term success of human rights: first, the upholding of the political and moral authority of the UN; and second the successful repelling of obsolete dogmas, such as the State being the only subject of international law, or the State being an end in itself, and with it the whole myth of unbridled sovereignty.[21]

IV Conclusions

One can easily see the modernity of these considerations. In view of the current evolutions in the world, a concentration on the main lines of defense of civilization should be favored. We should not get astray from our path, lest we divide ourselves and weaken our voice. The basic themes of Hersch Lauterpacht in 1947/1948 are unfortunately still not satisfactorily settled today, as other chapters in this publication illustrate. On the contrary, they remain the main stumbling blocks of a dignified human rights law placed beyond the fog and dust of the myriads of sometimes sectarian sub-problems which anxious, if not angry, fractions of contemporary humanity think it fit to call out of their confinement and thereafter to hail all too often in the lenitive spirit of self-proclaimed do-gooders or as depositaries of highest morality. Concerning human rights, we are certainly not any more in the shaky sands of 1947. But we are also disillusioned on the limits of human rights promotion and protection in the real world.

In such an often barren environment, the return to the basics is a call worth to be uttered. The very day of writing of this piece (25th of November 2018) a retrogressive initiative for the primacy of Swiss constitutional law (and perhaps also to some extent statute law) over international law has been defeated by the Swiss popular vote. For a time, it did not look obvious that the defeat could be obtained. The initiative was directed largely against the European Convention of Human Rights (1950) and its guardian, the Strasburg Court. It wanted to shake off any international control of Swiss legislation by 'foreign judges'. It is known that various circles in other States think in the same way, e.g. in the UK. The issue of the international machinery for the protection of human rights thus remains crucially with us, as does the constant reflex to raise domestic jurisdiction as a shield against any scrutiny. On the other hand, the militant excesses cloaked under the generous banner human rights law have

21 Ibid., 5 ff.

to be reduced or curbed if the human rights movement has to remain credible and if precisely the backslashes manifested in the hostile upsurges shall not be nourished. All the preceding considerations show just one thing: the utmost modernity of Hersch Lauterpacht's cautioning and effort.

CHAPTER 4

Pure Theory of Law Amidst the Tempest: Hans Kelsen, Democracy and Human Rights

Andrea Gattini

1 Introduction: Human Rights Enshrined in Kelsen's Systemic Theory

At first sight, nothing could seem more alien to Kelsen's pure theory of law (*reine Rechtslehre*) and positivism than attention to human rights. The theory's postulate, according to which the validity of any legal rule can be judged only according to formal legal criteria of its enactment irrespective of its content,[1] leads some scholars to maintain that Kelsen's doctrine could readily accommodate with Nazi rule or that it even paved the way to the latter's overtaking. Of course, this view is utterly wrong, grounded as it is at best on a fundamental misconception of Kelsen's doctrine, when not on an outright malicious distortion.[2]

1 Hans Kelsen, *Reine Rechtslehre: Einleitung in die rechtswissenschaftliche Problematik* (Deuticke 1934), 62 et seq.

2 The misconception dates back to Radbruch, who in 1946 in his famous juxtaposition between (unjust) positive law and (extra positivist) justice wrote, with a clear allusion to Kelsen's theory, that "positivism with its credo that 'law is a law' rendered the German legal profession defenceless against laws of arbitrary and criminal content", see Gustav Radbruch, 'Gesetzliches Unrecht and übergesetzliches Recht' (1946) 1 *Süddeutsche Juristenzeitung* 105, 107 (translation by Frank Haldenman, 'Gustav Radbruch vs. Hans Kelsen: A Debate on Nazi Law', (2005) 18 *Ratio Juris*, 162 at 163). For a later preposterous accusation of Kelsen having favoured with his pure theory of law the ascent of dictatorial regimes, see Heribert Köck, ,'Leben und Werk des österreichischen Rechtsgelehrten Alfred Vredross' (1991) 42 *Ősterreichische Zeitschrift für Őffentliches Recht und Völkerrecht* 31, 40: "Zurecht ist daher darauf hingewiesen worden, dass Kelsen mit seinem inhaltsleeren Rechtsbegriff gerade jenen Unrechtsordnungen Vorschub geleistet hat, über die er sich später so entrüstete". Köck's comment is even more malicious, if one considers that the protagonist of his celebration, Alfred Verdross, was the one who, despite being Kelsen's first pupil, in the first edition of his textbook published in 1937, just a year before the *Anschluss*, had written: "Wir haben schon früher darauf hingewiesen, daß es keine Menschen an sich, sondern nur Menschen bestimmter Art gibt. Die höchste natürliche menschliche Art bildet das Volkstum", see Alfred von Verdross, *Völkerrecht* (1 Aufl., Duncker & Humblot 1937) 39. On the complex and ambiguous relationship between Verdross' prewar acute nationalism and Nazi ideology, see Anthony Carty, 'Alfred Verdross and Othmar Spann: German Romantic Nationalism, National Socialism and International Law' (1995) 6 *European Journal of International Law* 78.

 | DOI:10.1163/9789004435650_005

It suffices to consider the logical implications of some fundamental tenets of Kelsen's doctrine to understand that the accusations are devoid of any ground. The first tenet, which Kelsen derived from Kant and the neo Kantian philosophy,[3] is the unity of the whole system descending from a single principle. From this it follows, in the first place, that domestic law is not essentially different from international law, and that the ultimate scope of both orders is the regulation of the conduct of individuals.[4] It follows also that the realization of a *civitas maxima* is not an illusionary project but is in the reach of positive (international) law and its dynamic character.[5]

This tenet also explains why a study of Kelsen's writings in international law should never lose sight of his writings in public law. As is well known, Kelsen conspicuously contributed to the drafting of the Austrian Constitution of 1920, one of the most advanced democratic constitutions of that time, and he was decisive for the creation of the Constitutional Court, of which he became a member from its inception until 1929, a year before he left Austria.[6] At a time when, in general, and in both domestic and international law, individuals had no direct voice and no direct tools for protecting their rights against the public authority, the idea of attributing to the Court the power of judicial review with regards to claims directly brought by individuals was a major and lasting achievement of Kelsen's farsightedness. Coherently with monism's premises,

3 Hans Kelsen, *Die philosophischen Grundlagen der Naturrechtslehre und des Rechtspositivismus. Vorträge der Kant-Gesellschaft Nr. 31* (Pan-Verlag Rolf Heise 1928).

4 See Hans Kelsen, *Das Problem der Souveränität und die Theorie des Völkerrechts* (Mohr 1920), 125 and 161; Hans Kelsen, 'Les rapports de système entre le droit interne et le droit international public' (1926) 14 *Recueil de cours de l' Académie de droit international de la Haye* 231, 283 et seq.; Hans Kelsen, 'Théorie générale du droit international public: problèmes choisis' (1932) 42 *Recueil de cours de l' Académie de droit international de la Haye* 121, 141 et seq.

5 Hans Kelsen, 'Les rapports de système', ibid, 319. For an assessment of the dynamic conception of international law in Kelsen's thoughts see Charles Leben, 'Hans Kelsen and the Advancement of International Law' (1998) 9 *European Journal of International Law* 287, 292 et seq.

6 See Stanley L. Paulson, 'On Hans Kelsen's Role in the Formation of the Austrian Constitution and His Defense of Constitutional Review', in Werner Krawietz et als. (eds.), *The Reasonable as Rational? On Legal Argumentation and Justification-Festschrift für Aulis Aarnio* (Duncker & Humblot 2000), 385. As pointed out by Clemens Jabloner, 'Kelsen and His Circle: The Viennese Years' (1998) 9 *European Journal of International Law* 368, 374–375, Kelsen's decision to leave Austria was mainly motivated by the increasing virulent opposition of clerical circles against the Constitutional Court and some of its decisions, to which he had greatly contributed.

Kelsen did not see any theoretical difficulty in extending this project to the international legal order.[7]

The second fundamental tenet of Kelsen's theory is his meta-ethical relativism. Far from being a sort of cynical nihilism, Kelsen's moral relativism constitutes the cornerstone of his pure theory of law and positivism. Discarding any indemonstrable natural law origin, for Kelsen legal norms are only those which are created by human beings for human beings through formal processes governed by logical inferences, and from which their sole validity derives. It is indeed through an exercise of inflexible logic that Kelsen traces the link between ethical relativism and positivism, and further from positivism to a normative commitment to democracy and human rights. Again, it is only through a systematic reading of both Kelsen's legal theory and political writings that his position on the issue of human rights becomes clear. This insight, already offered by Bobbio in his studies on Kelsen in the second half of last century,[8] is now becoming common staple among a new generation of scholars.[9]

2 Human Rights as Part and Parcel of the "essence and value" of Democracy

In an essay that Kelsen dedicated in 1920 to the essence and value of democracy,[10] which, albeit considered fundamental in his political writings was

7 H. Kelsen, 'La technique du droit et l'organisation de la paix' (1932) 2 *Journal des nations*. n. 135, 1. (German transl. 'Die Technik des Völkerrechts und die Organisation des Friedens' (1934) 14 *Zeitschrift fűr öffentliches Recht* 253).

8 Among the many essays of Bobbio dedicated to Kelsen, see especially Norberto Bobbio, 'Formalismo giuridico e formalismo etico' (1954) 45 *Rivista di filosofia* 255, for a defense of Kelsen's moral relativism against different strings of criticism, coming from followers of natural law doctrine or from Marxist philosophers; Norberto Bobbio, 'Kelsen e il problema del potere' (1981) 58 *Rivista internazionale di filosofia del diritto* 549, for the relationship between norm, power and the dynamic character of the legal system. Many of Bobbio's essays on Kelsen have been collected in Norberto Bobbio, *Diritto e potere. Saggi su Kelsen* (ESI 1992).

9 See Véronique Champeil-Desplats, 'Hans Kelsen's Work and the Modern Theories of Human Rights', in Peter Langford (ed.), *Kelsenian Legal Science and the Nature of Law* (Springer 2017) 173; Carlo Invernizzi-Accetti, 'Reconciling legal positivism and human rights: Hans Kelsen's argument from relativism' (2018) 17 *Journal of Human Rights* 215.

10 Hans Kelsen, 'Vom Wesen und Wert der Demokratie' (1920) 47 *Archiv für Sozialwissenschaft und Sozialpolitik* 50 (published in book form by Mohr- Tübingen 1920). This essay was amply revisited in a book form at the end of the decade (Hans Kelsen, *Vom Wesen und Wert der Demokratie* (2nd. ed Tübingen, Mohr 1929). English transl. *The Essence and Value of Democracy*, (Lanham MD: Rowman & Littlefield 2013).)

curiously neglected by legal scholars for a too long time,[11] Kelsen, faithful to his usual method of conceptual binary opposition, nimbly and concisely brought the issue to the point. Whereas a metaphysical absolutist *Weltanschauung* inevitably leads, at least in aspiration, to an autocratic political regime, a critical relativistic one equally inevitably leads to a democratic regime.[12] Again, once assumed that democracy is the political regime which better corresponds to a relativistic approach, it follows that the very concept of majority rule presupposes the existence of a minority, and again the existence of a minority presupposes its right to exist and hence its protection. The link between democracy and fundamental human rights, already clearly exposed in 1920,[13] found its consecration in 1929 in the following words: "the protection of the minority is the essential function of so-called freedoms and fundamental rights or human and civil rights, which are guaranteed by all modern parliamentary-democratic constitutions".[14] At a time when international lawyers were painfully struggling with the theoretical (and practical) accommodation of minorities as possible beneficiaries of international law norms and procedures, Kelsen, with his usual Olympian serenity and presenting it as a matter of the simplest logical inference, broke the taboo word of *Menschenrechte*.

Of course, Kelsen was too positivist to risk falling into his own trap and mistaking the *Sein* with the *Sollen*. The fact that his ethical relativism led him to recognize the "value" of democracy did not mean that only a democratic regime could aspire to being considered a legally valid one. Here we touch with Kelsen the limit of the legal thought. When the legal fabric is torn, what we see behind it is the Medusa-like gaze of naked power, and at that point each individual is left alone with his own choices of resignation, submissiveness or revolt. Being a Jew and discharged of his chair of Public Law at the University of Cologne in 1933, Kelsen's choice was an inevitable

11 See François Rigaux, 'Hans Kelsen on International Law' (1998) 9 *European Journal of International Law* 325, at 333 for the importance of what he nevertheless labels as a "pamphlet".

12 Hans Kelsen, 'Vom Wesen und Wert', ibid, 36 (2nd ed., at 101).

13 Hans Kelsen, 'Vom Wesen und Wert', *supra* note 10, at 12: "So fungieren die Grundrechte der Demokratie als Minoritätsschutz und sichern die Gleichberechtigung auch demjenigen, der nicht die politische, religiöse oder nationale Überzeugung der Mehrheit teilt".

14 Hans Kelsen, *Vom Wesen und Wert, supra* note 10, 53: "Dieser Minoritätsschutz ist die wesentliche Funktion der so genannten Grund- und Freiheits- oder Menschen- und Bürgerrechte, die in allen modernen Verfassungen parlamentarischen Demokratien garantiert sind" (at 67–68 engl. transl.).

one, and that was exile, first in Switzerland, then in the Czech Republic and finally in the USA.

Surely Kelsen's outstanding intellectual as well as moral integrity was out of tune with the mounting tide of cowardice, opportunism or outright fanaticism of most of his contemporaries in Austria or in Germany. A single example suffices to enlighten the greatness of his character and the vileness of that of Carl Schmitt. Despite the fact that Schmitt's political and legal theories were sharply opposed to Kelsen's owns and that Schmitt seemed to take a personal pleasure in attacking him, as the Dean at the Cologne Law School Kelsen unreservedly supported in 1932 Schmitt's appointment in his same Faculty, as a tangible proof of his attachment to the value of scientific freedom. When one year later, shortly after Hitler's seizure of power, Kelsen was removed from his position, Schmitt was the only colleague who refused to sign a letter sent by the whole faculty to the ministry in Berlin for the reconsideration of the measures taken against Kelsen.[15]

Kelsen's introduction to his *Reine Rechtslehre*, written in Geneva in May 1934 fourteen months after Hitler's seizure of power, is an everlasting monument of his equanimity and moral strength. With absolute lucidity, he wrote that "the ideal of an objective science of law and state can only have a chance of common recognition in an epoch of social balance".[16] Therefore, nothing looked more untimely in such an unraveled epoch than a pure theory of law. Without mentioning names, Kelsen seemed to have thought of Schmitt when he wrote that it was the spirit of the time, which allowed to raise "unabashed, loud and openly the call for a political theory of law ... extolling as a virtue, what could at most be pardoned as the expression of harshest personal misery".[17]

15 For a demystifying portrait of Schmitt's legal writings as tools for achieving the position *of Kronjurist* of the Reich, see Bernd Rüthers, *Entartetes Recht* (Beck 1988). See also Andrea Gattini, 'Sense and Quasisense of Schmitt's *Grossraum* Theory in International Law' (2002) 15 *Leiden Journal of International Law* 53.

16 Hans Kelsen, *Reine Rechtslehre, supra* note 1, at VI: "Das Ideal einer objektiven Wissenschaft von Recht und Staat hat nur in einer Periode sozialen Gleichgewichts Aussicht auf allgemeine Anerkennung".

17 Ibid., "während man sich nicht mehr scheut, laut und öffentlich den Ruf nach einer politischen Rechtswissenschaft zu erheben [...], so als Tugend preisend, was höchstens bitterste persönliche Not gerade noch entschuldigen könnte". For an enlightening insight on Kelsen's interest in psychoanalysis and on the subtle influences of psychoanalysis on his thoughts, see Clemens Jabloner, 'Kelsen and His Circle', *supra* note 6, 384, for a description of the personality character of democratic individuals in the Vienna of the twenties of the XX century.

3 Pure Theory of Law and the Punishment of the "most objectionable acts"

If Kelsen's normative commitment to democracy and human rights is a still relatively neglected aspect of his thought and action, more attention has been dedicated in the last decades to his writings on international criminal law and justice.[18] Kelsen had acted as judge advocate in the Austrian War Ministry during the First World War. Furthermore, the theme of individual criminal responsibility under international law had been the subject of a major work by one of Kelsen's disciples, Alfred von Verdross, commented by Kelsen in a short review published in a Viennese newspaper in 1920.[19]

Although nothing precluded Kelsen from accepting the idea that international law can directly regulate the conduct of individuals, a major difficulty for him to embrace the prospect of an individual criminal responsibility was due to his view of international law as a primitive legal order and to his adherence to the concept of act of state. With regard to the first point, Kelsen had already conceded in the thirties that the goal of international law would be in the long run to replace state liability with individual liability.[20] During the Second World War he further investigated how far and how quick international law could move in that direction regarding individual criminal responsibility.

18 See Andrea Gattini, 'Kelsen's Contribution to International Criminal Law' (2004) 2 *Journal of International Criminal Justice* 795; Kirsten Sellars, *Crimes Against Peace and International Law,* (Cambridge University Press 2013) 85 et seq.; Monica García-Salmones Rovira, *The Project of Positivism in International Law* (Oxford University Press 2013) 359 et seq.; Thomas Olechowsky, 'Hans Kelsen, the Second World War and the U.S. Government', in Jeremy Telman (ed), *Hans Kelsen in America – Selective Affinities and the Mysteries of Academic Influence* (Springer 2016) 101; Charles Leben, 'Hans Kelsen et le châtiment des criminels de guerre de l' Allemagne nazie' (2019) 102 *Droit et Société* 447; Monica García-Salmones Rovira, 'Not Just Pure Theory: Hans Kelsen (1881–1973) and International Criminal Law', in Frédéric Mégret, Immi Tallgren (eds.), *The Dawn of a Discipline: International Criminal Justice and its Early Exponents,* (Cambridge University Press forthcoming).

19 Alfred von Verdross, *Die völkerrechtswidrige Kriegshandlung und der Strafanspruch der Staaten,* (Engelmann 1920); Hans Kelsen, "Der völkerrechtliche Strafanspruch wegen völkerrechtlicheswidriger Kriegshandlungen", *Neue Freie Presse* 8 September 1920, 3.

20 Hans Kelsen, 'La technique du droit et l'organisation de la paix', *supra* note 7. The theoretical importance of this short contribution is stressed by Otto Pfersmann, 'De la justice constitutionnelle à la justice internationale: Hans Kelsen et la seconde guerre mondiale' (1993) 16 *Revue Française de Droit Constitutionnel* 761, 773. See also Jochen von Bernstorff, *Der Glaube an das universale Recht: zur Völkerrechtstheorie Hans Kelsens und seiner Schüler* (Nomos Verlag 2001), 128 (English transl: *The Public International Law Theory of Hans Kelsen* (Cambridge University Press 2010) 148).

But as late as 1944 Kelsen saw in the second concept, the act of state, an insurmountable barrier against the idea that a state could punish an act of war performed by an enemy soldier "even if the act in itself constituted a so-called war crime",[21] lest the foreign state would accept the jurisdiction of the former.

That was in all evidence the major stumbling block which prompted Kelsen to sharply criticize the Nuremberg Tribunal, on the establishment of which he had nevertheless discreetly worked as a legal adviser to the US War Crimes Office in the War Department in 1944 and 1945. Whereas, even at the price of some argumentative acrobatics, Kelsen was able to overcome the theoretical hurdle of a retroactive application of criminal law,[22] what he could not stomach was the lack of any disposition in the London Agreement of 8 August 1945, from which the consent of Germany could be deduced in any form whatsoever. In Kelsen's view, this fact caused the Tribunal's jurisdiction to rest on dubious grounds and tainted the Tribunal's output of the accusation of "victor's justice".[23] Kelsen's intransigency on the point may seem odd to a certain extent, if one thinks of the striking, and for Kelsen quite unusual, opening to considerations of "international morality" interspersed in his writings during the war, as well as his unmistakable condemnation of the "morally most objectionable"

21 Hans Kelsen, *Peace through Law* (University of North Carolina Press 1944), 81 et seq. Part II of the volume, entitled 'Peace Guaranteed by Individual Responsibility for Violations of International Law' reprinted an earlier essay, 'Collective and Individual Responsibility in International Law with Particular Regard to the Punishment of War Criminal', published in (1943) 31 *California Law Review* 530. Also after the war, Kelsen did not change his view on the dim perspectives of international law with regard to individual criminal responsibility, both because of the (alleged) primitive state of international law and because of the act of state obstacle. See Hans Kelsen, 'Collective and Individual Responsibility for Acts of State in International Law' (1948) 1 *Jewish Yearbook of International Law*, 226; Hans Kelsen, *Principles of International Law* (Rhinehart 1952), 128 et seq.

22 Hans Kelsen, 'The Rule against *ex post facto* Laws and the Prosecution of the Axis War Criminals' (1945) 2 *The Judge Advocate Journal*, third issue, 8. See Andrea Gattini, 'Kelsen's Contribution', supra note 19, 800 et seq. Among the technical devices referred to by Kelsen, one seems particularly debatable: that one of minimizing the revolutionary concept of crimes against humanity contained in Article 6 al. c of the London Agreement equating them to "ordinary" crimes "according to the municipal law of the persons to be accused, valid at the moment they were committed" (cit. at 10). On the point, see Charles. Leben, 'Hans Kelsen et le châtiment des criminels de guerre', *supra* note 19, 452. For a fascinating and accurate account of the major role played by Lauterpacht and by Lemkin in helping the concept of crimes against humanity to be accepted and finally consecrated in the London Agreement see Philippe Sands, *East West Street*, (Weidenfeld and Nicolson 2016).

23 Hans Kelsen, 'Will the Judgement in the Nuremberg Trial Constitute a Precedent in International Law?' (1947) 1 *International & Comparative Law Quarterly*, 153, 167.

acts committed in the Second World War by the Axis forces.[24] However, his sharp criticism of the Nuremberg Tribunal is the proof of how Kelsen remained faithful, all life long, to the unshakeable grounds of his legal theory.

4 Conclusion: Kelsen's Sense of Justice

This acknowledgment makes his lasting commitment to the liberal values of democracy even more impressive. Despite all the blows and disillusions of his life, Kelsen's personal choices always remained those of a liberal democrat, firmly believing in the values of freedom. In his farewell lecture as an active member of the University of California given in Berkeley in 1952, he once again rebutted the criticism according to which his ethical relativism would be incompatible with moral responsibility.

Taking up again the issue of the impossibility to determine the meaning of justice, a theme which intrigued him all his life, despite the appearances of an inescapable and definite irrelevance to his pure theory of law,[25] he came to this conclusion, which is his truest legacy: "Since science is my profession, and hence the most important thing in my life, justice, to me, is that social order under whose protection the search for truth prospers. "My" justice, then, is the justice of freedom, the justice of peace, the justice of democracy – the justice of tolerance".[26]

24 Hans Kelsen, *Law and Peace in International Relations* (Harvard Univ. Press 1942), 37: "Whatever is consider 'just' in the sense of international morality has at least the tendency of becoming international law"; Hans Kelsen, 'Will the Judgement in the Nuremberg Trial', ibid, 165.

25 See Hans Kelsen, *Das Problem der Gerechtigkeit*, appendix to the second edition of the *Reine Rechtslehre* (Deuticke Verlag 1960), 365 et seq. Significantly, the last edited text by Kelsen was *Die Illusion der Gerechtigkeit. Eine kritische Untersuchung der Sozialphilosophie Platons*, which was published only in 1985 edited by Karl Ringhofer and Robert Walter (Manz 1985).

26 Hans Kelsen, *What is Justice?* (California Univ. Press 1957), 24.

CHAPTER 5

Nikolaos Politis and the Legal Status of the Individual in the International Legal Order

Niki Aloupi

Nikolaos Politis was a very important Greek and French international lawyer during the inter-war period.[1] He was born in 1872 and died in 1942, just after having seen the world sink into chaos, betraying all his hopes and beliefs. He had started a brilliant academic carrier in France where he had been "agrégé" as a Law Professor in 1901, but he left during the Balkan wars having been called upon by E. Venizelos. He led a political carrier thereafter.

When someone is interested in the rising of the individual as a subject of international law and, by extension, in human rights, they are bound to come across Nikolaos Politis' doctrine. And it is indeed possible to refer to an actual "Politis' doctrine" on this subject matter, even though he did not theorize his whole vision in one monography dedicated solely to individuals in international law or to human rights. In order to thoroughly examine his views on this topic, it is thus necessary to look into several writings of his, which address – in

1 On Nikolaos Politis see: E. Lagrange, *Galerie des internationalistes de la SFDI*, online [http://www.sfdi.org/internationalistes/politis/]; R. Holsti, 'Nicolas Politis 1872–1942' (1942) *AJIL* 475; A. Geouffre de La Pradelle, *Maîtres et doctrines du droit des gens* (Les éditions internationales 1950) 371; M. Koskenniemi, *The Gentle Civilizer of Nations. The Rise and Fall of Modern International Law* (Cambridge University Press 2002), especially p. 30 and following; G. Sacriste, A. Vauchez, 'La guerre hors-la-loi. 1919–1930 Les origines de la définition d'un ordre politique international' (2004) 151 *Actes de la recherche en sciences sociales* 91; M. Papadaki, 'The 'Government Intellectuals': Nicolas Politis – An Intellectual Portrait' (2012) 23 (1) *EJIL* 221; U. Özsu, 'Politis and the Limits of Legal Form' (2012) 23(1) *EJIL* 243. See also M. Papadaki, *Nicolas Politis (1872–1942): La science au service de la construction d'une société internationale entre ordre et liberté*, Ecole des Hautes Etudes en Sciences Sociales, Phd, thesis defense on the 14th of October 2016; and 'Nicolas Politis, une approche biographique' (2015) 1(7) *Monde(s)*54 and 'L'action des juristes internationalistes au service de la paix internationale à la fin du XIXème siècle: le cas de Nicolas Politis (1872–1942)' (2015) 91 *Cahiers de la Méditerranée* 21. Finally, see Ph. Pazartzis' 'Préface' *in* N. Politis, *La justice internationale,* (Ed. Panthéon-Assas Paris II 2017). For an anlysis of Politis' doctrine concering topics similar to those adressed in this article see especially R. Kolb, 'Politis and Sociological Jurisprudence of Inter-War International Law' (2012) 32(1) *EJIL* 233; N. Tsagourias, 'Nicolas Politis' Initiatives to Outlaw War and Define Aggression, and the Narrative of Progress in International Law' (2012) 23(1) *EJIL* 255; A. Truyol y Serra, R. Kolb, *Doctrines sur le fondement du droit des gens* (Pedone 2007), 91 and following.

 | DOI:10.1163/9789004435650_006

different extents – the place and the role of individuals in the international legal order. This question is actually rather central, omnipresent even, in Politis' thinking. This is quite clear in at least three major pieces of writing, all of them printed in the mid-twenties: his course on abuse of rights at the Hague Academy "Le problème des limitations de la souveraineté et la théorie de l'abus des droits dans les rapports internationaux", published in 1925;[2] his monography of 1927 on the new tendencies of international law, which was also translated in English in 1928 and constitutes a summary of several conferences he gave in 1926 at Columbia University;[3] and from a more procedural point of view his book of 1924 on international justice.[4] This article will be mainly based on these three pieces of writing, and especially on the one about new tendencies of international law, which comprises a whole chapter (chapter II) on the individual's position in the international legal order.

The study of these three writings, but also of other Nikolaos Politis' publications, reveals a very complete and rich thinking on the different aspects of the place of individuals in international law. Pragmatic and realistic, Politis understands that individuals are still mostly at his time an *object* of international law. However, being a true believer of the need for a comprehensive international sociological theory putting human beings at the centre of the international legal order, he aspires to (and writes about) a system – already in motion according to him – to which individuals can be much more: namely the creators, subjects and sole true legal actors of the international legal order.

In order to briefly present the main aspects of Politis' doctrine, three separate but corollary questions will be addressed in this contribution. Their combination goes to show that Politis accorded to human rights a gradually growing importance in his writings. Such a tendency is perfectly coherent with Politis' general vision of international law. Major exponent of the French Sociological Law School,[5] he sees in individuals the true creators of international law, which will be the focus of the first section of this chapter. Furthermore, he considers that individuals are not only objects of international law, but also its subjects, entitled to rights and subjected to international obligations This evolution from objects to subjects of international law and the discrepancies that can be seen in Politis' views on this matter will be addressed in the second

2 N. Politis, 'Le problème des limitations de la souveraineté et la théorie de l'abus des droits dans les rapports internationaux' (1925) 6(1) *RCADI* 1.

3 N. Politis, *Les nouvelles tendances du droit international* (Librairie Hachette 1927); *The New Aspects of International Law* (1928).

4 N. Politis, *La justice internationale* (Ed. Panthéon-Assas Paris II 2017).

5 See R. Kolb, 'Politis and Sociological Jurisprudence of Inter-War International Law', supra note 1.

section. Finally, Politis also advocates for the individuals to be capable, competent subjects of international law, so as not only to be entitled to rights and subjected to obligations but also to be able to defend those rights and see their international responsibility engaged in front of international judges. The direct access of individuals to international justice and their capacity in front of international jurisdictions will be covered in section 3 of this contribution.

1 Individuals as Creators of International Law in Politis' Doctrine

The premises of Objective Socialism and of the French Sociological Law School are well known and there is no need to further insist on the presentation of these theories. Suffices it to say that as every sociological theory defender, Politis considers individuals to be the sole true actor of the law. Applying the objective sociological doctrine to the international legal order, he considers the state to be a "vain fiction"[6] behind the veil of which the only true person is the individual.[7] International law is created indirectly or even directly by human beings. Indirectly, since according to the basic premises of the sociological theory, the sole true source of the law is the juridical conscience of people; social solidarity is the true foundation of the mandatory character of international law. Thus, international rules are created by social solidarity needs and by the human conscience of the need to respect those rules: in other words, by the opinio juris sive necessitatis. But Politis goes even further seeing a direct interaction between individuals and the creation of international law. In "New tendencies of International law", he writes:

> relations between humans create economical and moral usages which become mandatory rules of law as soon as the interested persons acquire the sentiment that they must obey them.[8]

In brief, whichever the formal sources of international law may be, its true sources are always human conscience and solidarity. Individuals are thus the true creators of international law, which in turns governs the relations between

6 N. Politis, 'Le problème des limitations de la souveraineté et la théorie de l'abus des droits dans les rapports internationaux', supra note 2, 6.

7 Politis actually uses indifferentially the terms "fiction" and "abstraction" to refer to the state as opposed to human beings. However, if the state is indeed an abstraction compared to individuals, the legal personality of the latter is as much a fiction as the state's legal personality.

8 N. Politis, *Les nouvelles tendances du droit international*, supra note 3, 76.

them beyond the borders of one state. Indeed, Politis defines international law as "the set of rules that governs the relations between human beings belonging to different national groupings".[9] Thus, individuals are not only the indirect creators of international rules but also – and most importantly for Politis – their main subjects. He writes in his Hague course:

> the law of every relation, private, public or international, is always of the same nature, because, everywhere, it is aiming at the human being and only the human being.[10]

In a true monistic way of thinking, Politis considers that international law has the same roots, nature and subjects as municipal law.

Even though some of Politis views, especially concerning the uselessness, harmfulness and consequently end of state sovereignty,[11] have been proved wrong by the evolution of international law, his thinking is clearly visionary concerning human rights and the place of individuals as subjects of international law. It is nevertheless quite confusing to actually look into what Politis considers as proof of the fact that human beings are subjects of international law. Indeed, the examples that he takes as illustrations are not always clear as to whether the individual is a subject or rather an object of international law. Politis makes the distinction between the two at a theoretical level, but in a not always consistent manner as far as the practical examples are concerned. This is explained by the fact that he believes individuals to be the ultimate subjects of international law in any case; thus, even when international rules seem to be directed to states, the ultimately aim are humans. This will be shown in the second point of this contribution.

2 Individuals as Objects or as Subjects of International Law in Politis' Doctrine

In the international sociological theories, it is clear beyond any doubt that the individual becomes a subject of international law when the latter confers rights directly on him, as well as competences to defend those rights. However,

---

9 Ibid.

10 N. Politis, 'Le problème des limitations de la souveraineté et la théorie de l'abus des droits dans les rapports internationaux', supra note 2, 9 : "Le droit de tous les rapports, qu'ils soient privés, publics ou internationaux, a toujours la même nature, parce que, partout, il vise l'homme et rien que l'homme".

11 See especially 'Le problème des limitations de la souveraineté et la théorie de l'abus des droits dans les rapports internationaux', supra note 2.

there seems to be a discordance amongst scholars as to whether the individual is also a subject of international law when the latter imposes on states an obligation to confer such rights and competences to individuals, eventually invokable or actionable in the municipal legal order, but not in the international legal order. In other words, there seems to be a recurrent confusion between direct effect or invocability of an international norm – which nevertheless still aims at individuals as objects – and qualification of individuals as subjects of international law, as well as between cases in which the individual is taken into account by an international legal norm directed to a state and cases in which the individual is its direct recipient.

In Politis' writings the distinction between the individual as an object or as a subject of international law seems *prima facie* clear. However, it is in fact imprinted with ambiguity when the content of the international obligation has a link with human rights *lato sensu*. In such a case, Politis seems to consider the individual as a subject of international law, even when the rule is directed to the state only and the right is not invocable by the individual in the international legal order (or even in some cases in the municipal legal order), since he is not its legal beneficiary. Politis, who appeared for the *Mavrommatis* case in front of the Permanent Court of International Justice,[12] refers to the individual as an object of international law when he can "neither invoke nor undergo international law", but from this observation he goes on to add that in such a case "relations between individuals and foreign states are governed by the sole specially competent municipal law". Thus, "international law only indirectly concerns individuals: its prescriptions are translated in municipal rules (…) only by the intermediary of the state can individuals obtain an international protection".[13] In other words, Politis considers humans as objects of international law only when they are ignored by it, but not when they are taken into consideration by it, without being its recipients. Whilst he is clearly influenced by the "Mavrommatis fiction"[14] (before *Lagrand*,[15] *Avena*,[16] and *Diallo*[17],), which in fact he criticises severely, he seems

12 PCIJ, *The Mavrommatis Palestine Concessions*, judgment, August 30th, 1925, *Series A*, n° 2.

13 N. Politis, *Les nouvelles tendances du droit international*, *op. cit.*, p. 56.

14 I.e. when solely the state's right was taken into account for the needs of diplomatic protection with no reference to the individual's right.

15 ICJ, *Lagrand Case* (*Germany v. United States of America*), judgment, June 27th 2001, *I.C.J. Reports* 2001, p. 466.

16 ICJ, *Avena and other Mexican Nationals* (*Mexico v. United States of America*), judgment, March 31st 2004, *I.C.J. Reports* 2004, p. 12.

17 ICJ, *Ahmadou Sadio Diallo* (*Republic of Guinea v. Democratic Republic of the Congo*), preliminary objections, judgment, May 24th 2007, *I.C.J. Reports* 2007, p. 582.

to exclude the possibility of the individual being an object of international law in the cases where the latter governs its legal regime by addressing obligations to states. However, this is a topical illustration of individuals as objects of international law, as foreigners' law goes to show.

For Politis, the first subjects of international law are, by necessity, statelessness persons, since *they "belong to no country"*.[18] Starting from them, international law recognised in other cases as well the quality of "subject" to individuals. Politis goes on to explain that international law establishes for the individuals "objective" and "constructive" rules.[19] The first ones aim at protecting them or at forbidding some activities. The latter aim at giving them the possibility to defend their own legal interests by means of direct recourse to the international organisation, without having to resort to the intermediary of the state. If objective rules are directed to states, not to individuals, this does not mean that individuals are not subjects of international law, since such a conclusion "confuse[s] the intrinsic value of these rules with their application".[20] If they apply to states, it is only due to the present condition of international organisation, but in fact they directly and principally govern the individual.

Thus, the lines separating object from subject of international law become very blurred in Politis' thinking. This is even more obvious when we turn to the examples he uses to illustrate his ideas. He first explains that the aim of the objective rules is to:

> ensure respect and protection of the life, liberty, health, work, family, and intellectual and moral development of the individual, irrespective of nationality.[21]

Here, we have an unambiguous reference to human rights, with a very modern vision concerning their substance but also the eradication of any nationality condition. But right after Politis gives examples of such "objective rules": piracy, slave trafficking, drug and alcohol trafficking, the prohibition of obscene publications, humanitarian law, foreigner's expulsion, migration controls, minorities regimes. The confusion is complete: international obligations directed only to states unrelated to individuals (drug trafficking, obscene publications),

18 N. Politis, *Les nouvelles tendances du droit international*, supra note 3, 62.

19 See also for another analysis of the same idea N. Tsagourias, 'Nicolas Politis' Initiatives to Outlaw War and Define Aggression, and the Narrative of Progress in International Law'supra note 1, 263–265.

20 N. Politis, *The New Aspects of International Law*, supra note 3, 21–22.

21 Ibid., 64.

international obligations directed to states but taking human being as their object (foreigners law) and international human rights where international law takes individuals as its subjects are treated indifferently by Politis. Moreover, no distinction is made between cases where international law recognises the status of individuals as subjects of municipal law (which in turn can recognise their right to directly invoke the international legal rules concerned before the municipal judge), and cases where this quality is recognised to them directly in the international legal order.

Even if the illustrations chosen by Politis are not topical (and how could they be in the mid-twenties?), the idea that he defends is clearly visionary and prepares the rising of individuals as subjects of international law. Furthermore, Politis does not consider individuals as subjects only as far as human rights or humanitarian law are considered, but also in regards with international responsibility. Indeed, he believes in the need to establish international obligations aiming at individual criminal responsibility.[22] The state fiction is not a problem solely as far as human rights are concerned, but also when it prevents the true criminals, namely human beings, to be punished. According to Politis:

> by forcing those who govern to be (…) more respectful of international legality [individual criminal responsibility] will constitute a serious guaranty for peace.[23]

Human rights and individual criminal responsibility are thus the two domains where Politis view of individuals as subjects of international law is the most accurate. In both domains, not only does international law confer rights directly to individuals and subject them to obligations but also, thanks to constructive rules, gives them access to international justice, thus making them capable subjects of the international legal order.

3 Individuals as Capable Subjects in the International Legal Order in Politis' Doctrine

Politis considers the possibility of a direct judicial petition brought before international justice by individuals. He examines the few examples of such actions in the past (notably concerning the Central American Court of Justice between 1907 and 1917, mixed arbitral tribunals established by peace treaties

22 N. Politis, *La justice internationale,* supra note 4, 249–251.
23 N. Politis, *The New Aspects of International Law,* supra note 3, 45.

and international prize court) and expresses the wish to go much further. He believes that:

> it is because the individual does not have the means to defend himself that we still imagine that he does not have a place in the legal life of the nations and that only the intervention of his home country "internationalises" his interests. This is an illusion, which will be dissipated by the granting to the individual of the right of recourse in front of international justice.[24]

According to Politis, more often than not diplomatic protection is impossible or insufficient.[25] This fact, combined with the discretionary nature of diplomatic protection, goes to show the need and practical interest of direct recourse.[26] In the conclusion of his monograph on international justice,[27] Politis wishes for two additions to the international justice system: a transnational court allowing for the individuals to bring direct claims against the state that violated their human rights, and an international criminal court for individual responsibility. Thus, human beings, individual private persons but also governing persons, would have direct access to international justice in order to defend their rights against a state or to see their international responsibility engaged and be punished for their crimes, notably the crimes against the "laws of humanity". The modernity of Politis' views on individuals as subjects of international law is remarkable: not only does he believe in an international law that confers rights and obligations directly to humans, but also sees in them, as early as in the mid-twenties, competent, capable subjects of the international legal order, having their rightful place before the international justice.

4 Concluding Remarks

In conclusion, Politis' doctrine, at the dawn of the human rights era, is all at once: realistic and idealistic, visionary in a pragmatic view, but also on some aspects, utopian. The following passages testify that:

24 N. Politis, *Les nouvelles tendances du droit international,* supra note 3, 83.
25 Ibid., 87.
26 Ibid.
27 N. Politis, *La justice internationale,* supra note 42, 249–251.

> international law is in a phase of transition: if it is no longer exclusively the law of the states, it is not completely yet the one of men [...] international law will not really become the law of individuals until relations between people have lost their international character and have become properly speaking universal.[28]

It seems that Politis considers "the law of individuals" to be mainly international private law, transnational or even global law, since he believes that:

> relations between people are still, in principle, international. They are being practiced by the intermediaries of the states. But as the universal society forms, some relations are, exceptionally, already globalized. They take place directly between people from various countries. What is today still the exception will become one day the principle.[29]

In other words, the ultimate destination of international law and the "modern conception" of jus gentium is, for Politis, the end of the state as we know it (he is a fervent opponent of sovereingty) and the establishment of a human globalized community governed by global law. Human rights are thus only the beginning in the evolution aiming to place individuals in the absolute centre of the international legal order.

Whether we agree or not with Politis' views, whether time proved him right or wrong, it is certain that his doctrine is coherent. In expressing his ideas, Nikolaos Politis remains true to his ideals and his wish to combine "le souci de la verité scientifique" (the concern for the scientific truth) and "l'idéal de la solidarité et de la cooperation internationale" (the ideal of international solidarity and cooperation). The two of them are, after all, "closely linked" in his own words.[30]

28 N. Politis, *Les nouvelles tendances du droit international,* supra note 3, 91–92.

29 Ibid.

30 Ibid., avant-propos.

CHAPTER 6

International Institutional Protection of Human Rights: Achievements and Failures

Christian Tomuschat

Can one say anything new about the international institutional protection of human rights? Hundreds of books and articles have been written about the mechanisms designed to translate into concrete realities primarily the normative substance of the multilateral conventions covering that area as well as the other relevant legal standards not anchored in treaty instruments. Obviously, all those studies have clarified the main structures of that specific universe and have highlighted their main advantages together with their most significant shortcomings. And yet, quite a number of issues remain to be analyzed and will re-emerge again and again. There exists such a dynamism in the field of human rights that many of the lessons an observer may have learned just ten years ago appear already outmoded today, not in keeping any longer with the prevailing empirical data. Moreover, many studies confine themselves to considering just one specific aspect, one institution, one procedure – while the principal interest nowadays lies in comparing different mechanisms with similar objectives. And finally, there is one essential aspect often overlooked: the human rights as they are enshrined above all in the two International Covenants of 1966[1] have extremely ambitious objectives. *Grosso modo*, they seek to install paradise on earth – which mankind has never succeeded in performing. However, in order to advance mankind must set for itself lofty goals. The problem is to find some kind of fair compromise between ambitious aspirations and hard facts that cannot be talked away.

1 Substantive Human Rights Guarantees

The substantive basket is overwhelmingly rich and colourful. Nobody here needs to be reminded of the wealth of entitlements set out for the benefit of

1 The Office of the UN High Commissioner for Human Rights indicates nine core international human rights instruments, starting with the International Convention on the Elimination of all Forms of Racial Discrimination (1965) and ending with the Convention on the Rights of Persons with Disabilities (2006).

 | DOI:10.1163/9789004435650_007

the human person already in the Universal Declaration of Human Rights of 1948 (UDHR).[2] That document established a perfect marriage between the classic rights that have mainly grown up in Western societies in conjunction with the rule of law, and the more recent economic and social rights that lack such proud ancestral roots. While civil and political rights ensure a number of minimum guarantees essentially intended to check governmental arbitrariness, economic and social rights hold out promises the fulfilment of which requires an active and productive State machinery – which is not present everywhere in every country. The UDHR was no more than a manifesto, setting forth objectives to be attained in the future, 'un ideal commun à atteindre',[3] and its utopian character reflects itself particularly in Article 28 which provides that

> everyone is entitled to a social and international order in which the rights and freedoms set forth in this Declaration can be fully realized.

Eighteen years later, the two Covenants of 1966[4] translated almost all of the wishes expressed in the UDHR into legally binding substance, having been preceded by the International Convention on the Elimination of All Forms of Racial Discrimination (7 March 1966).[5] Only one example needs to be given to illustrate how optimistic the drafters were. In Article 11(1) of the Social Covenant the States Parties commit themselves to ensuring the right of everyone to 'the continuous improvement of living conditions'. The commitment of the State is fine – but the individual right to fulfillment is of course subject to all the vagaries of life and history.[6] In particular, respect for the natural environment of humankind that can be threatened by the striving of human beings for material welfare was not yet a matter of concern at that time more than half a century ago. Every well-informed observer knows today that an unrestrained rush for development in the sense of increased production of goods and services must finally end up in disaster for mankind.

2 GA Resolution 217 A (III).

3 The English version, 'a common standard of achievement', is less meaningful.

4 International Covenant on Civil and Political Rights (ICCPR) and International Covenant on Economic, Social and Cultural Rights (ICESCR), both adopted on 16 December 1966.

5 This article can only focus on the legal position at world level.

6 This critical comment applies also to the 2030 Agenda for Sustainable Development, GA Resolution 70/1, 25 September 2015, confirmed by the Political Declaration of the High-Level Forum on Sustainable Development, GA Resolution 74/4, 15 October 2019. Among the 17 development goals enunciated in the 2030 Agenda is the 'Eradication of extreme poverty' by 2030 (SDG 1).

II Institutional Mechanisms

1 *General Considerations*

From the very outset after the founding of the United Nations it was clear, though, that not every one of those lofty aims could be transformed into hard substance overnight. Therefore, the drafters distinguished carefully between rights that were to be guaranteed immediately, without any buffer period (civil and political rights),[7] and rights whose enjoyment was to be achieved in a process over an adequate period of time (economic, social and cultural rights).[8] As far as the implementation and observance of civil and political rights at national level is concerned, they enjoined States Parties to grant an appropriate remedy to all persons alleging a violation of their rights[9] while abstaining from such an injunction with regard to economic, social and cultural rights. While it is true that the rights under the ICESCR do not all pertain to the same class of entitlements, some being in fact suitable for direct application, such as the right to education (Article 13), it appears wrong generally to deny the difference in structure as consistently maintained by the Committee on Economic, Social and Cultural Rights, whose aim it is to equate the two categories of rights with one another.[10]

As far as the guarantee of the established rights at the international level is concerned, originally the great obstacle was Article 2(7) of the Charter which forbids the World Organization to intervene in matters 'which are essentially within the domestic jurisdiction of any state'. For a long time, this provision stood in the way of the UN institutions establishing themselves protective mechanisms without any specific authorization under the Charter. Yet it was absolutely contradictory to apply Article 2(7) to human rights since the Charter itself had included human rights within its programme of action. The international community, acting through the World Organization, was meant to be the guardian of the rights of the individual human person.[11] For that purpose, adequate procedures were required.

---

7 ICCPR, Article 2(2).

8 ICESCR, Article 2(1).

9 ICCPR, Article 2(3).

10 See General comment No. 9: the domestic application of the Covenant, E/C.12/1998/24, 3 December 1998.

11 This is now generally recognized. No government contends any longer that dealing with domestic implementation of human rights is not permitted for the UN.

2 *Monitoring by the Political Organs of the United Nations—the Early Period*

However, monitoring through the political bodies of the UN was slow and hesitant. The Commission on Human Rights, established in accordance with Article 68 of the Charter, originally did not have the courage of acting as the herald of human rights for the entire world. Obviously, it was a majority of the States members of the Commission that impeded any meaningful action. Concerns voiced about the human rights situation in a given country were originally processed only with regard to Israel and South Africa. Any complaint raised with regard to other countries was dismissed as lying outside the jurisdiction of the World Organization, and the petitioners were informed that the UN was unable to provide any remedy.[12] It was the military putsch in Chile of 1973 which eventually led to a breakthrough.[13] The atrocities committed by the new governmental junta under General Pinochet were so horrendous that the UN could not remain silent. A group of experts was established by the Human Rights Commission with the mandate to look into the situation.[14] For the first time, unanimity could be reached since the Socialist States, whose close ally President Allende had been, were eager to take revenge for the violent overthrow of the Chilean government. In the following years, with some hesitations and inconsistently, the new practice of investigating 'consistent patterns of gross and reliably attested violations of human rights'[15] consolidated itself. Yet many elements of contingency remained. The principal challenge was the choice of a country against which such massive allegations had been brought. Cuba had been placed on the list of States under observation in 1992[16] but succeeded after a couple of years to be removed from that list.[17] Still today, States are trying hard not to be mentioned as one of those countries submitted to close observation by UN bodies. The current practice is to establish commissions of inquiry, fact-finding missions or other investigative bodies to probe into extended patterns of non-respect for basic human rights, which may be placed under the authority of the Security Council, the General Assembly or

12 ECOSOC Resolution 75 (V) 1947.

13 For a detailed account of that development see Christian Tomuschat, *Human Rights – Between Idealism and Realism* (3rd. edn., OUP 2014) 186–191.

14 Human Rights Commission Resolution 8 (XXXI), 27 February 1975.

15 The formula was coined by ECOSOC Resolution. 1503 (XLVIII), 27 May 1970.

16 Human Rights Commission Resolution. 1992/61, 3 March 1992; GA Resolution. 47/139, 18 December 1992.

17 The last resolution criticizing Cuba for its practice of human rights was adopted by the General Assembly in 1997, Resolution 52/143.

the Human Rights Council. Currently (November 2019), seven such mandates exist for Venezuela, Myanmar, Yemen, Burundi, Syria, South Sudan and the Kasaï region in the Democratic Republic of the Congo.[18] The advantage of fact-finding missions is that they come into direct contact with the facts on the ground and may thus obtain a picture that is much closer to realities than by pursuing a dialogue with the representatives of the country concerned in the meeting rooms in Geneva or New York.

It is amazing to note, in particular, to what extent since a couple of years the Security Council takes care to pronounce itself about the essential requirements of a well-ordered polity, including the appropriateness of governmental institutions and the protection of human rights. The former inhibitions to deal with human rights issues have totally disappeared. The Security Council sees it as its legitimate task to interfere in all sectors of public life that directly affect the population, thus overseeing the whole breadth of governmental activities.[19] To date, it confines itself mostly to issuing recommendations in response to acknowledged human rights violations, shying away from resorting to Chapter VII of the Charter.

3 *The Expert Bodies within the Framework of the Core Human Rights Treaties*

After the entry into force of the International Convention on the Elimination of All Form of Racial Discrimination (ICERD) in 1969 and the two International Covenants on Human Rights in 1977 a more orderly procedure came into being. All States parties were placed under an obligation to submit, at regular intervals, reports about the way in which they implemented the obligations they had assumed. Yet it was obvious that the reporting procedure could apply only to those States that had committed themselves by ratification, and many States refused to accept the vast array of obligations laid down in those three instruments. China is the most prominent State of those that have remained aloof from the ICCPR, and many conservative Arab States still keep deliberately away from that instrument,[20] while the United States consistently refuses to join the International Covenant on Economic, Social and Cultural Rights. Obviously, where a monitoring mechanism is based on a conventional instrument it can be easily avoided just by remaining passive. On the other hand, where any of the human rights treaties provides for individual communications such

18 https://www.ohchr.org/EN/HRBodies/HRC/IIMM/Pages/Index.aspx.

19 A particularly illustrative example is provided by SC Resolution 2458 (2019), 28 February 2019, on Guinea Bissau.

20 Oman, Saudi Arabia, United Arab Emirates.

additional remedy must be specifically accepted,[21] and the number of States parties is generally much lower than the number of States parties to the main substantive instrument.[22] Moreover, the number of applications sent to the expert body concerned remains generally fairly low, probably because people realize that the outcome of such proceedings amounts to no more than a simple recommendation which the State concerned may simply reject or even ignore completely,[23] although all the expert bodies have attempted their best to establish follow-up procedures.[24] Lastly, visits on the spot constitute a rare exception.[25]

One of the great achievements of the treaty bodies is the practice of General comments, a legal instrument that originally was not provided for in the text of the ICCPR and the ICESCR. While during its first years of activity the Human Rights Committee was unable to conclude its examination of State reports by hard substantial conclusions, progressively the sentiment emerged that something had to be done to bring to fruition the general experiences gained in examining those reports. Taking advantage of the phrase in Article 40(3) ICCPR that after the study of such reports it is to send 'general comments' to the States parties, the Committee decided that it would indeed condense the lessons learned in the form of such 'General comments'.[26] First of all, advice was imparted to States parties on how to draft the reports due to be submitted.

21 Optional Protocol to the ICCPR, 16 December 1966, currently 116 States parties; Optional Protocol to the ICESCR, 10 December 2008, currently 24 States parties.

22 Thus, the Optional Protocol to the ICESCR, 10 December 2008, counts currently only 24 States parties whereas the ICSCR has been accepted by 170 States. Regarding the ICERD, the number of States parties to the individual communication procedure under Article 14 remains as low as 58, compared to 182 States parties.

23 The Human Rights Committee has been seized by 3,624 communications in the course of 42 years (Report of the Human Rights Committee, GAOR A/74/40, p. 4, para. 25), while the Committee on Economic, Social and Cultural Rights has received 63 communications since the Optional Protocol came into force on 5 May 2013, (2018) Report of the Committee on Economic, Social and Cultural Rights, E/2019/22, p. 14, para. 76.

24 See, e.g., for the Human Rights Committee the latest Follow-up report on individual communications, CCPR/C/122/R.2, 29 May 2018.

25 The Convention against Torture and Other Criminal, Inhuman or Degrading treatment or Punishment provides for country visits in agreement with the government concerned (Article 20(3)). Many States, however, have rejected even this potential competence of the Committee against Torture from the very outset (Bahamas, China, Equatorial Guinea, Eritrea, Fiji, Israel, Laos, Pakistan, Poland, Samoa, Saudi Arabia, Syria, United Arab Emirates, Viet Nam), as permitted by Article 28. The later Optional Protocol to the Convention against Torture, 18 December 2002, has meanwhile attracted 90 ratifications.

26 Decision of 24 March 1992, *Official Records of the Human Rights Committee 1991/92*, Vol. II, 275, para. 45.

Thereafter, the main subject of 'general comments' were general explanations on the implementation of the rights under the ICCPR and, last not least, on the scope and meaning of the relevant individual guarantees. One of the most famous ones of the 'general comments' dealt with nuclear weapons and the right to life,[27] which was highly controversial in political terms. To date, the Human Rights Committee has adopted 36 General comments, which now encompass at least the most important civil and political rights. The Committee on Economic, Social and Cultural Rights has adopted 24 of such comments. Lastly, the 35 General recommendations of the CERD Committee deserve close attention. In departure from their original purpose, the General comments of the Human Rights Committee are not based any longer only on experiences gained with the consideration of State reports but refer additionally to its jurisprudence – and other international materials – in dealing with individual communications.[28]

The general comments are taken into account anywhere in the world where institutions are tasked with ensuring respect for and observance of human rights. In particular, the general comments defining the specific substance of a given right are regularly canvassed by regional human rights bodies. In their jurisprudence, they rely on the comments by the Human Rights Committee as guidelines for the interpretation of the same or similar rights so that a truly universal groundwork of interpretive articulations of human rights is steadily growing. Unfortunately, the Human Rights Committee has to some extent undermined its recognition as an independent and neutral institution by overruling the European Court of Human Rights regarding the wearing of the face-hiding *niqab* according to some Muslim traditions. A French Law that had been declared being in harmony with the ECHR[29] was denounced by it as contrary to the ICCPR.[30]

III Universal Periodic Review

This disparity within the international community was one of the grounds why in 2006, more than half a century after the adoption of the UDHR, the Universal

27 General comment No. 14 (1984). It has recently been replaced by General comment No. 36 on the right to life, CCPR/C/GC/36, 3 September 2019.

28 General comment No. 36 with its 272 footnotes is particularly instructive in this regard.

29 ECtHR, *S.A.S. v. France*, Application No. 43835/11, 1 July 2014. Later, the ECtHR also rejected applications against a similar prohibition enacted in Belgium: *Dakir v. Belgium*, Application No. 4619/12, 11 July 2017; *Belkacem and Oussar v. Belgium*, Application No. 37798/13, 11 July 2017.

30 *Sonya Yaker v. France*, Communication No. 2747/2016, 17 July 2018.

Periodic Review (UPR) was established.[31] UPR is discharged by the Human Rights Council but every UN member is entitled to take part in the proceedings. UPR has no conventional foundation. It was launched by a resolution of the General Assembly[32] and therefore lacks any binding effect. Nonetheless, all States members of the UN have voluntarily accepted to be examined as to their performance with regard to human rights, the yardstick being not only the treaties a State has accepted but also the UDHR – which amounts to a tremendous upgrading of this instrument.[33] A four year cycle was originally established, which permitted indeed to cover all UN member States within that time span; after a while, the cycle was extended to a period of four-and- half years. Thus, general accountability according to perfect equality was introduced. No State remains exempt from the critical eyes of its peers, and the permanent members of the Security Council enjoy no privilege whatsoever. Assessment of a country's performance in open meetings on the basis of reports has become the standard procedure. An individual complaint procedure continues to exist alongside that standard procedure[34] but it plays only a marginal role at world level.

When comparing in particular the scrutiny by the treaty-based treaties and UPR a first observation comes up immediately: the method applied in both instances consists of nothing else than dialogue, of which it is hoped that it will be constructive. No measures of constraint are provided for. Both procedures end up with acts that lack any bindingness. The hope is that arguments will be heard, that good reason prevails and that, having listened to well-reasoned criticism, a State will desist from its objectionable conduct. It is true that at the very last the Security Council may determine to resort to measures under Chapter VII of the Charter.[35] But this is highly improbable, and it has happened only once, in the Libya situation, since UPR was introduced.[36] Thus, it is indeed the exchange of views or, to put it in a more drastic way, the battle of words that constitutes the main tool relied upon to enforce the splendour of

31 For an overview of the UPR see, in particular, Hilary Charlesworth and Emma Larking (eds.), *Human Rights and the Universal Periodic Review: Rituals and Ritualism* (CUP 2015); Christian Tomuschat, 'Universal Periodic Review: a New System of International Law with Specific Ground Rules?', in Ulrich Fastenrath *et al.* (eds.), *From Bilateralism to Community Interest. Essays in Honour of Judge Bruno Simma* (OUP 2011) 609–628.

32 GA Resolution 60/251, 15 March 2006.

33 HRC Resolution 5/1, 18 June 2007, Annex, para. 1.

34 HRC Resolution 5/1, 18 June 2007, Section IV.

35 By its resolution 60/1, World Summit Outcome, 16 September 2005, para. 139, the GA has explicitly legitimated the Security Council to resort to Chapter VII measures in case a country does not act in accordance with its responsibility to protect.

36 SC Resolution 1973 (2011), 17 March 2011.

the human rights enshrined in the instruments elaborated under the auspices of the UN.

Apart from this common feature, many other features could hardly be more different.

In the first place, the UPR finds itself at a great advantage vis-à-vis the review process in the hands of the treaty bodies. Each one of the treaty bodies has a limited scope of inquiry, according to the scope of the treaty concerned. Although civil and political rights have a wide field of application, and the same is true, even to a greater extent, of economic, social and cultural rights, it remains that the Human Rights Committee is mandated only to look into civil and political rights, and, mutatis mutandis, the same is true of the Economic and Social Committee and the other expert bodies under the nine core instruments. In the UPR, the unity of human rights is maintained. China, which has many shortcomings in respect of civil and political rights, can boast its achievements regarding economic and social rights and may – rightly – receive praise for this positive record[37] which has no relevance in dealings with the Human Rights Committee. Thus, in the UPR the balance sheet may become better equilibrated.

The treaty-based bodies are committees composed of experts, persons who act according to their conscience, not bound by any instructions. This is their advantage but also their weakness. Their legitimacy derives from their nomination by governments and additionally from their election by the respective conferences of States parties. But, on the whole, they remain nothing else than experts riveted to the principles of truth and objectivity, not supposed to follow the political mainstream. By contrast, in UPR a State encounters its peers, a political reality that brings with it the entire spectrum of tensions, of friendship and enmity. The States parties intervening in UPR are a more powerful interlocutor than any high-qualified expert body. They are able to exert pressure through denouncing any shortcomings and violations – which an expert body is unable to do in a direct fashion although its findings will generally be taken into account by governments and may thus eventually entail far-reaching consequences.

37 In proceedings under the UPR, many countries emphasize the achievements of the Chinese government with regards to economic and social rights. Curiously enough, the report on the review of China, A/HRC/40/6, 26 December 2018, which took place on 6 November 2018, does not reproduce that positive acknowledgment by other States, confining itself to reproducing the self-praise by China, apparently due to lack of space because of the large number of recommendations addressed to China which the report also had to indicate.

Another significant difference is inherent in the modality of examination. Before the expert bodies the State under consideration stands alone. It may look like a defendant before its judges, notwithstanding all the good words about a 'constructive dialogue' being conducted. This is a bilateral relationship where the State concerned must try to maintain itself with its own intellectual capacities, without the support of its friends and allies. In the UPR, the situation is totally different, the exercise taking place in the presence of all the other States, under the eyes of the international community. Every State is at the same time prosecutor and defendant, everyone knows that a question it raises may soon be turned against it. Support may be provided by friends and allies through specific questioning by highlighting the achievements reached by the State under consideration. Thus, the UPR inevitably turns into a discourse on human rights within the entire international community, not limited to the exchange of views between the intervening States and the State under review.

In both procedures, one can observe a certain amount of reticence vis-à-vis NGOs.[38] Thus, the Human Rights Committee does not allow NGOs to intervene when State reports are being examined; the NGOs are confined to providing individual members with information material. Within UPR, the UN Secretariat is mandated to condense the submissions collected from NGOs in a document of no more than 10 pages which is destined for general circulation.[39] During the 3 and a half hours of the oral exchange of views they are excluded, being granted an opportunity to express themselves orally during half an hour before the definitive adoption of the report[40] – which makes no real sense. It goes without saying, however, that NGOs enjoy unlimited freedom to establish contacts with governmental delegations as they see fit.

The duration of the review displays tremendous differences. Before the treaty bodies, the examination of a report may take a whole day. It does not last forever, but the minutes are not counted. The experts can express their views in appropriate detail. Questions can be put, and answers are expected. In the UPR, the allocated time is limited to 3 and a half hours, 210 minutes. Where interest is great in participating in the exercise – when China was questioned on

38 See Natalie Baird, 'The Role of International Non-Governmental Organizations in the UPR of Pacific Island States' (2015) 16/2 *Melbourne Journal of International Law* 550–587; Mie Roesdahl, 'Universal Periodic Review and its Limited Change Potential: Tracking the Complexity of Multiple Actors and Approaches to Human Rights Change' (2017) 9 *Journal of Human Rights Practice* 401–423.

39 HRC Resolution 5/1, 18 June 2007, Annex, para. 15(c).

40 HRC Resolution 5/1, Annex, 18 June 2007, para. 31.

6 November 2018 no less than 150 delegations intervened[41] – the time available may be reduced to less than two minutes. This does not seem to make good sense. Critical authors have spoken of a purely formal ritual.[42] But the time constraints compel delegations to focus on the State under review, on the essentials, without entering into political rhetoric. And if numerous States highlight the same issues, it becomes clear where the real problems of the country concerned lie. On the other hand, no genuine dialogue takes place. In most instances the State under review, which has in any event the last word, reserves its position, preferring instead to respond at a later date in writing. And when a State declares that a specific proposal 'has its support', little is achieved.[43] Essentially, the UPR resembles to little more than a huge brainstorming process.

Lastly, the final outcome differs enormously. The concluding observations of the treaty bodies encompass an accurate diagnosis of the country concerned. All the former hesitations have disappeared. For many years the Human Rights Committee had not dared to bring its examination of a country report to a definite conclusion by pronouncing itself on the deficits found or the progress noted in promoting the human rights under the instrument concerned. Two major obstacles stood in the way of such an assessment. On the one hand, Article 40(3) ICCPR is formulated in the most unfortunate way by stating that after the examination of a report the Human Rights Committee is to 'transmit its reports, and such general comments as it may consider appropriate' to the States parties. Did that proviso permit or prohibit a general assessment? The second obstacle was the resistance of the Committee members from the socialist States. They argued that looking into the practice of human rights within the domestic legal order amounted to forbidden intervention in internal matters. Only after the demise of socialism as a general doctrine for

41 A/HRC//40/6, 11 July 2018. A few months earlier, the review of Cuba had motivated 143 delegations to take the floor, A/HRC/39/16, 11 July 2018. The procedure depends on the interest shown by the members of the UN to engage themselves which cannot be taken for granted. Thus, e.g., in the review of Grenada on 26 January 2015 only 44 delegations took the floor, A/HRC/29/14, 9 April 2015.

42 Walter Kälin, 'Ritual and ritualism at the Universal Periodic Review: a preliminary appraisal' in Hilary Charlesworth and Emma Larking (eds.), *Human Rights and the Universal Periodic Review: Rituals and Ritualism* (CUP 2015) 25–41; J.K. Cowan, 'The UPR as a public audit tribunal', *ibid.*, 42–62.

43 Thus, Eritrea submitted its response to the recommendations made to it during its review on 28 January 2019 in a note where it declared without any additional comment that 131 of all the 261 recommendations had its support while the remainder of 130 recommendations were simply 'noted'. Not much can be expected of such a statement that was issued without any careful consideration: Report of the Working Group on the UPR, Addendum, A/HRC/41/14/Add.1, 20 June 2019.

international relations could this obstacle be removed. For the first time on the occasion of the consideration of the Algerian report did the Human Rights Committee decide to express itself without any restrictions on the evidence it had found to exist. This practice has subsequently been adopted by all other treaty bodies.

This was a great step forward, which prevented the procedure of examining country reports from sinking into meaningless routine. The language is now generally clear and without any diplomatic mollification. The assessment of the treaty bodies may be trusted – except in very rare instances where a treaty body confounds its role with that of an activist NGO.[44] In the UPR, on the other hand, there is no collective assessment. As already pointed out, it is the State under review that has the last word – but it is expected that it will take a stance on each and every one of the recommendations that have been made to it.[45]

Monitoring of compliance with the recommendations expressed and the promises made has generally been established. What was said should not be forgotten immediately. All the bodies concerned come back to the previous sessions of review. But repetitive exhortations do not increase in strength.

IV Conclusion

What is the power of words – this is the key question. It has already been pointed out that through the soft procedures of the human rights institutions no State can be compelled to abandon positions of principle that mark its identity. Thus, it seems really useless to remind China that it should ratify the International Covenant on Civil and Political Rights, the core instrument that forbids any kind of political discrimination. Yet in the UPR that recommendation is reiterated time and again – certainly a senseless ritual.[46] Nor will a truly

44 An example of that kind is provided by the opinion of the CERD Committee in the case of *TBB – Turkish Union in Berlin / Brandenburg v. Germany*, Communication No. 48/2010, 26 February 2013, with dissenting opinion Carlos Emanuel Vázquez, and the comment by the present author, 'Der „Fall Sarrazin“ vor dem UN-Rassendiskriminierungsausschuss', (2013) 40 *Europäische Grundrechte-Zeitschrift* 262–265.

45 For an example of a State that examined the recommendations addressed to it one by one see Viet Nam, Report of the Working Group on the UPR, Addendum, A/HRC/41/7/Add.1, 26 June 2019.

46 Yet, when the latest review of China's performance in the field of human rights took place, a recommendation to ratify the ICCPR was made no less than 26 times, Report of the Working Group, A/HRC/40/6, 9 November 2018.

authoritarian regime, disrespectful of human rights, be brought back to the rule of law by such vocal criticism alone.

However, the positive aspects of the UN processes should not be overlooked. The treaty bodies have brought light into many issues that had not even been noticed beforehand. Most States are prepared to remedy inconsistencies that have no great importance for their political positions of principle, and which are mainly attributable to negligence and administrative oversight. Many injustices have been repaired in that way. On the other hand, many States are prepared to listen and to proceed to change if practices are denounced that have their roots in traditions inherited from a past where discrimination was regarded as an element of normal life. Thus, some States have become aware of the unbearable situations in their prisons, and many governments have realized that the practice of FGM amounts to a fundamental violation of female dignity which only archaic groups of the population oppose. Then, all of a sudden, a problem originally attributed to the State machinery becomes a problem of society. As we know, no institutions exist that are tasked with altering the fundamental characteristics of societies. Our only hope and trust is that eventually freedom of opinion and expression, coupled with a deep sense of common humanity, will prevail inside any human community.

CHAPTER 7

The Promise of International Criminal Justice: Achievements and Failures in Protecting Human Dignity

Micaela Frulli

1 A Few Preliminary Remarks

Nothing like international criminal justice is loaded with so much hope and high expectations and nothing like it is in constant danger of dashing them.[1] When I started to plunge into this field of studies, about 25 years ago, I also had my personal and very idealistic expectations about the potential role of international criminal justice to deal with the consequences of mass atrocities, undoubtedly powered by the crucial moment coinciding with the first steps of the two *ad hoc* international criminal tribunals created by the UN Security Council: the International Criminal Tribunal for the former Yugoslavia (ICTY) and the International Criminal Tribunal for Rwanda (ICTR). After many years, while trying to carry out an assessment of achievements and failures of international criminal justice in ensuring respect for human dignity, I realized that I had to come to terms with these expectations. These short personal notes are due to the fact that I have found in legal literature heavy traces of similar attempts at constantly reshaping expectations about international criminal justice. On the one hand, one finds the advocates of international criminal justice depicting it as an epic struggle against evil, but still having to confront the paucity of recent results. At the other end of the spectrum are the sceptical voices who see international criminal justice just as a tool for prosecuting individuals for serious violations of international law and constantly curb its role, even when addressing the most relevant accomplishments. Expressing a balanced appraisal and finding a middle ground is not indeed an easy task.[2] More

1 See the very interesting reflections of Frédéric Mégret in 'International Justice as a Peace Project' (2018) 29 *EJIL* 835–858.

2 It is impossible to give account of the variety of scholarly positions at both ends of the spectrum and of the many that are placed in-between. For a couple of interesting reflections on the topic, see again Frédéric Mégret, 'The Anxieties of International Criminal Justice' (2016) 29 *LJIL* 197–221 and less recently Mirjan Damaška, 'What Is the Point of International Criminal Justice?' (2008) 83 *Chicago Kent Law Review* 329. For a comprehensive

 | DOI:10.1163/9789004435650_008

humbly, I will focus on one momentous achievement and one patent failure of international criminal justice, which also assume an exemplary value regarding the protection of human dignity, being conscious that brevity carries with it a certain amount of over-simplification of very complex issues. Of course, both the fulfilled promise and the broken promise of international criminal justice ought to be read in light and shades.

2 The Fulfilled Promise: the Development of Substantive Law to Enhance the Protection of Human Dignity

2.1 *The First Stage (1945–1993): Setting the Normative Process for the Protection of Human Dignity*

After the birth of international criminal justice and the delivery of the judgments of the Nuremberg and Tokyo Tribunals,[3] the international community was full of hopes about the subsequent developments of the law.[4] The promise of international criminal justice was at its peak and the awareness and attention of States and of the public opinion were extremely high, although States already held very different views on the way forward[5] and eminent scholars uttered very sharp critical opinions.[6]

overview, see Christine Schwöbel (ed) *Critical Approaches to International Criminal Law* (Routledge 2014).

3 Robert B. Walkinshaw, 'The Nuremberg and Tokyo Trials: Another Step Toward International Justice', (1949) 35 *American Bar Association Journal*, 299; Guénaël Mettraux (ed). *Perspectives on the Nuremberg Trial* (OUP 2008) Neil Boister; Robert Cryer, *The Tokyo International Military Tribunal: A Reappraisal* (OUP 2008).

4 UN doc. A/CN.4/5, *The Charter and Judgment of the Nürnberg Tribunal – History and Analysis: Memorandum submitted by the Secretary-General, Part II e Part III*, available at https://digitallibrary.un.org/record/160809/files/A_CN.4_5-EN.pdf (February 2020).

5 The early attempts of codification of international crimes carried out within the United Nations disclosed a strong friction between the advocates of codification governed exclusively by States - as for other traditional areas of international law – and those supporting the idea of taking into account the jurisprudence of the Nuremberg and Tokyo Tribunal for the codification of international crimes. Both paths were eventually followed, but the tension between the two approaches had a durable impact on the development of substantive law. On the codification of international criminal law within the UN see Micaela Frulli, 'Le Nazioni Unite e la codificazione del diritto internazionale penale', in Alessandra Annoni, Serena Forlati, Francesco Salerno (eds.), *La codificazione nell'ordinamento internazionale e dell'Unione europea* (Editoriale Scientifica, 2019) 111–141.

6 See the critical views of Hans Kelsen 'Will the Judgment in the Nuremberg Trial Constitute a Precedent in International Law?'(1947) 1 *ICLQ* 164: "That the London Agreement is only the expression, not the creation, of this new law, is the typical fiction of the problematical doctrine purpose is to veil the arbitrary character of the acts of a sovereign law-maker"

In the age of youth of international criminal justice, the greatest outcome in terms of development of substantive rules was quite obviously the legal definition of genocide, eventually included in the 1948 UN Convention on the prevention and repression of the crime of genocide. This was the one objective that could not be missed from a political point of view.[7] After the shock of the Holocaust, there had to be a strong reaction and it should entail the definition of the crime of genocide only partially described in the Nuremberg judgment.[8] The Convention provided a legal definition of the 'crime of crimes' and became a symbol that embodied the will of States to prevent future mass atrocities.[9] However, the rush to conclude the negotiations brought States to sacrifice at least two of the features that could have made the treaty effective: universality of jurisdiction and the creation of an international criminal tribunal.[10] Universality was dropped in favor of territoriality and the task to draft a project for the

... and also "The judgment of Nuremberg, even if it complied with all the formal requirements of a true precedent, will hardly be considered as worthy to be followed. For there are some serious objections against the appropriateness of the adjective as well as the substantive law applied by it". (...) "And even more objectionable than the fact that the London Agreement has the character of a *privilegium odiosum* imposed upon vanquished States by the victors is that the tribunal established by the Agreement was composed exclusively of representatives of victorious States directly affected by the crimes over which this tribunal had jurisdiction. Not only representatives of the vanquished States, but also-what is more important- representatives of neutral States were excluded from the bench." at 170.

7 "Genocide is a denial of the right of existence of entire human groups, as homicide is the denial of the right to live of individual human beings; such denial of the right of existence shocks the conscience of mankind, results in great losses to humanity in the form of cultural and other contributions represented by these human groups, and is contrary to moral law and to the spirit and aims of the United Nations. Many instances of such crimes of genocide have occurred when racial, religious, political, and other groups have been destroyed, entirely or in part. The punishment of the crime of genocide is a matter of international concern", A/RES/1/96, 11 December 1946, Preamble.

8 For an overview of the impact of the Nuremberg Tribunal and its jurisprudence on the development of international criminal law Guénaël Mettruax (ed.), *Perspectives on the Nuremberg Trial* (OUP 2008).

9 For a comprehensive account of the preparatory works of the Genocide Convention see Hirad Abtahi, Philippa Webb, *The Genocide Convention. The Travaux Préparatoires* (Nijhoff 2008). See also William Schabas, *Genocide in International Law. The Crime of Crime* (2nd ed. CUP 2009) 14–51.

10 Although very critical statements were made by some delegates: 'The representative of France regarded the creation of such a court as the essential purpose of the Convention on genocide, since, for the reasons already given, it was impossible to leave to each individual State the responsibility for punishing acts of genocide committed in its own territory. The Convention would be a mere accumulation of entirely ineffective formulas, if such a court were not established within a reasonable period'. (Charles Chaumont, France, General Assembly, VI Committee, UN doc. A/C.6/SR.95).

future creation of an international criminal tribunal was entrusted to the newborn International Law Commission (ILC), but separately from the task of codifying the crimes against pace and security of mankind. Actually, the very early stages of the debate on these issues revealed a major divide between two lines of thought. On one side, there were States and scholars who believed that there was not yet much to codify.[11] According to them, the major task ahead was to elaborate new rules in this field with the greatest caution; in short, they were already satisfied with the adoption of the Genocide Convention. There was no reason to stress the importance of Nuremberg case-law because States were to be the masters of this law-making process. On the other side, there were States and scholars who considered the jurisprudence of the Nuremberg and Tokyo tribunals as an indispensable starting point and that it should play a crucial role in developing the law and in building a system of international criminal justice.[12] The tension between these two approaches generated a cleavage in the codification of primary and secondary rules that partially stalled the development of the law and also precluded the building of an international criminal justice system for 45 years.[13]

11 See for instance the debate going on in ECOSOC sub-committees, UN doc. E/AC.7/W.14, *Summary Record of the Drafting Sub-Committee of the Social Committee*, 24 March 1947. See also the account of the negotiations of the early stages of the genocide convention codification process in William Schabas, *Genocide in International Law. The Crime of Crimes* (2nd ed. CUP 2009) spec. 14–51.

12 Eventually no reference to the Nuremberg case law was inserted in the final text, see Yuval Shany, 'The Road to the Genocide Convention and beyond', in Paola Gaeta (ed), *The UN Genocide Convention. A Commentary* (OUP 2009) 9–10.

13 It is very interesting to read the sceptical remarks of Brierly during the meetings of the *International Law Commission*: 'If an international court were established but could not function, it would be not only ineffectual, but it would also create dangerous illusions among the nations', *ILC 42nd meeting*, 8 June 1950, *Yearbook of the International Law Commission*, 1950, vol. I, 16. And also with foretelling words he stressed that it seemed: 'impossible to draft a convention under which all States would undertake to bring their nationals accused of crimes before an international tribunal. Even if they did undertake to do so, it was extremely probable that when the time came they would not honour their signatures. And after all, crimes against humanity were committed by individuals not of their own accord, but with the acquiescence of their governments. How then could it be hoped that those governments would agree to the accused persons being summoned before an international tribunal? Would the establishment of such an organ in 1930 have prevented the crimes of genocide perpetrated by Germany? An international criminal court would not be required to judge cases covered by national laws since if a government disapproved of the criminal activities of one of its nationals, it could summon him before a national tribunal. On the other hand, if it approved of his activities, it would not bring him before an international court. To prosecute a criminal without the co-operation of his government, an international court would have to have at its disposal,

Once the objective of concluding a Convention on Genocide was reached, the protection of human dignity through international criminal justice faded in the background. Nonetheless, the normative processes occurred in this long phase were also pursuing the objective to enhance the safeguard of human dignity – especially in the field of international humanitarian law and more specifically the development of provisions on war crimes[14] – and were decisive to allow the international criminal tribunals created at a later stage to concretely develop and apply the law and to foster accountability for mass atrocities.

2.2 *The Years of Maturity: Developing and Applying the Law to Enhance the Protection of Human Dignity*

It took the establishment of the two *ad hoc* international criminal tribunals in the 1990s to revitalize the promise of international criminal justice and to trigger new developments of substantive law, once again brought by virtue of jurisprudence, as it occurred with the case-law of Nuremberg and Tokyo. The role of the *ad hoc* tribunals in developing substantive law, and in particular the definition of the elements of the so-called core crimes, was unprecedented.[15]

---

in the international sphere, a full-scale police organization comparable to that possessed by States on the national scale for the prevention of crimes. It was impossible to reconcile all those factors', *ibidem* 17.

14 On the 1949 Geneva Conventions see Andrew Clapham, Paola Gaeta, Marco Sassòli, *The 1949 Geneva Conventions: A Commentary* (OUP 2015). On the 1949 Conventions, the 1977 Additional Protocols and other IHL treaties see the International Committee of the Red Cross (ICRC) commentaries available on the website at https://www.icrc.org/en/war-and-law/treaties-customary-law/geneva-conventions (visited 10 February 2020).

15 A lot has been written, also in very critical terms, on judicial creativity of the judges of the ICTY and ICTR and on its merits and pitfalls. The debate often grew around the questions of where and how to draw the line between evolutive interpretation and the creation of new rules by the judges and consequently on the amount of judicial creativity to be considered acceptable for international criminal law to be consistent with the principle of legality. A complete bibliography on this topic cannot fit the size of a footnote and it is beyond the scope of this article, see for a general overview of the issues Shane Darcy; Joseph Powderly (eds), *Judicial Creativity at the International Criminal Tribunals* (OUP 2010). Without entering into this debate, it is difficult to deny that the developments brought about by the ICTs' jurisprudence to the definition of the crimes is to be considered the major outcome of international criminal justice in this second period. From the qualification of serious violations of IHL as war crimes in internal conflicts with all the consequences it entailed, to the delineation of the untested elements of the crime of genocide to be applied to concrete cases, to the definition of the contextual/threshold element of crimes against humanity identified as: 'widespread or systematic attack directed against any civilian population'.

One of the most relevant examples of the contribution of the ICTs' case law to the development of substantive law and to its concrete application stands in the definition of rape and other sexual offences as war crimes, crimes against humanity and acts of genocide. These developments marked an enormous progress for the protection of human dignity, mainly but not exclusively that of women and children, by far the most vulnerable and targeted categories. Without the focus of international criminal justice on sexual violence in armed conflict and in other situations of widespread violence, rape and other sexual offences, although prohibited by several international humanitarian law conventions and human rights treaties, would most likely still be seen as a by-product of war or as inevitable consequences of situations of unrest.

The impact of the ICTY[16] and ICTR case law on the definition of sexual and gender-based crimes was enormous.[17] Their jurisprudence has been a point of reference for other internationalized criminal tribunals, such as the Special Court for Sierra Leone, which had to confront the specific practice of exploiting 'bush wives' and the crime of forced marriage,[18] and eventually a lot of their findings paved the way for the inclusion of several sexual and gender-based crimes in the Statute of the International criminal court (ICC). The Statute includes crimes such as rape, sexual slavery, enforced prostitution, forced pregnancy, enforced sterilization, and other forms of sexual violence. It also established that persecution on the basis of gender may be labelled as a crime against humanity.[19]

16 Serge Brammertz, Michelle Jarvis (eds), *Prosecuting Conflict-Related Sexual Violence at the ICTY* (OUP 2016).

17 The *ad hoc* tribunals identified a wide range of sexual and gendered conducts as outrages upon personal dignity, for instance forced nudity (including forced public nudity), threats of sexual mutilation, rape, sexual violence, sexual exploitation (including the sale of victims to others as sexual slaves) and the constant fear of being subjected to sexual violence. Although the legal literature on sexual and gender-based crimes before international criminal tribunals is very extensive, references here are limited to a few recent works: Valerie Oosterveld, 'The Legacy of the ICTY and ICTR on Sexual and Gender-Based Violence', in Milena Sterio, Michael Scharf (eds) *The Legacy of Ad Hoc Tribunals in International Criminal Law* (CUP 2019) 197–220; Claire Bradford Di Caro, 'Call it what it is: Genocide Through Male Rape and Sexual Violence in The Former Yugoslavia and Rwanda', in (2019) 30 *Duke Journal of Comparative & International Law*, 57.

18 See Micaela Frulli, 'Advancing International Criminal Law: The Special Court for Sierra Leone Recognizes Forced Marriage as a "New" Crime against Humanity', (2008) 6 JICJ 1033; Michael P. Scharf, 'Forced Marriage as a Separate Crime against Humanity', in Charles C.Jalloh (ed.) *The Special Court for Sierra Leone and its Legacy* (CUP 2014) 193.

19 There is a very extensive literature on the topic is very extensive. Just a few selected references: Kelly D.Askin, 'Prosecuting Wartime Rape and Other Gender-Related Crimes

Of great significance in terms of improving the safeguard of human dignity are the side effects of the development of substantive law in this area: the elaboration of policies and procedures on investigation of sexual and gender-related crimes, the progressive inclusion of highly experienced investigators with expertise in gender-based violence and human rights violations, and the prioritization of the prosecution of these crimes. It took some time for these side effects to occur[20] – it is hard to overturn decades of inaction and to cope with the lack of expertise in this field – and the turning point was the *OTP Policy Paper on Sexual and Gender-Based Crimes* released in 2014.[21] It is worth mentioning also the *OTP Policy on children* of 2016 where it is stated that 'children may be impacted differently by crimes based on their sex, gender, or other status or identities'[22] and that they are 'particularly vulnerable to sexually violent crimes'[23] and 'may also be persecuted on intersecting grounds, such as ethnicity, religion and gender'.[24] Moreover, the OTP referenced Article 54 of the Rome Statute, which requires that the Prosecutor, in conducting investigations and prosecutions, respect the interests and personal circumstances of victims, particularly where the crime involves sexual violence, gender violence, or violence against children.

These documents were instrumental in incorporating a gender-perspective in the early stages of investigations and contributed to bring about convictions for sexual and gender-based crimes against women and men, for instance in

Under International Law: Extraordinary Advances, Enduring Obstacles', (2002) 21 *Berkeley Journal of International Law*, 288; Valerie Oosterveld, 'The Definition of "Gender" in the Rome Statute of the International Criminal Court: A Step Forward or Back for International Criminal Justice', in (2005) 18 *Harvard Human Rights Journal*, 55; Solange Mouthaan S. 'The Prosecution of Gender-based Crimes at the ICC: Challenges and Opportunities', (2011) 11 *International Criminal Law Review* 775.

20 On the poor record in terms of prosecution of sexual and gender based crimes at the ICC in the first period see Mannix Bridget, 'A Quest for Justice: Investigating Sexual and Gender-Based Violence at the International Criminal Court' (2014–2015) 21(7) *James Cook University Law Review* 19.

21 ICC, Office of the Prosecutor 'Policy Paper on Sexual and Gender-Based Crimes' (June 2014) 3, available at https://www.icc-cpi.int/iccdocs/otp/OTP-Policy-Paper-on-Sexual-and-Gender -Based-Crimes--June-2014.pdf (visited on 17 January 2020). See Rosemary Grey, *Prosecuting Sexual and Gender-Based Crimes at the International Criminal Court* (CUP 2019).

22 ICC, Office of the Prosecutor 'Policy on Children' (November 2016) 2 and 12, available at https://www.icc-cpi.int/iccdocs/otp/20161115_OTP_ICC_Policy-on-Children_Eng.PDF . (visited on 17 January 2020)

23 *Ibidem*, 6.

24 *Ibidem*, 24.

the *Bemba* case in 2016.[25] This judgment was considered a milestone decision that 'sends a strong signal that commanders will be held responsible for international crimes committed by those under their authority'.[26] However, the trial judgment was overturned on appeal in 2018 attracting strong criticism[27] and although the acquittal of Bemba was not due to reasons related to the charges of sexual and gender based crimes, the case turned out being a half a victory and no reparations order for compensations to the victims could be issued by the Court.[28]

A definite step forward is instead represented by the trial judgment in *Prosecutor v. Ntaganda*, the first international conviction for sexual slavery.[29] The case is a very important precedent for the preliminary decisions on the confirmation of charges for sexual and gender-based crimes. The defence lawyers challenged the jurisdiction of the Court to pronounce on the charges of rape and sexual slavery of child soldiers by the same militia group arguing that, according to the ICC Statute, members of an armed force may not commit war crimes against members of the same group.[30] The Trial Chamber, stressing that

25 *Prosecutor v. Jean-Pierre Bemba Gombo*, Case No. ICC-01/05-01/08, Judgment Pursuant to Article 74 of the Statute (Mar. 21, 2016), see Niamh Hayes, 'The Bemba Trial Judgement – A Memorable Day for the Prosecution of Sexual Violence by the ICC', 21 March 2016, *PhD Studies in Human Rights* http://humanrightsdoctorate.blogspot.com/2016/03/hayes-bemba-trial-judgement-memorable.html; Janina N. Clark, 'The First Rape Conviction at the ICC: An Analysis of the *Bemba* Judgment', (2016) 14 JICJ 667.

26 Statement attributable to the Spokesperson of the Secretary-General on judgment of the International Criminal Court regarding Jean-Pierre Bemba, 22 March 2016, https://www.un.org/sg/en/content/sg/statement/2016-03-22/statement-attributable-spokesperson-secretary-general-judgment.

27 *Prosecutor v. Jean-Pierre Bemba Gombo* (Appeals Judgment) ICC-01/05-01/08, 8 June 2018. Diane M. Amann, 'In Bemba and Beyond, Crimes Adjudged to Commit Themselves' *EJILTalk!* 13 June 2018 https://www.ejiltalk.org/in-bemba-and-beyond-crimes-adjudged-to-commit-themselves/; Joseph Powderly, Niamh Hayes, 'The Bemba Appeal: A Fragmented Appeals Chamber Destabilises the Law and Practice of the ICC', 26 June 2018, *PhD Studies in Human Rights* https://humanrightsdoctorate.blogspot.com/2018/06/the-bemba-appeal-fragmented-appeals.html, Leyla N. Sadat, 'Prosecutor v. Jean-Pierre Bemba Gombo', (2019) 113 AJIL 353.

28 *Prosecutor v. Jean-Pierre Bemba Gombo* (Final decision on the reparations proceedings), ICC-01/05-01/08-3653, 3 August 2018.

29 *Prosecutor v Ntaganda* (Judgment), ICC-01/04-02/06-2359 08 July 2019.

30 *Prosecutor v Ntaganda* (Application on behalf of Mr Ntaganda challenging the jurisdiction of the Court in respect of Counts 6 and 9 of the Document containing the charges), ICC-01/04-02/06, 1 September 2015 an later (Appeal on behalf of Mr Ntaganda against Trial Chamber VI's "Second decision on the Defence's challenge to the jurisdiction of the Court in respect of Counts 6 and 9"), ICC-01/04-02/06-1707, 10 January 2017. For all other documents submitted by the Defence team to challenge the Court's Jurisdiction see the

ICC Statute does not provide that victims of war crimes of rape and sexual slavery should have any particular status, held that the submission of the defence undermines the rationale of international humanitarian law, which seeks to mitigate the suffering resulting from armed conflict. It ruled that members of the same armed forces are not excluded as potential victims of the war crimes of rape and sexual slavery.[31] The Appeals Chamber confirmed the trial chamber's finding.[32] Eventually Ntaganda, known as 'Terminator', was convicted as an indirect co-perpetrator for rape and sexual slavery against child soldiers belonging to his own group (including an instance of rape against a girl of approximately nine years of age), and sentenced to 30 years of imprisonment.[33] The case could indeed represent a breakthrough in the prosecution of gender-based crimes.[34]

The case was meaningful also because more than 2000 victims participated in the trial proceedings and the ICC registry is currently mapping the beneficiaries of reparations after Bosco Ntaganda's conviction.[35]

ICC website at https://www.icc-cpi.int/Pages/record.aspx?docNo=ICC-01/04-02/06-1707 and https://www.icc-cpi.int/Pages/record.aspx?docNo=ICC-01/04-02/06-1256 (visited 11 February 2010).

31 *Prosecutor v Ntaganda* 'Decision on the Defence's challenge to the jurisdiction of the Court in respect of Counts 6 and 9' Trial Chamber, ICC-01/04-02/06, 9 October 2015 and 'Second decision on the Defence's challenge to the jurisdiction of the Court in respect of Counts 6 and 9', ICC-01/04-02/06-1707, 4 January 2017.

32 *Prosecutor v Ntaganda* (Judgment on the appeal of Mr Ntaganda against the "Second decision on the Defence's challenge to the jurisdiction of the Court in respect of Counts 6 and 9") ICC-01/04-02/06-1962, 15 June 2017.

33 *Prosecutor v Ntaganda* (Sentencing judgment) ICC-01/04-02/06-2442, 07 November 2019.

34 See Còman Kenny, Yvonne McDermott, 'The expanding protection of members of a party's own armed forces under international criminal law' (2019) 68 *ICLQ* 943. Some scepticism has been expressed by other scholars: Luca Poltronieri Rossetti, 'Intra-party sexual crimes against child soldiers as war crimes in Ntaganda. 'Tadić moment' or unwarranted exercise of judicial activism', (2019) 60 QIL, *Zoom-in*, 49–68 at http://www.qil-qdi.org/intra-party-sexual-crimes-against-child-soldiers-as-war-crimes-in-ntaganda-tadic-moment-or-unwarranted-exercise-of-judicial-activism/.

35 *Prosecutor v Ntaganda,* 'Order for preliminary information on reparations', ICC-01/04-02/06, 25 July 2019, Judge Chang-ho Chung, Single Judge. The judge noted that there were 2129 victims who had been authorized to participate in the proceedings under article 68(3). The judge ordered the Registry to submit information on three questions: information on and a methodology for identifying victims (not yet participating) in the proceedings, observations on whether experts should be appointed to assist the Chamber and an update on security in the Congo (para. 4). See James Hendry, 'Early submissions about how Ntaganda reparations hearings should proceed', *Global Justice Journal,* 6 November 2019, available at https://globaljustice.queenslaw.ca/news/early-submissions-about-how-ntaganda-reparations-hearings-should-proceed.

3 The Broken Promise of International Criminal Justice: the Impossibility to Bring to Justice Incumbent Heads of States and High-Ranking State Officials

On the dark side of the picture, one of the major failures of international criminal justice, casting a long shadow on its future accomplishments, on its credibility and on its ultimate objective – that is, bringing to justice those who bear the greatest responsibility of mass atrocities – has been the actual impossibility to remove personal immunities of sitting high-ranking state officials before international criminal tribunals.

It is widely shared that, under customary international law, incumbent heads of state and other high-ranking state officials are entitled to personal immunity from arrest and from the criminal jurisdiction of foreign states, even when facing charges of international crimes. On the contrary, personal immunities should not constitute a bar to the exercise of criminal jurisdiction by international criminal courts.[36] Art. 27, para 2 of the ICC Statute, represents the culmination of the development of the law in this respect.[37]

The possibility to prosecute the most responsible of atrocious crimes before an international criminal tribunal, all the more so heads of state and governments still in office and potentially continuing to order the commission of appalling crimes, is one of the most promising aspects of international criminal justice and potentially one of the cornerstones of an effective system. Mass crimes are the expression of systemic criminality and the prosecution of those occupying high-ranking positions is one of (if not the) very purposes underlying the creation of an international criminal justice system. The inability to arrest incumbent high-ranking state officials, as the Omar Al Bashir saga clearly shows, seriously undermined the functioning and the credibility of the ICC

36 For a comprehensive and recent overview on the issue of immunities accruing to state officials see Tom Ruys: Nicolas Angelet; Luca Ferro (eds), *The Cambridge Handbook of Immunities and International Law* (CUP 2019), especially Part IV on Individual Immunities. See also Gerhard *Werle*, Andreas *Zimmermann* (eds.), The International Criminal Court in Turbulent Times (Asser/Springer 2019) insisting in several chapters on the controversial issue of immunities of state officials before the ICC.

37 "Art 27.1. This Statute shall apply equally to all persons without any distinction based on official capacity. In particular, official capacity as a Head of State or Government, a member of a Government or parliament, an elected representative or a government official shall in no case exempt a person from criminal responsibility under this Statute, nor shall it, in and of itself, constitute a ground for reduction of sentence. 2. Immunities or special procedural rules which may attach to the official capacity of a person, whether under national or international law, shall not bar the Court from exercising jurisdiction".

and most likely also contributed to a more general backwards movement in the law of immunities of state officials from criminal jurisdiction.[38]

Various elements support the existence of a customary exception to personal immunities of state officials prosecuted before an international criminal court. The International Court of Justice (ICJ) on its part, in the *Arrest Warrant* case, established that 'an incumbent or former Minister of Foreign Affairs may be subject to criminal proceedings before certain international criminal courts'[39] although without any further clarification. The rationale of this exception stands in the fact that, whereas at the 'horizontal' level – amongst States – the need to protect state officials from the possible abuse of jurisdiction by foreign states still prevails, at the 'vertical' one the exercise of jurisdiction by international criminal tribunals may not be assimilated to an exercise of authority of a state upon that of another state, and fulfilment of the task entrusted to these tribunals (i.e., the prosecution of the most serious crimes under international law) overcomes any immunity issue. In fact, no state protested when the ICTY indicted Milošević, sitting president of the Federal Republic of Yugoslavia, nor when Charles Taylor – sitting head of State of a third-state party with respect to the treaty establishing the tribunal – was indicted by the Special Court for Sierra Leone. The same holds true (at least partially) for the indictment and arrest warrant of the President of Sudan, Omar Al-Bashir.[40]

However, international criminal courts do not have enforcement powers, and they have to rely on the cooperation of national authorities in order to get their warrants enforced. In practice, States parties are still claiming that at the horizontal level the obligation to respect personal immunities prevails on the obligations to cooperate with the ICC and prevents them to enforce the arrest warrant, issued against a national of a State that is not party to the Statute. In fact, both Milošević and Taylor were arrested and tried respectively before the ICTY and the SCSL only after having been removed from power. Omar al Bashir remained in office for almost 10 years since he was first indicted by the ICC (and yet he has not been surrendered to the Court

38 A backward movement emerges clearly from the analysis of the recent works of the ILC on immunity of state officials from domestic criminal jurisdiction.

39 International Court of Justice, *Case concerning the arrest warrant of 11 April 2000 (Democratic Republic of the Congo v. Belgium)*, 14 February 2002, para.61.

40 On the contrary, Claus Kress stated that '[i] t is very doubtful whether a compelling defence (for a customary law basis in respect of the complete demolition of immunities before international courts) is possible at this stage of the development of the law' (Claus Kreß, 'The International Criminal Court and Immunities under International Law for States Not Party to the Court's Statute ' in Morten Bergsmo and Ling Yan (eds.), *State Sovereignty and International Criminal Law* (FICHL Publication Series, No. 15, 2012) 263).

after being removed from office) because States, including state parties to the ICC, refused to enforce the warrant in light of their obligations to respect immunities accruing to a sitting head of state (of a State that is not party to the ICC Statute).

In fact, the most controversial issue, which generated a series of decisions by the ICC Pre-Trial Chamber and a vigorous discussion among scholars, is not whether there is a customary exception to the rules on personal immunities whenever jurisdiction is exercised by the ICC but, more specifically, the question whether states parties would violate their obligations to respect personal immunities by enforcing the ICC request to surrender an incumbent head of a State that is not party to the Statute.

The ICC Pre-Trial Chamber (PTC) was confronted with several cases of refusal to cooperate in enforcing the arrest warrant against Al Bashir and adopted several decisions on this matter. In 2011, the ICC took the view that Malawi and Chad had failed to comply with the Statute.[41] It simply argued that because heads of state of non parties to the ICC Statute may not invoke personal immunity from the jurisdiction of the ICC by virtue of the customary exception, states enforcing an arrest warrant and surrendering an indicted head of state to the Court would not violate their obligations under international law. In other words the Court's Judges took the view that article 98(1) of the Statute does not apply. But they did not explain why and how the lack of immunity in the vertical relationship among the ICC and states automatically extend to the horizontal level. Subsequently, in decisions concerning the refusal to cooperate by the Democratic Republic of Congo, the Pre-Trial chamber followed a different line of reasoning and stated that the Security Council, by issuing Resolution 1593(2005), had decided that the 'government of Sudan ... shall cooperate fully with and provide any necessary assistance to the Court and the Prosecutor pursuant to this resolution'.[42]

---

41 *Prosecutor v. Al Bashir*, Decision Pursuant to Article 87(7) of the Rome Statute on the Failure by the Republic of Malawi to Comply with the Cooperation Requests Issued by the Court with Respect to the Arrest and Surrender of Omar Hassan Ahmad Al Bashir, PTC I,ICC- 02/ 05- 01/ 09- 139, 13 December 2011; Décision rendue en application de l'article 87- 7 du Statut de Rome concernant le refus de la République du Tchad d'accéder aux demandes de coopération délivrées par la Cour concernant l'arrestation et la remise d'Omar Hassan Ahmad Al Bashir, PTC I,ICC- 02/ 05- 01/ 09- 140, 13 December 2011. See also already in 2004 *Prosecutor v. Taylor*, Decision on Immunity from Jurisdiction, SCSL- 2003- 01- I, 31 May 2004.

42 *Prosecutor v. Al Bashir*, Decision on the Cooperation of the Democratic Republic of the Congo Regarding Omar Al Bashir's Arrest and Surrender to the Court, PTC II, ICC- 02/ 05- 01/ 09, 9 April 2014, para. 29.

In legal scholarship, well before these decisions were issued by the ICC PTC, there were several studies tackling this topic, with scholars expressing two main positions. According to the first, the treaty establishing the ICC derogates from the rules of customary international law on personal immunities with respect to the exercise of jurisdiction by national authorities, including the execution of an arrest warrant issued by the ICC, but only with respect to the relationship among contracting states. Article 98 recognizes that state parties are obliged to respect international rules on personal immunities accruing to officials of states that are not parties to the ICC Statute.[43] Therefore, states parties are not compelled to execute the ICC request for surrender of President Al-Bashir – who belongs to a third state – and can lawfully decide not to comply with it. On the contrary, the arrest and surrender of a serving head of state of a state party by the authorities of another state party would not, under Article 98(1), violate obligations under international law. According to a different position, the referral to the ICC of the situation of Sudan by the UN Security Council would have rendered the ICC Statute applicable to Sudan as if it were a state party. As a consequence, not only Sudan is obliged to cooperate with the Court and to arrest Al-Bashir, but the same holds true for all state parties to the ICC Statute. In addition, by virtue of the referral, third states are allowed to cooperate with the ICC for the enforcement of the arrest warrant without incurring international responsibility, although they have no obligation to do so.[44]

Leaving aside that neither of these solutions is entirely satisfactory,[45] in more recent decisions on non-compliance by States parties the Court opted

43 Kimberly Prost & Angelika Schlunck, 'Article 98', O. Triffterer (ed.) *Commentary on the Rome Statute of the International Criminal Court. Observers' Notes, Article by Article* (Nomos 1999) 1131.

44 Dapo Akande, *The Legal Nature of Security Council Referrals to the ICC and Its Impact on Al Bashir's Immunities*, (2009) 7 *JCIC* 333, at 340–42. There is also a slightly different position according to which Security Council Resolution 1593 implicitly removed personal immunities, Sophie Papillon, 'Has the United Nations Security Council Implicitly Removed Al Bashir's Immunity?', (2010) *10 ICLR* 275–88; Marko Milanovic, 'ICC Prosecutor Charges the President of Sudan with Genocide, Crimes against Humanity and War Crimes in Darfur', (July 28, 2008) *12 ASIL Insight*, available at http://www.asil.org/insights080728.cfm. For a recent general comment on the inconsistencies of the Court's decision see Dapo Akande, 'The Immunity of Heads of States of Non-Parties in the Early Years of the ICC?', (2018) 112 *AJIL Unbound*, 172.

45 For a detailed set of critical comments see Nerina Boschiero, 'The ICC Judicial Finding on Non-cooperation Against the DRC and No Immunity for Al-Bashir Based on UNSC Resolution 1593' 2015 13 JICJ 625. See also Micaela Frulli, 'Piercing the Veil of Head-of-State Immunity: The Taylor Trial and Beyond' in Charles C. Jalloh (ed.), *The Special Court and its Legacy: The Impact for Africa and International Criminal Law* (CUP 2014) 325.

for the 'Security Council Route',[46] both in the 2017 decision concerning South Africa[47] and in the decisions regarding refusal to cooperate by Jordan.[48] However, in the latter case Jordan appealed the decision and in the judgment, rendered in May 2019, the ICC partially abandoned the 'Security Council Route' and went back, amid much criticism, to the customary exception argument.[49] Another critical feature lies in the fact that, although the Court unanimously held that Jordan violated its obligation not to arrest Bashir, the majority decided not to refer Jordan to the UN Security Council reversing the Pre-Trial Chamber on this point.[50]

Omar al Bashir was overthrown in April 2019 and yet Sudan has not surrendered him to the Court as requested. On 11 February 2020 the spokesman for the Sudanese government, Mohammed Hassan al-Taishi, said that 'Justice cannot be achieved if we don't heal the wounds' and announced that Bashir and three others would be handed over to the ICC.[51] However, being the surrender part of the peace negotiations with Darfur rebels it cannot be granted that it will happen anytime soon.[52] Eventually also the arrest of a former head

46 Talita de Souza Dias, 'The 'Security Council Route' to the Derogation from Personal Head of State Immunity in the Al-Bashir Case: How Explicit must Security Council Resolutions be?', *EJILTalk!*, 19 September 2018, at *https://www.ejiltalk.org/the-discussion-of-the-security-council-roots-to-the-derogation-from-personal-immunities-in-the-al-bashir-case-how-explicit-must-security-council-resolutions-be/#more-16485* (visited 10 February 2020).

47 *Prosecutor v. Al Bashir* , , Decision under article 87(7) of the Rome Statute on the non-compliance by South Africa with the request by the Court for the arrest and surrender of Omar Al-Bashir, PTC II, ICC-02/05-01/09, 6 July 2017.

48 *Prosecutor v. Al Bashir* , Decision under Article 87(7) of the Rome Statute on the Non-compliance by Jordan with the Request by the Court for the Arrest and Surrender of Omar Al Bashir, PTC II, ICC-02/05-01/ 09, 11 December 2017, para. 55.

49 *Prosecutor v Al-Bashir*, Judgment in the Jordan Referral re Al-Bashir Appeal, Appeals Chamber, ICC-02/05-01/09 OA2, 6 May 2019.

50 Dapo Akande, *ICC Appeals Chamber Holds that Heads of State Have No Immunity under Customary International Law Before International Tribunals*, *EJILTalk!*, 6 May 2019, https://www.ejiltalk.org/icc-appeals-chamber-holds-that-heads-of-state-have-no-immunity-under-customary-international-law-before-international-tribunals/.

51 *Omar al-Bashir: Sudan agrees ex-president must face ICC*, BBC News, 11 February 2020 https://www.bbc.com/news/world-africa-51462613.

52 'The Sudanese delegation negotiating with rebels in Darfur has made a key concession to victims of the Darfur conflict by agreeing that all those wanted by the ICC should be handed over to the court to stand trial. The surrender of former President Bashir is, in fact, something that Sudan's top military general Abdel Fattah al-Burhan alluded to at a meeting in December with victims of the conflict. But there is no guarantee that it will happen – the generals may renege on the deal. If it does happen, it is unlikely to be anytime soon, as talks to end the conflict still have a long way to go and the transfer of the wanted men – from both sides of the conflict – would have to be part of a broader peace deal', *ibidem*. Other possible options have been analyzed, see Mark Kersten, '*What Happens Now*

of state who does not enjoy any longer personal immunities proves to be no easy step.[53]

However, one of the interesting aspects about this endless affair is precisely the struggle of the victims of the crimes to bring Bashir to justice before the ICC. After he was ousted, he was tried and sentenced for corruption and the authorities said that they would try him also for other crimes before domestic courts. However the victims of grave abuses in Darfur have never stopped clamouring for justice and insist to hold perpetrators accountable to show that no one is above the law.[54] The tough battles of the victims of appalling crimes tragically show that the failure to bring sitting heads of states (and other rulers in office) to trial is indeed an unfulfilled promise of international criminal justice, especially in the perspective of upholding human dignity, since in the eyes of the victims "as long as impunity continues, the pain remains".[55]

4 International Criminal Justice at a Crossroad: Looking Ahead

What are the prospects for international criminal justice? As to the development of the law, the crimes are now defined in a more precise manner in the ICC Statute. Having been crystallized in a treaty negotiated by States, the definitions carry a certain degree of ambiguity and some backward-looking elements reflecting the divergent opinions of States. The negative side-effect is the freezing of the law: a perfect example is represented by the Draft articles on crimes against humanity recently adopted on first reading by the ILC as a

---

with Omar Al-Bashir?', 20 February 2020, Justice in Conflict, https://justiceinconflict.org/2020/02/20/what-happens-now-with-omar-al-bashir/.

53 Mohammed Amin, '"Suspect still at large": Why Sudan hasn't handed Omar Bashir over to the ICC' The Middle East Eye, 12 March 2020, https://www.middleeasteye.net/news/sudan-why-omar-bashir-icc-international-criminal-court.

54 *Human Rights Watch*, 'Interview: Finally, Sudan's Ex-Dictator al-Bashir May Face Justice' 13 February 2020, https://www.hrw.org/news/2020/02/13/interview-finally-sudans-ex-dictator-al-bashir-may-face-justice. For his part, Jamal Mohamed said: 'We felt comfortable when Bashir fell, and now we feel that we are recovering (from the effects of the war), after the decision to hand him over to the International Criminal Court, this is a prerequisite for us', 'Darfur camps express joy at the decision to hand Bashir over to the International Criminal Court', *Teller Report*, 16 February 2020, https://www.tellerreport.com/news/2020-02-16---darfur-camps-express-joy-at-the-decision-to-hand-bashir-over-to-the-international-criminal-court-.rJfyYp4D7L.html.

55 Interview with Rita Yvonne Tobón, survivor of atrocious crimes in Colombia, *Comisión Intereclesial de Justicia y Paz*, 27 April 2015, available at https://www.justiciaypazcolombia.com/mientras-continue-la-impunidad-el-dolor-seguira-latente-rita-yvonne-tobon/.

first step on the road to a future Convention.[56] The text reproduces *verbatim* the definition of crimes against humanity contained in the ICC Statute notwithstanding some shortcomings highlighted by many parts and the developments occurred in the meantime. In addition, it is also evident that when the development of the law goes back, to a great extent, in the hands of States the pace of evolution rapidly gets slower: it took 20 years to have a definition of the crime of aggression and to allow the ICC to exercise its jurisdiction over it.

As to the impossibility to remove personal immunities and the consequences it entailed on the functioning of international criminal justice, it seems to be part of a more general trend to safeguard sovereignty over the protection of fundamental rights and the prosecution of international crimes. Looking at the law of immunities in a comprehensive manner, it may easily be inferred that the rules in this field are one of the last defences through which States try to avoid accountability for some of the most serious violations of international law. The difficulty to affirm a human rights exception to State immunity, a regressive attitude of many states and scholars towards functional immunity of state officials and the impossibility to remove personal immunities of sitting heads of State before the ICC are all part of the same picture. We are trapped in a catch-22 situation, where States are calling for the application of immunities for the sake of protecting sovereignty when what is at stake is the application of international rules which protect individuals from the abuses of States' sovereignty, often committed through their state officials, including top ones.

Unfortunately, the Al Bashir saga briefly described above and the impossibility to bring major leaders to trial played a major role in aggravating the sharp contrast between the African Union (AU) and the International criminal court,[57] thus endangering the future of international criminal justice. On one hand, the AU adopted the Malabo Protocol which extends the jurisdiction of the proposed African Court of Justice and Human Rights (ACJHR) to include international and transnational crimes,[58] including those covered in the Rome Statute, thus potentially placing the ACJHR in direct competition with the ICC. On the other hand, there was a withdrawal campaign of African countries from

56 UN doc. A/72/10, 11 September 2017, 9–127 (*Draft Articles with Commentary*).

57 Gino Naldi, Konstantinos Magliveras, 'The International Criminal Court and the African Union: A Problematic Relationship', in Charles C. Jalloh & Ilias Bantekas (eds), *The International Criminal Court and Africa* (OUP 2017) 111.

58 Protocol on Amendments to the Protocol on the Statute of the African Court of Justice and Human Rights (Malabo Protocol), available on the website of the AU at: https://au.int/sites/default/files/treaties/36398-treaty-0045_-_protocol_on_amendments_to_the_protocol_on_the_statute_of_the_african_court_of_justice_and_human_rights_e-compressed.pdfFort.

the ICC. Burundi withdrew from the ICC; other African countries attempted or threatened to do so, with spillover effects outside the African continent since the Philippines also denounced the treaty and withdrew from the system.

The Malabo Protocol has not come into force yet because it is short of the 15 ratifications it needs to become law. However, one of the critical features of the Protocol is precisely the immunities clause for incumbent state officials,[59] that it is seen by some as a shield from prosecution.[60] Without entering into the debate among the supporters and the detractors of this provision,[61] it is interesting to note that the criticism it attracted reinforces the idea of how crucial it is to deal with this issue in order to foster the objectives of international criminal justice.[62] A possibility highlighted by some scholars rests on interpreting the Malabo Protocol as a tool of a positive complementarity approach among African States and the ICC. They argue that including regional jurisdictions such as ACJHR within the principle of complementarity will contribute to the ongoing development of a robust system of international criminal justice.[63] The principal merit of this approach that draws on the applicability of the complementarity principle, initially conceptualized with respect to the obligations of States Parties to the ICC, to successfully regulate the jurisdictional relationship also with regional criminal courts[64] rests in the fact that it focuses on the

---

59 Article 46A *bis*: 'No charges shall be commenced or continued before the Court against any serving AU Head of State or Government, or anybody acting or entitled to act in such a capacity, or other senior State officials based on their functions, during their tenure in office'.

60 Amnesty International, *The Malabo protocol. Legal and Institutional Implications of the Merged and Expanded African Court*, 2016, available at https://www.refworld.org/pdfid/56a9ddcf4.pdf.

61 For a critical overview of various positions see Dire Tladi, 'Immunities (Article 46 A bis)' in Gerhard Werle, Moritz Vorbaum (eds), *The African Criminal Court. A Commentary on the Malabo Protocol* (Springer 2017) 203. See also Charles C Jalloh, 'Reflections on the Indictment of Sitting Heads of State and Its Consequences for Peace, Stability and Reconciliation in Africa', (2014) 7 *Afr. J. Leg. Stud.* 43 and Adejoké Babington Ashaye, 'International Crimes, Immunities and the Protocol on Amendments to the Protocol of the Merged African Court: Some Observations' in Charles C Jalloh and Femi Elias (eds) in *Shielding Humanity: Essays in Honor of Judge Abdul G Koroma* (Brill 2015) 406.

62 See Gerhard Kemp 'Immunity of High-Ranking Officials before the International Criminal Court – Between International Law and Political Reality' in Gerhard Werle, Andreas Zimmermann (eds), *The International Criminal Court in Turbulent Times* (Springer 2019) 61.

63 Sara Ningman, 'TheMalabo Protocol, the ICC, and the Idea of "Regional Complementarity"' (2019) 17 JICJ 1005.

64 See Charles C Jalloh arguing that by fostering this approach to complementarity no amendment to the Rome Statute would be required. He affirms that as the international human rights system which is composed of a multilayered national, regional, and

joining forces to fight impunity for international crimes. It also highlights the need not overburden the ICC with overarching ambitions and expectations.

The risk of a mass withdrawal of African countries from the ICC also posed a serious threat to the future prospect of international criminal justice. The AU campaign against the ICC began after the Court issued arrest warrants for Omar al-Bashir and increased radically after the ICC Prosecutor brought cases against Kenyan politicians Uhuru Kenyatta and William Ruto in 2011, who then became Kenya's president and deputy. The campaign succeeded in passing successive resolutions that urged non-cooperation with ICC in the arrest of al-Bashir and suspension of ICC cases involving crimes in Darfur and Kenya, and ultimately requested an AU strategy on the ICC that included the issue of withdrawal.[65] Three States parties to the ICC at the time of the adoption of the strategy had notified or announced their withdrawal, namely Burundi,[66] South Africa,[67] and Gambia;[68] also the National Assembly of Kenya had passed a motion of withdrawal.[69] Eventually, only Burundi withdrew from the Statute on 27 October 2017. As for Gambia, the new President elected in 2017 withdrew the country notice of withdrawal[70] and in South Africa the withdrawal notice was ruled as unconstitutional by the High Court[71] and the government revoked

international enforcement system, international criminal law could most likely benefit from a similar multilevel system of accountability, C.C Jalloh, 'The Place of the African Court of Justice and Human and Peoples' Rights in the Prosecution of Serious Crimes in Africa', in C Jalloh, Kamar M Clark, Vincent O Nmehielle (eds) *The African Court of Justice and Human and Peoples' Rights in Context development and challenges* (CUP 2019), 57.

65 See the African Union Assembly, Draft Decision on the International Criminal Court, 30–31 January 2017, Assembly/AU/Draft/Dec.1(XXVIII)Rev.2, at https://au.int/sites/default/files/decisions/32520-sc19553_e_original_-_assembly_decisions_621-641_-_xxviii.pdf.

66 See Burundi, Withdrawal from the Rome Statute of the International Criminal Court, 27 October 2016, C.N.805.2016. TREATIES-XVIII.10 (Depositary Notification).

67 See South Africa, Declaratory Statement on the Decision to Withdraw from the Rome Statute of the International Criminal Court, 19 October 2016, C.N.786.2016. TREATIES-XVIII.10 (Depositary Notification).

68 See Gambia, Withdrawal from the Rome Statute of the International Criminal Court, 10 November 2017, C.N.862.2016. TREATIES-XVIII.10 (Depositary Notification).

69 *Kenya parliament votes to withdraw from ICC.MPs vote to withdraw country from jurisdiction of International Criminal Court, as president and deputy face charges*, Al Jazeera, 5 September 2013, available at https://www.aljazeera.com/news/africa/2013/09/201395151027359326.html.

70 See Gambia, Withdrawal of Notification of Withdrawal from the Rome Statute of the International Criminal Court, 10 February 2017, C.N.62.2017. TREATIES-XVIII.10 (Depositary Notification).

71 South African High Court at Pretoria – Gauteng Division, *Democratic Alliance v. Minister of International Relations and Cooperation and Others (Council for the Advancement of*

it accordingly.[72] In another context, the Philippines notified their withdrawal from the ICC statute,[73] which became effective on 17 March 2019.

The risk of mass withdrawal is stemmed for the time being. However, this as well fosters reflections and proposals on how to resize expectations on the role of the ICC and at the same time on finding alternative ways to pursue the repression of international crimes as a means for protecting human dignity. As to the negative appraisal of the work of the ICC – and more generally as to the scepticism surrounding international criminal justice – it ought to be stressed once again that the failure of states to cooperate with the court caused major problems, as it already happened in the past with other international criminal tribunals. On the positive side, the creation of the ICC and the ratification of its Statute by many States brought about the adoption and/or revision of domestic laws and tools for the prosecution of international crimes. The court itself, as briefly outlined above, has begun to add to the body of international criminal law.

Unfortunately, the ICC is entering into adulthood at the time of a global crisis for multilateralism. It is also true, as highlighted in the introductory remarks, that the expectations of the international community, especially civil society and NGOs working with the victims of mass atrocities, about the potential of international criminal justice have been so high that no court would be able to meet them. It is thus important to start shaping realistic yet ambitious expectations, devising pragmatic strategies to improve the work of the ICC but also working on the elimination of the obstacles hindering a culture of accountability.

the South African Constitution Intervening), Case no. 83145/2016, Order, 22 February 2017, [2017] ZAGPPHC 53.

72 See South Africa, Withdrawal of Notification of Withdrawal from the Rome Statute of the International Criminal Court, 7 March 2017, C.N.121.2017. TREATIES-XVIII.10 (Depositary Notification).

73 Philippines, Withdrawal from the Rome Statute of the International Criminal Court, 17 March 2018, C.N.138.2018. TREATIES-XVIII.10 (Depositary Notification).

CHAPTER 8

Human Dignity in International Labour Rights

Matteo Sarzo

1 Introduction

The reference to human dignity is contained in many international conventions and it is widely accepted that such concept occupies a dominant role in the realm of international human rights law.[1] Some commentators, however, argued that the lack of a uniform definition of human dignity and its vagueness would render it 'dangerous' to use in the context of international human rights law.[2] Although the same criticism may be made regarding other 'vague' or 'open-ended' international rules, nevertheless the inevitable leeway in interpreting or applying such rules should not be confused with lack of normative value. Given that international human rights law is a set of provisions with binding force, which afford rights to individuals while imposing obligations upon States, nothing prevents us using dignity as an equally binding standard, if couched in legal terms.

The core of the philosophical notion of human dignity demands respect in a relationship between two persons, as Kant, the most prominent scholar who first addressed this topic comprehensively, pointed out.[3] In this context, the

1 A list of the international conventions on human rights containing the term dignity has been provided by Christopher McCrudden, 'Human Dignity and Judicial Interpretation of Human Rights' (2008) 19 EJIL 656, 668–672.

2 The criticisms have been summarized by Paolo G Carozza, 'Human Dignity' in Dinah Shelton (ed), *The Oxford Handbook of International Human Rights Law* (OUP 2013), 345–346. Interestingly, both the scholars who criticize the use of dignity and those who support it commonly acknowledge that the notion is vague and open to a broad interpretation. See Doron Shulztiner and Guy E Carmi, 'Human Dignity in National Constitutions: Functions, Promises and Dangers' (2014) 62 Am J Comp L 461, 462. Also the investigation made by McCrudden on the international legal texts led to the conclusion that dignity 'is a shorthand way of summing up how a complex, multi-faceted set of relationships involving Man is, or should be, governed: relationships between man and man, man and God, man and animals, man and the natural environment, man and the universe'. See McCrudden, 'Human Dignity' (n 1), 675.

3 According to the Kantian view, dignity entails a duty of self-esteem that every human being (as person and not as mere *homo phaenomenon* belonging to the system of nature) must owe to himself as a moral being, because he possesses an 'absolute inner worth by which he exacts *respect* for himself from all other rational beings in the world'. As a consequence, the 'recognition of *dignity* (*dignitas*) in other human beings' is 'the *respect* that I have for others

 | DOI:10.1163/9789004435650_009

leading role that human dignity might play in economic rights is with respect to labour rights. On the one hand, the relationship between the employer and the worker is not, nor it may ever be, equal on its own; it needs to be regulated by the State accordingly.[4] From this standpoint, the legal notion of dignity can explain the important legal limitations on the powers that typically rest with any employer and may be directed against the workers as the weaker parties in any employment relationship.[5] On the other hand, dignity may indicate a condition or status of living which any individual might achieve through labour. In this case, States have the duty to take any action deemed necessary to remove the substantial impairments or inequalities so that everyone may have the same chances to strive for a dignified life.[6]

These considerations can be supported not only by history, but also by present day life conditions: labour may be a means of oppression and even extermination as well as a means of attaining a dignified standard of living. And it is precisely because of this concern that Article 23, paragraph 3 of the Universal Declaration of Human Rights expressly provides that any worker 'has the right to just and favourable remuneration ensuring for himself and his family an existence worthy of human dignity, and supplemented, if necessary, by other means of social protection'. From such provision it can be deduced that States are entrusted with a very delicate task.[7] They have the duty to enact laws and regulations aimed at ensuring compliance with the 'minimum core' of dignity in the framework of labour relationships, thus bolstering the general duty of every individual to recognize and respect 'the intrinsic worth' of another person.[8]

---

or that another can require from me'. The object of such recognition is a 'worth that has no price, no equivalent for which the object evaluated (*aestimii*) could be exchanged'. See Immanuel Kant, *The Metaphysics of Morals* (Mary Gregor trs and ed, CUP 1996), 186–187, 209.

4 It has been noted that the regulation by the State of labour relationships has a pivotal role in the implementation of international obligations protecting labour rights. See Olivier De Schutter, 'Human Rights in Employment Relationships: Contracts as Power' in Filip Dorssemont and others, *The European Convention on Human Rights and the Employment Relation* (Hart Publishing 2013), 127–129.

5 Oscar Schachter, 'Comment: Human Dignity as a Normative Concept' (1983) 77 AJIL 848, 851.

6 In its social dimension, human dignity 'requires recognition of a minimal concept of distributive justice that would require satisfaction of the essential needs of everyone'. Ibid 853.

7 It has been suggested that Article 23, paragraph 3 of the Universal Declaration of Human Rights calls for State action which should ensure the achievement of a certain quality of life. See Klaus Dicke, 'The founding function of human dignity in the Universal Declaration of Human Rights' in David Kretzmer and Eckart Klein (eds), *The Concept of Human Dignity in Human Rights Discourse* (Kluwer Law International 2002), 118.

8 As for the notion of 'minimun core', see McCrudden, 'Human Dignity' (n 1), 679.

However, at the same time, States are extremely careful not to limit their freedom of choice as to which economic policies and objectives of growth they may develop or pursue. In their view, such leeway cannot be severely curtailed by stringent international rules.[9] Caught between this potential conflict of needs, judges are often called upon to determine whether they are in a position to deliver a decision in the light of human dignity, which might strike down the policies developed by parliaments or governments.[10]

Against this background, two issues will be focused on in this Chapter. The second section will seek to investigate the relevant norms of some international conventions encompassing both dignity and labour rights. The analysis aims at finding out whether and how dignity is couched in an international legal provision which affords protection to workers. For the sake of comparison, a brief investigation on some comparable rules contained in national constitutions will be carried out. The third section of this Chapter will illustrate the interpretation given by some international bodies, including judges, to those legal provisions.

---

9 It has been argued that many international standards on labour rights embody the relevant economic theories commonly shared at the moment of their draft, thus ignoring other approaches to economy. Notably, Article 1 (1) of the European Social Charter of 1961, which provides that States must attain the 'full employment', reflects the Keynesian understanding that States can successfully regulate their level of domestic employment. By contrast, other economic theories, which deny such premise, did not find echo in Article 1. See Colm O'Cinneide, 'The Right to Work in International Human Rights Law' in Virginia Mantouvalou (ed), *The Right to Work: Legal and Philosophical Perspectives* (Hart Publishing 2014) 113. For instance, in the framework of 'financial crisis management strategies, labour market governance norms manifest a rejection of the right to work, at least insofar as it is conceptualized in terms of obligations by the state to directly provide opportunities for work or to backstop rising incomes and better terms and conditions of work'. See Kerry Rittich, 'The Right to Work and Labour Market Flexibility: Labour Market Governance Norms in the International Order' in Virginia Mantouvalou (ed), *The Right to Work: Legal and Philosophical Perspectives* (Hart Publishing 2014) 320ff.

10 As for the several methods, including the test of proportionality, used by the courts when they have to settle a case involving human dignity, see McCrudden, 'Human Dignity' (n 1), 714–719. It has been argued that, through the recourse to human dignity and 'the intrinsic worth of every person', many human rights may be extended and strengthened 'by formulating new rights or construing existing rights to apply to new situations'. However, such approach should not imply that, 'as a rule', dignity has to be enhanced 'through legal action and the assertion of rights' in judicial fora, but – better – through 'social processes such as education, material benefits, political leadership and the like'. See Oscar Schachter, 'Comment: Human Dignity' (n 5) 853–854.

2 Legal Texts

At the national level, many European constitutions contain provisions referring to human dignity.[11] The most remarkable example is Article 1, §1 of the Basic Law for the Federal Republic of Germany of 1949, which provides the inviolability of human dignity and the 'duty of all state authority' to respect and ensure it. As for the Italian Constitution of 1948, the term dignity is included in Article 3, which sets forth the principle of equality before the law ('all citizens shall have equal social dignity and shall be equal before the law') and in Article 41, paragraph 2, which assigns a central task to dignity in the labour relationships. In fact, this rule states that 'private economic enterprise' shall not be carried out against human dignity. Another illuminating example is Article 23 of the Belgian Constitution, which stipulates that the domestic laws are required to guarantee economic, social and cultural rights, including labour rights, with the aim of securing to everyone the right to lead a life in keeping with human dignity.[12] It is evident that these rules do not exactly indicate the measures that public authorities should enact in order to ensure respect for human dignity. From the standpoint of a constitutional judge, the standard of review provided by these provisions (the compliance with human dignity) appears very broad.

By contrast, at the international level, the notion of human dignity is not commonly mentioned together with, or linked to, certain economic, social and cultural rights, including labour rights. The term dignity appears only twice in the International Covenant on Economic, Social and Cultural Rights (ICESCR) of 1966, which currently represents the most important legal instrument with a universal approach in this field. The preamble asserts that the rights herein laid down 'derive from the inherent dignity of the human person', and only a short reference is made in Article 13, paragraph 1, stating that 'education shall

---

11 It has been demonstrated that, since the Second World War, the notion of human dignity has been increasingly incorporated in the constitutions, thus becoming a 'universal feature'. In many of them, dignity is directly connected to labour rights. Doron Shulztiner and Guy E Carmi, 'Human Dignity in National Constitutions' (n 2) 465, 468, 477–478. See also Aharon Barak, *Human Dignity : The Constitutional Value and the Constitutional Right* (CUP 2015), 51–65.

12 Article 23 reads as follows : « Chacun a le droit de mener une vie conforme à la dignité humaine. À cette fin, la loi, le décret ou la règle visée à l'article 134 garantissent (...) 1° le droit au travail et au libre choix d'une activité professionnelle dans le cadre d'une politique générale de l'emploi, visant entre autres à assurer un niveau d'emploi aussi stable et élevé que possible, le droit à des conditions de travail et à une rémunération équitables, ainsi que le droit d'information, de consultation et de négociation collective ».

be directed to the full development of the human personality and the sense of its dignity'.

This limited space accorded to human dignity within the text of the Covenant is stunning, especially if one considers that Articles 6 to 9 actually lay down many obligations purporting to ensure and enhance just and favourable conditions of work as well as the right to form and join to trade unions and right to social security. There are, however, some exceptions, such as Article 70 of the International Convention on the Protection of the Rights of All Migrant Workers and Members of Their Families of 1990. Under this provision, State are required to accord the national treatment to migrant workers, whose working and living conditions have to respect the 'principles of human dignity'.

As for the multilateral treaties targeted at the protection of labour, only a few of the approximately 190 ILO conventions contain specific provisions embodying the notion of dignity. In a first group of such treaties, dignity is included in the preamble, which recalls the text of the Declaration of Philadelphia adopted by the International Labour Conference on 1944.[13] This is the case in the Discrimination (Employment and Occupation) Convention of 1958 (No. 111), the Employment Policy Convention of 1964 (No. 122) and the Workers with Family Responsibilities Convention of 1981 (No. 156).[14] The preamble of the recent Violence and Harassment Convention of 2019 (No. 190), not yet entered into force, slightly differs because it recognizes that 'violence and harassment in the world of work affects a person's […] dignity'.[15]

The second group of ILO Conventions do something more than a plain *renvoi* to the Declaration of Philadelphia in the preamble. The term dignity is couched in a specific provision, which lists some conducts that cannot be considered in compliance therewith. For instance, Article 2 of the Indigenous and Tribal Populations Convention of 1957 (No. 107) affirms that the 'primary

13 Article II, par. (a) of that Declaration provides, in general terms, that 'all human beings […] have the right to pursue both their material well-being and their spiritual development in conditions of freedom and dignity'.

14 Convention (No. 111) concerning discrimination in respect of employment and occupation. Adopted by the General Conference of the International Labour Organisation at its forty-second session, Geneva, 25 June 1958, UNTS 362 (1960), 32; Convention (No. 122) concerning employment policy, adopted by the General Conference of the International Labour Organisation at its forty-eighth session, Geneva, 9 July 1964, UNTS 569 (1966), 66; Convention (No. 156) concerning equal opportunities and equal treatment for men and women workers: workers with family responsibilities. Adopted by the General Conference of the International Labour Organisation at its sixty-seventh session, Geneva, 23 June 1981, UNTS 1331(1983), 296.

15 <www.ilo.org/dyn/normlex> accessed 5 May 2020.

objective' of the actions, which States are required to take in order to protect such populations, must be the 'the fostering of individual dignity' thereof.[16] Furthermore, Article 3, paragraph 8 (a) of the Seafarers' Identity Documents Convention (Revised) of 2003, as amended (No. 185) provides that the biometric data must be collected 'without any invasion of privacy of the persons concerned [...] or offence against their dignity'.[17]

It is not only UN Conventions that seem to be reluctant to enshrine human dignity in specific provisions protecting labour rights. At the regional level, even the European Convention on Human Rights (ECHR) is silent about the concept, with the sole exception of the preamble of Protocol 13 concerning the abolition of death penalty. With specific regard to labour rights, no provision of the original European Social Charter of 1961 mentioned dignity until the entry into force of the Revised Charter of 1996, whose Article 26 eventually included the notion.[18] This rule ensures the 'right to dignity at work' to all workers and imposes upon the State parties the duty to prevent sexual and moral harassments in the workplace and to protect the workers from such acts.[19]

Two considerations may be drawn from this pattern. In the first place, only a few international treaties analysed above embody the notion of dignity in provisions aimed at protecting labour rights, whereas most of them confine any reference to dignity to their preambles.[20] Second, only a couple of conventions

16 Convention (No. 107) concerning the protection and integration of indigenous and other tribal and semi-tribal populations in independent countries. Adopted by the General Conference of the International Labour Organisation at its fortieth session, Geneva, 26 June 1957, UNTS 328 (1959), 252.

17 Convention 185: Convention revising the Seafarers' Identity Documents Convention, 1958 UNTS 2304 (2007), 125.

18 During the *travaux préparatoires* of the European Social Charter of 1961, in the drafters' view the notion of dignity of the workers was more suitable for expressing a value and not a right. Accordingly, no provision on the dignity of the workers was eventually embodied in the final draft. See Mariann Arany Tóth, 'The Right to Dignity at work: Reflections on Article 26 of the Revised European Social Charter' (2008) 29 Comp Lab L & Pol'y J 275, 288–289.

19 Article 26 reads as follows: 'With a view to ensuring the effective exercise of the right of all workers to protection of their dignity at work, the Parties undertake, in consultation with employers' and workers' organisations: 1. to promote awareness, information and prevention of sexual harassment in the workplace or in relation to work and to take all appropriate measures to protect workers from such conduct; 2. to promote awareness, information and prevention of recurrent reprehensible or distinctly negative and offensive actions directed against individual workers in the workplace or in relation to work and to take all appropriate measures to protect workers from such conduct'.

20 It has been stated that many constitutions include the notion of dignity in their preamble rather than in substantive provisions. This would be explained by the fact that the

spell out the conduct or course of conduct which a State should comply with in order to ensure the respect of human dignity in the framework of an employment relationship.

It is tempting to conclude that the caution surrounding the use of dignity in substantive international rules betrays the intention of the drafters to limit the margin of appreciation of any international body, which eventually might be empowered to directly apply them. In fact, not only is the reference to dignity generally confined to the preambles of most conventions, but also the detailed phrasing of the international rules, which actually contain the term 'dignity', is not comparable to the more open-ended language used in certain national constitutions. This may suggest that human dignity should be better conceived as a canon of interpretation rather than an obligation binding upon States, whose breach could entail the international responsibility.[21] Such consideration may be supported by Article 31, paragraph 2 of the Vienna Convention of the Law of Treaties, providing that the rules of a treaty must be construed in their context, including the preamble.

However, one may wonder whether such textual limitations might successfully narrow the scope of review. Apparently, as will be illustrated in the following section of this Chapter, they do not. In fact, the international actors, and especially judges and quasi-judicial bodies, may use the notion of human dignity not only to justify the broad construction of a right or to highlight its importance, thus prohibiting possible exceptions to it, but also in order to bring 'new content to the treaty norms through interpretation'.[22]

3 Practice of International Judicial and Quasi-Judicial Bodies

Before focusing on the interpretation given by international judges or supervisory bodies, this section briefly examines the domestic case-law concerning the application of dignity to labour rights.

---

values herein enshrined, albeit not enforceable, nonetheless 'contribute to affect the constitutional discourse in a more diffused manner' alongside with other values, which can be antithetical. Doron Shulztiner and Guy E Carmi, 'Human Dignity in National Constitutions' (n 2) 73–476.

21 As for the use of the notion dignity as an interpretive tool in the international practice, see Ginevra Le Moli, 'The Principle of Human Dignity in International Law' in Mads Andenas and others (eds), *General Principles and the Coherence of International Law* (Brill Nijhoff 2019), 365–367.

22 See Carozza, 'Human Dignity' (n 2), 357–358.

Many decisions delivered by the Italian Constitutional Court regarding Article 41 of the Constitution demonstrate that, within the purview of constitutional scrutiny, some domestic provisions regulating the employment relationships have been examined in the light of the notion of human dignity. For instance, the Court pointed out that the violation of the rules, which set forth the conditions enabling the lawful dismissal of workers, is not in keeping with the dignity of workers.[23] In the same vein, the Court held that the set of provisions dictating the requirements for the lawful exercise of the power of sanction, which any employer may direct against employees, must effectively ensures the respect of the dignity of the workers.[24] Furthermore, the obligation incumbent on employers to control and prevent hazards in the workplace is to be meant as a reflection of human dignity.[25] The Court also maintained that the human dignity of the workers is ensured by the legal obligation of the employer to allow weekly rest, according to Article 36 of the Constitution.[26] If this brief glance at the constitutional practice shows that the judicial review of national rules on labour rights in the light of human dignity can be very accurate in the domestic legal order, one may wonder whether the same applies to international adjudication.[27]

At the international level, the task of interpreting the ICESCR is entrusted with the Committee on economic, social and cultural rights (CESCR), which has issued several General Comments with the purpose of strengthening the implementation of the Covenant in the domestic legal orders. The General Comment no. 18 of 24 November 2005 provides the construction of Article 6 of

23 Corte cost n 309 (18 giugno–1° luglio 1992), para 3. All decisions are available on <https://www.cortecostituzionale.it> accessed 5 May 2020.

24 Corte cost n 586 (13–29 dicembre 1989), paras 2–3.2; n 427 (8–25 luglio 1989); n 394 (25 novembre–4 dicembre 1998) para 2.1.

25 Corte cost n 312 (18–25 luglio 1996), para 2.

26 Corte cost n 111 (5 aprile 1974), para 3.

27 This brief overview of the constitutional scrutiny seems to confirm the argument that, from the standpoint of domestic adjudication, dignity is commonly meant as a notion closer to obligations than rights. In fact, it has been remarked that dignity has been increasingly used by national judges to impose obligations binding upon individuals rather than to protect a right thereof, as it was with the dwarf-throwing prohibition upheld by the French Supreme Administrative Court in 1995. In these cases, the national judges usually determine that human dignity 'as such' is violated, as it was 'an abstract and completely objectivized' entity not belonging to anyone. This would demonstrate that the contemporary application of dignity aims at protecting 'humanity as a matter of rank' and it is accordingly closer to the ancient concept of *dignitas*. See Stéphanie Hennette-Vauchez, 'A human dignitas? Remnants of the ancient legal concept in contemporary dignity jurisprudence' (2011) 9 IJCL 32, 36–41.

the ICESCR. In the view of the Committee, the very notion of human dignity is enshrined in 'the freedom of the individual regarding the choice to work' and States are required to respect immediately such core obligation, thus assuring 'individuals their right to freely chosen or accepted work, including the right not to be deprived of work unfairly'.[28] It is evident that the obligation not only provides to the States very specific indications, but also a manageable standard to the CESCR, should it been called upon to examine an individual communication under the Optional Protocol of 10 December 2008. However, the Committee has not yet adopted any view on Article 6 because the only complaint lodged by an individual so far, which included the alleged violation of such provision, was dismissed on procedural grounds.[29]

At the regional level, the European Court of Human Right has been using the concept of human dignity in the reasoning of many of its decisions since the leading case *Tyrer v. United Kingdom* of 1978, notwithstanding the abovementioned silence of the European Convention in this regard. It has been convincingly argued that the Court makes recourse to human dignity in two main contexts, either in cases involving serious violations of the rights enshrined in the Conventions (notably, those regarding Article 3) or as an interpretative tool aimed at reinforcing the reasoning of a judgment.[30]

Turning to labour rights, the Convention does not directly protect them by means of specific provisions, with the sole exception of Article 4, which prohibits servitude, slavery and forced labour, including – through an extensive reading given by the Court – trafficking.[31] Under this rule, the States parties

28 CESCR, 'The right to work: General Comment No. 18', E/C.12/GC/18, para 4, at 3. See also Colm O'Cinneide, 'The Right to Work' (n 9) 108–109. See Yuval Shany, 'Stuck in a Moment in Time: The International Justiciability of Economic, Social and Cultural Rights' in Daphne Barak and others, *Exploring Social Rights: Between Theory and Practice* (Hart Publishing 2007), 90. It has been argued that the 'more open-ended character' of Article 6, targeted at the protection of human dignity, gives to the CESCR a broader leeway in the interpretation thereof in respect of the narrower technical standards contained in many ILO Conventions. See Ben Saul, David Kinley, Jacqueline Mowbray, 'Article 6' in Ben Saul and others (eds), *The International Covenant on Economic, Social and Cultural Rights: Commentary, Cases, and Materials* (OUP 2014), 277.

29 CESCR, Views adopted by the Committee at its sixty-third session (12–29 March 2018), concerning communication No. 7/2015, E/C.12/63/D/7/2015, 26 March 2018, para. 9 at 11. The Committee affirmed the existence of a special link between dignity and other rights enshrined in the Covenant, for instance the right to housing and the right to culture. See Carozza, 'Human Dignity' (n 2), 355–356.

30 Jean-Paul Costa, 'Human Dignity in the Jurisprudence of the European Court of Human Rights' in Christopher McCrudden (ed), *Understanding Human Dignity* (OUP 2013), 400ff.

31 It has been noted that the Court has occasionally protected labour rights *par ricochet*, when – for instance – she found a violation of Article 8, as it may be the case with

have also the duty to take all appropriate measures, including legislative and administrative ones, to effectively prohibit and punish those acts. However, to date the Court has never deemed contrary to human dignity the inaction of the State which eventually amounted to a violation of such positive obligations, even if the Court recognized – at the same time – that the material acts giving rise to servitude, forced labour, slavery and trafficking did affect human dignity in the case at hand.[32] Clearly, nothing would prevent the Court from considering that the inaction of a State eventually results in a breach of human dignity, but this finding might appear inappropriate in all the cases where the State is not the material author of the acts committed exclusively by private individuals.[33] It may be that the breach of a positive obligation aimed at securing the horizontal effect of the rights enshrined in the Convention is not deemed contrary to human dignity as such because, in the Court's view, the responsibility of the State appears less serious than the underlying violations actually perpetrated by private individuals.[34]

---

dismissal due to a sex-based discrimination, or Article 10, in case of a firing grounded on the expression of criticisms. See Eva Brems, 'Indirect Protection of Social Rights by the European Court of Human Rights' in Daphne Barak-Erez and Aeyal M. Gross, *Exploring Social Rights: Between Theory and Practice* (Hart Publishing 2007), 153.

32 *Rantsev v. Cyprus and Russia*, App no 25965/04, paras 282–390 (ECtHR, 07 January 2010). In this case, the Court recognized that 'trafficking threatens the human dignity' under Article 4 of the Convention but did not find that the inactions of the State were contrary to human dignity, albeit in breach of that provision. For a similar approach, see *C.N. v. the United Kingdom*, App no 4239/08, paras 75-28 (ECtHR, 13 November 2012); *Chowdury and Others v. Greece*, App no 21884/15, paras 92–128 (ECtHR, 30 March 2017); *S.M. v. Croatia*, App no 60561/14, paras 51–81 (ECtHR, 19 July 2018). As for a comparable decision concerning servitude and forced labour, see *Siliadin v. France*, App no 73316/01, paras 140–149 (ECtHR, 26 October 2005). The Court extended the scope of application of Article 4 by imposing upon States parties the obligation of prevention in order to effectively ensure the protection afforded by the Convention in horizontal relationships between private individuals. See Olivier De Schutter, 'Human Rights in Employment Relationships' (n 4) 108, n 7.

33 In such a case, the responsibility of the State party is 'derivative', because it stems from the failure to adequately fulfill the obligation to prevent (or due diligence) that a given act is perpetrated by private individuals, without any involvement of the State. See ibid 105ff. This kind of derivative responsibility, and the corresponding positive obligations binding upon State, is quite common with regards to some rights enshrined in the ECHR and relates to the matter of the horizontal effect of some human rights.

34 It has been suggested that, when the ECtHR determines the violation of a positive obligation concerning private relations, the standard of review (the so called 'proportionality test') substantially implies the assessment of an 'excessive inaction' of the State. See Dean Spielmann, 'Chapter 14: The European Convention on Human Rights' in Dawn Oliver and Jörg Fedtke (eds), *Human Rights and the Private Sphere: A Comparative Study* (Routledge-Cavendish 2007) 435–436.

While the application of human dignity to provisions on labour rights cannot but play a very limited role in the case-law of ECtHR for the reasons given, surprisingly neither did such a role become leading in the jurisprudence of European Committee of Social Rights (ECSR), which is the quasi-judicial body empowered to hear collective complaints under the Revised European Social Charter.[35] In fact, the notion of human dignity has been used so far by the ECSR to construe or apply many provisions of the Charter other than those securing labour rights.

The recourse to dignity in the case-law of the ECSR traces its history back to the decision of 2004 in the case *International Federation of Human Rights Leagues* (FIDH) *v. France* regarding the interpretation of Article 17 of the Charter, which entitles children to social, legal and economic protection. Even if paragraph 1 of the Appendix to the Charter restricts *ratione personae* the enjoyment of most rights therein enshrined only to foreigners which are 'nationals of other Parties lawfully resident or working regularly within the territory of the Party concerned', nevertheless the Committee deprived such exclusion of any meaning in the light of the principle of human dignity.[36] The ESCR held that, under Article 17 of the Charter, France had the obligation to provide medical treatment also to migrants in irregular situations, especially children, given that the restriction set out in the paragraph 1 of the Appendix currently affected 'a right of fundamental importance' aimed at securing 'the very dignity of the human being'.[37] It then concluded by stating that such limitation could not be applied in the case at hand because the 'health care is a prerequisite for the preservation of human dignity', which constitutes a

35 Holly Cullen, 'The Collective Complaints System of the European Social Charter: Interpretative Methods of the European Committee of Social Rights' (2009) 9 HRLR 61, 69–76, 77–78. The recommendations of the Committee as well as the official documentation relating to the Charter is available on <https://hudoc.esc.coe.int/eng > accessed 5 May 2020.

36 The paragraph 1 of the Appendix reads as follows: 'Without prejudice to Article 12, paragraph 4, and Article 13, paragraph 4, the persons covered by Articles 1 to 17 and 20 to 31 include foreigners only in so far as they are nationals of other Parties lawfully resident or working regularly within the territory of the Party concerned, subject to the understanding that these articles are to be interpreted in the light of the provisions of Articles 18 and 19'.

37 As for the consideration of dignity which inspired the Committee in such decisions, see Giuseppe Palmisano, 'On the limits of the European Social Charter in terms of persons protected' in Bernardo Cortese (a cura di), *Studi in onore di Laura Picchio Forlati/Essays in Honour of Laura Picchio Folati/Etudes en l'honneur de Laura Picchio Forlati/Festschrift Laura Picchio Forlati* (Giappichelli Editore 2014), 92–93.

'fundamental value and indeed the core of positive European human rights law'.[38]

Even if this line of argument fostered a strong dissent among members of the ECSR, which eventually adopted the ruling by a majority of seven votes to six, this landmark decision initiated a discussion on how to develop and extend the legal discourse on human dignity to other provisions of the Charter.[39] In some cases, by means of the notion of human dignity, the Committee imposed additional obligations upon States parties, as in the case of Article 31§2 of the Charter (right to housing), which provides the duty 'to take measures designed [...] to prevent and reduce homelessness with a view to its gradual elimination'. In the view of the Committee, under such a provision the States parties are not only bound by the obligation to carry out evictions 'in conditions that respect the dignity of the persons concerned', by circumscribing them within scheduled time or seasons, but they are also required to make available an 'alternative accommodation'.[40] In another case, the ECSR held that the decision of a

---

38 Decision on the merits, 8 September 2004, *International Federation of Human Rights Leagues (FIDH) v. France*, Complaint No. 14/2003, para 26–32. Such approach gave the Committee the pathway to create a sort of presumption according to which 'restrictions on rights are to be read restrictively, i.e. understood in such a manner as to preserve intact the essence of the right and to achieve the overall purpose of the Charter', when a vulnerable category of persons is at stake, including migrants in irregular situation. See ibid, para 29. In a subsequent case relating to the same matter, the Committee pointed out that the 'teleological approach' followed in *International Federation of Human Rights Leagues (FIDH) v. France* explained its decision to narrow the scope of application of the Appendix. See Decision on the merits, 20 October 2009, *Defence for Children International (DCI) v. the Netherlands*, Complaint No. 47/2008, para 34–38. See also Decision on the merits, 11 September 2012, *Médecins du Monde – Internationalv. France*, Complaint No. 67/2011, para 34–35. By means of the same rationale, the Committee extended the enjoyment of some other rights enshrined in the Charter to migrants in irregular situation as is the case with the right to shelter granted by Article 3, para 2. See Decision on the merits, 2 July 2014, *European Federation of National Organisations working with the Homeless (FEANTSA) v. the Netherlands*, Complaint No. 86/2012, para 61ff.

39 The representatives of some States parties maintained that the interpretation given by the Committee to paragraph 1 of the Appendix is *contra legem*. See Klaus Lörcher, 'Interpretation' in Niklas Bruun and others (eds), *The European Social Charter and the Employment Relation* (Oxford Hart Publishing 2017), 53. On 2011, the Committee submitted to the States parties a proposal which substantially encouraged the repeal of paragraph 1 of the Appending by means of unilateral declarations. However, such proposal was generally rejected by States. See Giuseppe Palmisano (n 37), 94–95.

40 Decision on the merits, 7 December 2005, *European Roma Rights Centre v. Italy*, Complaint No. 27/2004, para 41; Decision on the merits, 5 December 2007, *International Movement ATD Fourth World v. France*, Complaint no. 33/2006, para 150; Decision on the merits, 5 December 2007, *European Federation of National Organisations working with the Homeless (FEANTSA) v. France*, Complaint No. 39/2006, para 85, Decision on the merits, 21 March

State to approve or allow the use of the textbooks on sexual health education, which contained some statements directly affecting the human dignity of non-heterosexual persons, resulted in the breach of its obligation under Article 11, paragraph 2 (right to protection of health) 'to provide advisory and educational facilities for the promotion of health and the encouragement of individual responsibility in matters of health' having regard to the 'non-discrimination clause of the Preamble to the Charter'.[41] The Committee pointed out that the violation of human dignity committed by the official endorsement from the State of the defamatory statements was not in keeping with the Charter.

Beside this rich case-law, just two complaints regarding both dignity and labour rights have been examined by the ECSR to date. In the first case, the Committee determined that an amendment to the Bulgarian Social Assistance Act was not in conformity with Article 13, paragraph 1 of the Revised Charter in so far as it lowered the time period for the entitlement to social assistance benefits, which had been previously unlimited and only conditional on the effective needs of unemployed individuals.[42] Remarkably, the Committee interpreted the meaning of the term 'adequate assistance' laid down in Article 13, paragraph 1 in the light of human dignity, concluding that such assistance must enable 'the person concerned to continue to live in manner compatible with their human dignity'.[43] From this decision it may be said that the States parties are required to provide those 'adequate' social benefits that enable individuals to live with dignity. It is evident that such additional guidelines dictated by the ECSR serve the purpose of enriching the narrower standard of adequateness laid down in the Charter.

The only other relevant recommendation in which the ECSR determined the violation of a provision containing the notion of dignity coupled with labour rights, was in the case *Confederazione Generale Italiana del Lavoro* (CGIL) *v. Italy* of 2015. The complaint originated from the improper application of the

2012, *International Federation of Human Rights (FIDH)v. Belgium*, Complaint No. 62/2010, para 164.

41 Decision on the merits, 30 March 2009, *International Centre for the Legal Protection of Human Rights (INTERIGHTS) v. Croatia*, Complaint No. 45/2007, paras 58–66.

42 Article 13, para. 1 reads as follows: 'With a view to ensuring the effective exercise of the right to social and medical assistance, the Parties undertake ensure that any person who is without adequate resources and who is unable to secure such resources either by his own efforts or from other sources, in particular by benefits under a social security scheme, be granted adequate assistance, and, in case of sickness, the care necessitated by his condition'.

43 Decision on the merits, 18 February 2009, *European Roma Rights Centre (ERRC) v. Bulgaria*, Complaint No. 48/2008, paras 37, 43.

domestic law regulating the conscientious objection of medical practitioners in relation to abortion services, which resulted in a heavier workload on the few non-objecting practitioners. Furthermore, the non-objecting praticitioners also alleged to be victims of moral harassment by their colleagues in breach of the right to dignity enshrined in Article 26, paragraph 2.

As already seen in the previous section, under this provision, States parties have the duty not only to protect workers from harassment, but also to prevent such acts, even if they are not required to enact legislation pursuant to the Appendix to Article 26.[44] With regard to the obligation of protection, by means of the Statement of interpretation of 2007 the Committee narrowed the scope of application of the Appendix by affirming that States parties are not under an obligation to enact legislation that makes 'express reference to harassment', provided however that domestic laws still encompass 'measures making it possible to afford employees effective protection', including shifting of the burden of proof in domestic claims concerning harassment.[45] By contrast, the Statement of interpretation did not spell out which measures should be taken to comply with the obligation of prevention stemming from Article 26, paragraph 2 in addition to the vague phrasing of this clause, which expressly embodies the duty to 'promote awareness, information and prevention'. Unfortunately, the Committee missed the glaring opportunity given by the case at hand of clarifying the pivotal issue of the duty of prevention.[46] After determining that actual harassment had not been convincingly substantiated by the complainant, the Committee nevertheless found the violation of Article 26, paragraph 2 as a result of the failure of Italy to take any 'preventative action, training or awareness raising' measure in order to prevent the moral harassment, of which the non-objecting medical practitioners are likely to be victims.[47]

44 Text to n 19. The Appendix to Article 26 reads as follows: 'It is understood that this article does not require that legislation be enacted by the Parties'. See Csilla Kollonay-Lehoczky, 'The Right to Dignity at Work' in Niklas Bruun and others (eds), *The European Social Charter and the Employment Relation* (Oxford Hart Publishing 2017) 439, 447.

45 According the Statement of interpretation of article 26, para. 2, the protection provided by domestic laws must include 'the right to appeal to an independent body in the event of harassment, the right to obtain adequate compensation and the right not to be retaliated against for upholding these rights'.

46 The scope of application of the obligation of prevention is controversial between the members of the Committee, who hold divergent views as to whether Article 26 imposes upon State the duty to enact legislation even in the absence of any provision in the domestic orders. See Csilla Kollonay-Lehoczky, 'The Right to Dignity at Work' (n 44) 449 and Mariann Arany Tóth, 'The Right to Dignity at work' (n 18) 296–297.

47 Decision on admissibility and the merits, 12 October 2015, *Confederazione Generale Italiana del Lavoro (CGIL) v. Italy*, Complaint No. 91/2013, paras 289–298. Before assessing

This approach resembles self-restraint rather than 'quasi-judicial' activism, of which the Committee has given some evidence in other cases. Moreover, once called upon to assess the follow-up of its previous decision, the ECSR simply kept the same stance by urging Italy to 'inform workers about the nature of the behaviour in question and the available remedies'.[48] This conclusion appears too weak against the conceptual core of Article 26, which is aimed at prohibiting serious violations of dignity in the workplace.[49] However, a possible explanation for this self-restraint may the fact that the violation of an obligation of prevention entails a less serious responsibility of the State in the light of the canon of human dignity, as it is the case with the ECtHR case-law on Article 4 mentioned above.[50]

4 Conclusion

The analysis of the relevant legal texts and the practice of some international judicial or quasi-judicial bodies unveil surprisingly weak ties between the protection of labour rights and the concept of human dignity. Contrary to some national constitutions, this notion is commonly embodied in the preambles of many international conventions on human rights instead of being couched in substantive provisions. Such limited use may be explained by the fact that States consider the concept of dignity more suitable for a canon of interpretation than for a binding legal standard, whose breach could entail international responsibility. The practice of international bodies partially confirms this intention of States. Some international jurisdictions (as the ECtHR) use dignity in the context of labour-related rights to emphasize the seriousness of a violation, whereas other international quasi-judicial bodies (as the CESCR) use it as an interpretive tool, which strengthens the standards laid down in the Covenant with a view to future application to individual complaints. The case law of the ECSR demonstrates an ever-increasing use of the

the violation of the obligation of prevention, the Committee ascertained the conformity of domestic laws with the obligation of protection, ibid para 293.

48 Assessment of follow-up: *Confederazione Generale Italiana del Lavoro (CGIL) v. Italy*, Complaint No. 91/2013.

49 It has been stated that the reference to dignity contained in Article 26 requires 'gravity in the act' perpetrated in the workplaces, and not only slight offences. See Csilla Kollonay-Lehoczky, 'The Right to Dignity at Work' (n 44) 441.

50 As for the issue of positive obligations in the case-law of the ECtHR, see n 34. Furthermore, as already illustrated, in the view of the Committee the complainant did not convincingly demonstrated that acts of moral harassment actually occurred. See n 47, para 296.

notion of human dignity, which occasionally has allowed the Committee to interpret some rights enshrined in the Charter beyond the limits strictly established in the Appendix. However, such an activist interpretation appears less pervasive in the context of labour rights.

There are some reasons which may explain this distinction. It may be that some violations of labour rights are not consistently perceived by an international body as so serious as to jeopardize human dignity, but this explanation relies on the personal cultural background of each member rather than being an objective assessment. It is more probable that self-restraint in matters concerning labour rights is dictated by the need to avoid a strong disagreement among the members on the expansion of such rights, whose interpretation largely relies also on ideological premises. From a legal standpoint, one explanation for the limited use of the concept of human dignity could be that, in all cases concerning the breach of an obligation of prevention, the State may not be directly involved in the underlying acts giving rise to the 'substantive' violation.

However, in the present writer's opinion, the main reason may be that labour rights are inextricably linked to the economic policy of States, which involves intricate political and social arrangements as well as choices on redistributive justice. Constitutional courts, because of their position, are legitimately empowered to read any labour right in the light of the underlying concept of human dignity shared by the national community. However, the authority of international judges or quasi-judicial bodies rests on more fragile grounds, and they are called to act within narrower limits. Accordingly, in matters concerning labour rights, they prefer to maintain a certain (perhaps wiser) self-restraint, thus avoiding a broad use of a concept such as human dignity, which may foster opposing views between judges or members and eventually complicate the domestic compliance with the decision.

CHAPTER 9

The "Poor Cousins": What, If Anything, Can International Law and Lawyers Do for Social Rights?

Octávio Luiz Motta Ferraz

1 Introduction

Scepticism about the effectiveness of international human rights law seems to be at a high point. Perhaps the highest it has ever been since its early days after the second world war. Much higher, at any rate, than it was in the more hopeful days at the end of the 1980s and beginning of the 1990s, when history was supposed to "have ended" according to some interpretations of that period.[1] Recent books proclaiming the futility of international human rights law ("IRHL") have generated a great deal of attention and a lively debate in academia and beyond.[2] They question the worth of the IHRL system and the wisdom of continuing to invest in it as a major strategy in global efforts to improve the world.

In this chapter, I want to engage in this discussion with a particular focus on so-called *social and economic rights* such as *health, education, housing, food and water* ("social rights" for short). My aim is to revisit the older and more longstanding scepticism about social rights in light of this newer scepticism about the human rights system as a whole (I call it "wholesale scepticism"). That will hopefully illuminate both debates and show where, in my view, both types of scepticism are to a great extent misguided.

My argument, in brief, is this. The current wave of wholesale scepticism about the effectiveness of IHRL has always been the default mode among social rights supporters, who have traditionally seen social rights as *neglected* in comparison to civil and political rights – their "poor cousins" as they are sometimes referred to.[3] But both wholesale and social rights scepticism are to

1 F Fukuyama "The End of History?" (1989) 16 *The National Interest* 3.

2 E Posner, *The Twilight of Human Rights Law* (Oxford University Press 2014), S Moyn, *The Last Utopia* (Harvard University Press 2012), S Hopgood, *The Endtimes of Human Rights* (Cornell University Press 2013).

3 P Alston, "Phantom rights: the systemic marginalization of economic and social rights", Open Global Rights, 6.8.2016, https://www.openglobalrights.org/phantom-rights-systemic-marginalization-of-economic-and-social-rights/ accessed on 15.5.2020.

 | DOI:10.1163/9789004435650_010

a great extent misguided. Their main problem is to equate the persistent occurrence of human rights violations across the world, which is of course real, to a *failure* of the IHRL system. As I will contend, this assumes a mode of operation of that system that is at the same time unrealistic in terms of what the system can and ought to do and underappreciative of what the system has actually achieved so far. If my arguments stand up, a much more optimistic view of international human rights law emerges, as well as a useful role for international human rights lawyers to play.

2 Scepticism about the Effectiveness of Human Rights

Scepticism about the effectiveness of human rights is of course not new and has probably always been a widespread position, with the exception perhaps of the short period of optimism that occurred between the end of the Cold War and the beginning of the "War on Terror".[4] Whether the current wave of scepticism is stronger is hard and probably too early to tell. But what underlies all waves of scepticism is mostly a feature of the IHRL system that it shares with most other areas of international law, namely a lack of strong enforcement mechanisms of international norms and decisions of international institutions. To borrow from Jack Donnely, IHRL is "normatively strong" but weak in implementation and enforcement.[5] For those who automatically link effectiveness to strong enforcement mechanisms, i.e. mechanisms of the type found in domestic law such as courts and police, this feature of IHRL makes it inherently ineffective, and thus the significant efforts and energy placed on creating and extending stronger enforcement mechanisms, i.e. international courts or quasi-courts in order to enhance the effectiveness of the system.[6]

---

4 See for instance P Sands, *Lawless World. Making and Breaking Global Rules* (Penguin 2005) and C Gearty, *Can Human Rights Survive?* (Cambridge University Press 2006).

5 J Donnelly, "International Human Rights: A Regime Analysis". (1986) 40(3) International Organization 599.

6 It is of course true that international adjudicatory bodies still lack the capacity of enforcing their decisions, but they are seen nonetheless as a move in the right direction of strengthening IHRL. See EA Posner and JC Yoo, *"Judicial Independence in International Tribunals"* (2005) 93 CALIF. L. REV. 1 See also AT Guzman, *"International Tribunals: A Rational Choice Analysis"*, (2008) 157 U. PA. L. REV. 171 ("International dispute resolution and international tribunals are all the rage. On the one hand, many international lawyers celebrate them as a powerful tool in the effort to bring order to our anarchic world. On the other hand, critics view these tribunals – perhaps inconsistently – as both a threat and a waste of resources").

This faith in adjudication as the main strategy to combat the perceived ineffectiveness of the IHRL system can be well illustrated through the history of the adoption of the Optional Protocol to the ICESCRs in 2009, which finally established, after decades of campaigning, a quasi-judicial mechanism of adjudication of social and economic rights at the United Nations (the “ICESCR-OP”). As one can read in its preamble, the mechanism was regarded as necessary “in order further to achieve the purposes of the Covenant and the implementation of its provisions”.[7] The main rationale, which was at the core of the campaign for the protocol which stretched back officially to 1990 (but earlier in academic debates) was that the lack of an adjudication mechanism deprived those rights of “teeth” and placed them at a position of inferiority (the “poor cousins”) vis a vis civil and political rights, whose adjudication has been a part of the UN system since the adoption of the optional protocol to the ICCPR in 1966 (entering into force in 1976).[8] That asymmetry between the two categories of rights also contradicted, it was argued, the idea of indivisibility of human rights, proclaimed several times since the Universal Declaration in 1948.[9]

Now that this adjudication imbalance between civil and political rights and social and economic ones has been finally eliminated from the system, the energy and efforts of social rights campaigners has moved towards ratification of the ICESCR-OP (currently ratified by only 24 countries), most of them from Latin America and Western Europe.[10]

As mentioned earlier, the campaign for the adoption (and now ratification) of the ICESCR-OP illustrates well the widespread faith in adjudication as a crucial element for the effectiveness of the IHRL system. In my view, this faith is misguided. This excessive focus on adjudication overestimates its ability to enhance rights’ enjoyment in the real world and diverts attention from other mechanisms of implementation of IHRL which are much more relevant for

7 The protocol, which entered into force in May 2013. https://www.ohchr.org/EN/ProfessionalInterest/Pages/OPCESCR.aspx.

8 ESCR Net, *“Timeline of the Campaign for the OP-ICESCR”* https://www.escr-net.org/timeline-campaign-op-icescr accessed on 15.5.2020.

9 The well-known General Comment n.3 of the Committee on Economic, Social and Cultural Rights tried to clarify the nature of state obligations related to social and economic rights and give them some teeth through the concept of the minimum core. See CESCR General Comment No. 3: The Nature of States Parties’ Obligations (Art. 2, Para. 1, of the Covenant). *Adopted at the Fifth Session of the Committee on Economic, Social and Cultural Rights, on 14 December 1990 (Contained in Document E/1991/23).*

10 For the full list of countries see https://treaties.un.org/pages/ViewDetails.aspx?src=TREATY&mtdsg_no=IV-3-a&chapter=4&clang=_en.

effectiveness but are often overshadowed by adjudication, such as legislation and policy, as I will elaborate later on in this chapter.

Ironically, this misguided faith in adjudication seems to underlie both the "envy" of social rights campaigners towards the alleged higher effectiveness of civil and political rights and the current wave of wholesale scepticism about IHRL mentioned earlier. Whereas many civil and political rights campaigners have become disillusioned with international adjudication for its supposed lack of teeth, social and economic rights' supporters are still betting on it as the solution against the perceived ineffectiveness of the IHRL system.[11]

Both views are misguided, I repeat, for placing excessive faith in international adjudication as an essential instrument of IHRL's effectiveness while paying little attention to other more relevant tools, mostly domestic politics, and to how rights are actually enjoyed in the real world (which I call the empirical reality of human rights). The next sections elaborate on this point.

3 The Empirical Reality of Human Rights

The problem of focusing too much on the judicial enforcement of human rights legal norms (adjudication for short) is that it is a poor indicator of the actual effectiveness of these norms. This is probably true of any type of legal norm, not just human rights ones. Judicial enforcement and effectiveness are not the same thing, yet many legal experts tend to confuse them or, worse, many tend to confuse effectiveness with *success in court*, which is neither the same as judicial enforcement nor the same as effectiveness. This is hardly surprising given the focus of legal education on abstract legal argument and individual case

11 With the gradual correction of that asymmetry both at the domestic level with the increasing number of national courts accepting to adjudicate them and at the international level with the entry into force of the protocol, this kind of scepticism tends to diminish or migrate to the perennial problem of obstacles to enforcement, where scepticism about IHRL as a whole has always focused. Once social rights' justiciability supporters start to realise the limited (and often pernicious) effects of justiciability, scepticism will tend to rise again, as it seems to have already started to in the domestic realm. See OLM Ferraz, Health as a Human Right. The Politics and Judicialization of Health in Brazil (Cambridge University Press 2020) for the growth of scepticism in Brazil in the field of health. We are likely to see, thus, an interesting convergence between social rights and civil and political rights sceptics in their scepticism grounded on lack of enforcement.

analysis and almost no attention given to the empirical study of the impact of legal norms on the reality on the ground.[12]

Yet, if we are interested on the effectiveness of IHRL, we need to distinguish it both from success in court and from judicial enforcement. Success in court and judicial enforcement are easy to distinguish. Anyone familiar with litigation knows that winning a case is no guarantee that the successful litigant will actually enjoy whatever the decision delivered. And this is not true only of defective legal systems with weak enforcement mechanisms. Even in the most developed countries there is always the risk of wining in court but not profiting in real life. And this is in large part why litigation is rarely a good investment (except for lawyers themselves, of course).

The potential causes of such disconnect between winning and gaining are many, often involving the incapacity or unwillingness of the defeated party to comply with the judicial decision. In this latter case, a properly functioning system may be able to solve the issue, but barriers like costs, time, etc, may get in the way and leave judicial orders unenforced. For illustrations, think of the creditor who wins in court against a debtor gone bankrupt and thus incapable of paying the debt or of the divorced parent who wins in court the right to access his or her children yet continues to face the obstruction of the other parent. In the human rights field "winning but not gaining" is far from a rare phenomenon, especially at the international sphere and even in the most developed regional systems. Here are a couple of examples. Prisoners in the UK have won their case in the ECtHRs against their legislative ban to vote back in 2005 and to this date the decision has not been fully complied with.[13] In 2010, victims of the Brazilian dictatorship won their case in the IACtHR to declare void the legislative amnesty that prevented crimes like torture, murder and disappearances from being prosecuted in Brazilian courts.[14] Again, to this date,

12 So-called sociolegal studies is perhaps an exception that proves the rule. Moreover, while still representing a fringe in most law school departments, even sociolegal scholars are often not very familiar or interested in conducting empirical research.

13 Although a compromise was reached 12 years after the decision https://www.theguardian.com/politics/2017/dec/07/council-of-europe-accepts-uk-compromise-on-prisoner-voting-rights accessed on 15.5.2020.

14 See Gomes Lund et al. (Guerrilha do Araguaia) v. Brazil IACHR 2010. The decision states the following in paragraph 3: "(The provisions of the Brazilian Amnesty Law that prevent the investigation and punishment of serious human rights violations are not compatible with the American Convention, lack legal effect, and cannot continue as obstacles for the investigation of the facts of the present case, neither for the identification and punishment of those responsible, nor can they have equal or similar impact regarding other serious violations of human rights enshrined in the American Convention which occurred in Brazil.)"

the decision has not been implemented. If we extend our survey to decisions of the UN Human Rights Committee, lack of enforcement is even more widespread. It seems clear, thus, that success in court cannot be used as a proxy for effective enforcement.

More complex is the distinction between judicial enforcement and effectiveness. Judicial enforcement, as I understand it, has to do with the actual implementation of the judicial decision. Take, again, the example given earlier about immunity from criminal prosecutions in Brazil for crimes committed during the military dictatorship. If the Brazilian legislature or the Supreme Court had revoked the Amnesty law that establishes that immunity, allowing thus lower courts to receive and process charges against perpetrators, the decision would have been enforced. Would it have been also *effective*? Not necessarily. That would depend on several additional factors, including how members of the Brazilian Public Prosecutions' Office reacted to that development. Assume, for the sake of the argument, that none, or very few prosecutors decided to investigate those crimes and only a few charges were actually brought to the courts. Effectiveness of IHRL would have been rather low, despite the victory at the IACtHRs and enforcement through legislation or judicial order. Lack of interest (whatever the reasons) by the only actors capable of initiating criminal prosecutions in Brazil, i.e. public prosecutors, would have thwarted effectiveness. Imagine, now, the opposite scenario, i.e. that lots of public prosecutors decided to investigate those crimes yet, after such a long time from the perpetration of the crimes, they managed to gather very little evidence in order to support viable charges, or that only a handful of perpetrators were still alive. Again, we would be forced to conclude that, in that case, IHRL was not very effective. Effectiveness is thus broader and much more complex than judicial enforcement. As a consequence, it demands access to much more detailed and often difficult to find empirical data.

It is not surprising, thus, that lawyers tend not to venture into this arena, yet this confusion between effectiveness and judicial enforcement leads to inaccurate conclusions about the former in both directions: over-celebration of victories in court and underestimation of other avenues of human rights' implementation. Let me focus on this latter danger now, as it underlies, in my view, both scepticisms discussed earlier.

As we saw, scepticism about the effectiveness of IHRL, in the fields of both civil and political and social and economic rights, stem mostly from the accurate observation that judicial enforcement of IHRL is notoriously feeble. If decisions are not even enforced, the reasoning goes, IHRL is all but ineffective. But this, as already mentioned earlier and as I will explain in more detail now, is an unwarranted (though understandable) move. It focuses too much on judicial enforcement and overlooks other potential, and in my view stronger, routes to effectiveness. It dismisses too quickly the possibility that IHRL may still be effective despite total lack of enforcement mechanisms and/or enforcement capacity at the international level.

How might that happen? Through several routes that totally bypass or interact with international adjudicatory mechanisms. The most prominent one is the use of IHRL standards as tools of political mobilization in the domestic arena. Examples of such effective mobilization abound in the short history of IHRL. The fight against apartheid is perhaps the clearest and most prominent. It wasn't until 1994, after the end of apartheid, that South Africa started to ratify human rights treaties such as the CERD and the ICCPR. And yet the existence of the IHRL system was critical in energising and providing legitimacy to the anti-apartheid struggle way before 1994.[15] The same can be said of the fight against military dictatorships in South America, in particular on the issue of torture. Again, no South American state had ratified the Convention Against Torture or the ICCPR at the time of the worst abuses in those regimes, and yet the IHRL system proved a crucial supporting tool in their struggle. It is of course hard, almost impossible, to measure the effectiveness of IHRL in these complex historical developments. How less violent were the South African and South American regimes than they would have been if IHRL did not exist? Would these regimes have lasted longer if IHRL did not exist? How much longer? These are impossible questions to answer with any degree of precision. It seems plausible to claim, however, that the existence of IHRL made some difference for the human rights' struggles in these domestic settings and this is a type of effectiveness that cannot be captured by looking simply at the judicial enforcement of legal norms, let alone court's decisions.

Attempts to measure effectiveness more precisely have started to emerge in the social sciences (mostly non-legal) literature more recently trying to assess the relationship between ratification of IHRL treaties and the situation of human rights in the ratifying countries. The challenges of data collection are significant, but some innovative methods have been devised and the results are interesting if far from conclusive. The pioneer in this type of research was probably Oona Hathaway, finding no connection between ratification of treaties and improvements on the ground, and even some deterioration in some countries.[16] Others have questioned such studies and have found more

---

15 S Wheatley, *"How the 1960 Sharpeville massacre sparked the birth of international human rights law", The Conversation, 20.3.2020.*

16 OA Hathaway, "Do Human Rights Treaty Make a Difference", 111 Yale LJ 1935. But note that her focus was on a handful of civil and political rights (genocide, torture, fair trial, civil liberty and political equality of women).

positive results, such as Beth Simmons, especially in certain types of countries, i.e. those transitioning from authoritarian to democratic regimes, and certain types of rights, such as gender discrimination, children' rights and torture.[17] More studies, including my own on the right to health in Brazil discussed in the next section, seem to corroborate Simmons' argument that IHRL's effectiveness vary from place to place yet, when it works, it is mostly through local mobilization, i.e. by strengthening domestic pressure groups and not through direct enforcement.[18]

4 Advances in Social and Economic Rights

Not many studies have focused on social and economic rights, yet here, as I will argue, the connection between IHRL and domestic improvement may be even stronger. This will sound surprising, or even implausible, to many social rights supporters. As mentioned earlier, many tend to see social rights as neglected in comparison to civil and political rights, the "poor cousins"! But this, I repeat, is due to the narrow, and in my view misguided emphasis on adjudicatory mechanisms and judicial enforcement as a crucial element of effectiveness and a lack of attention to empirical data on the situation of human rights enjoyment on the ground. Once we move beyond that narrow frame and explore the other potential routes to effectiveness, as discussed in the previous section, we start to realise that the "poor cousin" narrative is not very plausible.

A good place to start, as Kathryn Sikkink has done in her book *Evidence for Hope*,[19] is by looking at the raw data on social and economic indicators of the past few decades. Whatever indicator one chooses on education, health, poverty, etc, the vast majority of countries in the world have witnessed significant improvements in all of them, and most notably after the second world war, which is of course when IHRL started to develop. Take, as an example, child mortality rates which, as the chart below shows, have decreased significantly almost everywhere since the second half of the last century.

17 See also AM Clark and K Sikkink, "Information Effects and Human Rights Data: Is the Good News about Increased Human Rights Information Bad News for Human Rights Measures?" (2013) 35(3) Human Rights Quarterly 539.

18 BA Simmons, *Mobilizing for Human Rights. Intenrational Law in Domestic Politics* (Cambridge University Press 2009).

19 K Sikkink, Evidence for Hope. Making Human Rights Work in the 21st Century (Princeton University Press 2017).

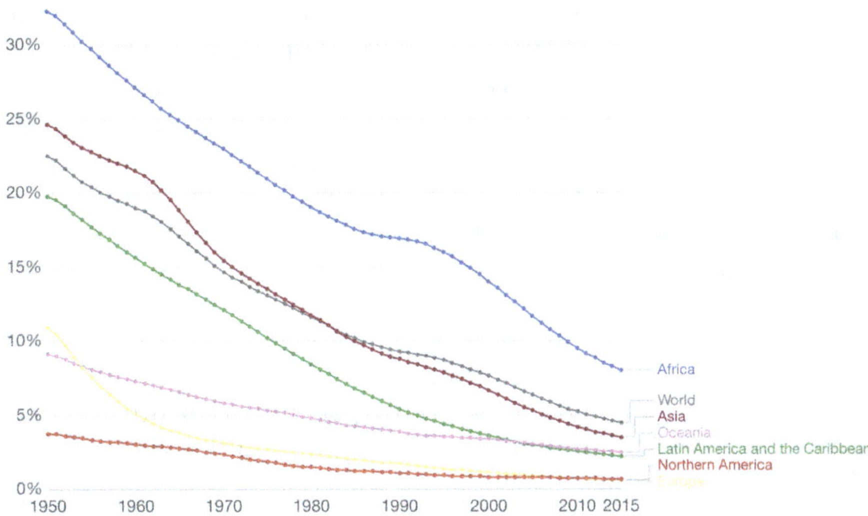

FIGURE 9.1 Child Morality-Share of children, born, alive, dying before they are five years old
SOURCE: UN POPULATION DIVISION (2017 REVISION). OURWORLDINDATA.ORG/CHILD-MORTALITY. CC-BY.

A similar picture would emerge of all main social and economic indicators. Improvements in these indicators do not of course prove that IHRL is effective, as the causal determinants of such improvements are very complex and may well exclude IHRL altogether, i.e. it is of course possible (though not plausible as I will argue shortly) that such improvements have occurred without any input from IHRL. But the mere fact that significant improvements have indeed taken place weakens significantly the sceptical narratives we are discussing here. Recall that the sceptical view is grounded on the perception that the world is worse or stagnant in terms of human rights violations in spite of the existence of IHRL. Once this perception is formed, the understandable inference is that IHRL is ineffective. Yet when we look at the empirical data and realise that the world is *not* worse (nor stagnant), but in fact way better than it has ever been (even if far from ideal of course), in particular in terms of social and economic conditions, this particular sceptical narrative collapses. There may still be other reasons, of course, to be sceptical about IHRL. One may still claim, for instance, that the world has improved *despite* the existence of IHRL, i.e. that IHRL played no part whatsoever in the significant improvements that occurred, coincidentally, in the same period that IHRL has developed. But this is a very different type of sceptical narrative, much weaker, and one whose accuracy is much more difficult to assess.

To know if and how IHRL has played a part in such improvements we need to carry out a much more in depth and focused investigation than simply observing a correlation between the existence, or even ratification of IHRL and improvement of the human rights situation on the ground.[20] An in depth analysis of the factors that led to improvements in a particular context needs to be conducted and, even then, it is unlikely that a very clear-cut answer either way will be possible. But this is of course a limitation of most scientific endeavours, in particular social sciences ones. We ought to be aware of these limitations but still try to advance towards plausible, if always inevitably tentative conclusions.

This is precisely what I have tried to do in my research on the effectiveness of the right to health in Brazil, which I will summarise here as an illustration of the kind of endeavour that may shed more light on the debate on effectiveness and on the role of international law and lawyers.[21] Although my main focus was not IHRL but rather the role played by the right to health recognised in the 1988 Constitution, I believe that some of my findings strengthen the hypothesis that IHRL can and probably does play an important role in advancing the enjoyment of the right to health on the ground. It is just not the role envisaged by sceptics, who focus too much on international adjudication.

As I argue in that study, the significant improvement of the health conditions of the Brazilian population in the past three decades (see, as an example among many, the figure on infant and child mortality below) could not be appropriately explained without the inclusion of the right to health in the 1988 constitution. As I also argue, however, those improvements were not a consequence of the availability of domestic adjudication for the judicial enforcement of that right. They were the upshot of civil society pressure and legislative action catalysed and strengthened by the existence of the right to health in IHRL and, after 1988, by the inclusion of that right in the national constitution. After 1988, the Brazilian state adopted a myriad of health policies, through primary and secondary legislation and executive regulations, which have had a demonstrable effect in improving the health conditions of the population, such as the creation of the Unified Public Health System in 1990 (the SUS, a universal system funded by taxation), the Family Health Strategy which

20 A Palmer, J Tomkinson, C Phung *et al*, "Does ratification of human-rights treaties have effects on population health?", (2009) 373 The Lancet 1987; N. Pillay, "Ratification of human rights treaties: the beginning not the end", (2009) The Lancet 374(9688):447; T Risse, SC Ropp, K Sikkink K, BA Simmons, "From Ratification to Compliance: Quantitative Evidence on the Spiral Model", in T Risse, SC Ropp, K Sikkink K (eds), *The Persistent Power of Human Rights: From Commitment to Compliance* (Cambridge University Press 2013).

21 OLM Ferraz, Health as a Human Right. The Politics and Judicialization of Health in Brazil (Cambridge University Press 2020).

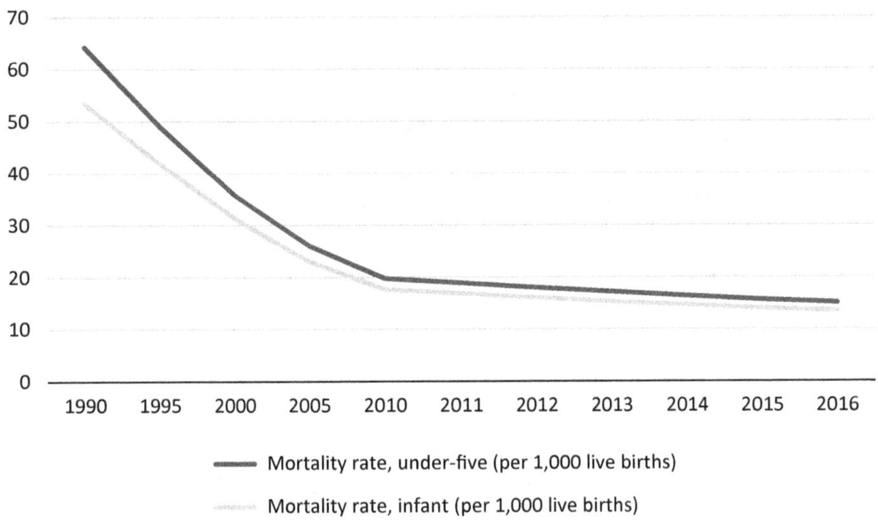

FIGURE 9.2 Infant and child mortality in Brazil
SOURCE: UNITED NATIONS DEVELOPMENT PROGRAMME, HUMAN DEVELOPMENT REPORTS

extended primary care to more than a hundred million people, mostly poor, and several others I discuss at length in that study.[22]

This mechanisms of guaranteeing the effectiveness of rights' through political mobilization rather than judicial enforcement operate both at the national and international level and to a great extent independently from ratification of international treaties or domestic legalization or constitutionalization of rights. Formal recognition in treaties and domestic legal instruments can of course strengthen the political campaign towards effectiveness, as I argued was the case in Brazil after 1988. Yet the mere existence of the IHRL system can provide important support for domestic political struggles for the improvement of human rights. I have already mentioned the South Africa (apartheid) and Latin America (torture) cases earlier. Let me add here, by way of conclusion of this section, a note on the right to health in Brazil. The campaign for health improvements started of course way before the constitutionalization of the right

22 The availability of judicial enforcement, on the contrary, has been actually disrupting the actual implementation of that right by transferring scarce resources of the public system to litigants whose claims are by and large successful yet unjustified according to well established principles of fair allocation of health resources. See Ferraz, ibid (n23), and OLM Ferraz, "The right to health in the courts of brazil: worsening health inequities?" (2009) 11(2) Health and Human Rights, An International Journal.

to health in 1988, during the military dictatorship (1964–1985). At that time, Brazil had not ratified any UN human rights law treaty that includes the right to health.[23] Yet, in my view, the mere recognition of that right in international instruments such as the World Health Organisation Constitution of 1948, the Universal Declaration of Human Rights (1948), the International Covenant on Economic, Social and Cultural Rights (1976) and the Alma Ata Declaration of (1978) provided crucial political force to the Brazilian campaign for that right to be also recognised and implemented domestically, before and after 1988.[24]

5 Conclusion: the Role of International Law and Lawyers

I have tried to show, in this short piece, that scepticism about the effectiveness of international human rights law, currently at a high level, perhaps the highest ever so far in its brief history, is misguided. This false perception results from a combination of flawed views and attitudes that reinforce each other: i. the conflation between *occurrence* of human rights violations and *failure* of the international human rights legal system; ii. an exaggerated faith in adjudication (i.e. judicial enforcement) as a relevant instrument of effectiveness; and iii. a lack of attention to empirical data on the actual enjoyment of human rights by real people.

Once these mistakes are corrected, the following, more plausible conclusions in my view, seem to follow: i. Human rights enjoyment, in particular social and economic rights, have seen significant improvement in the past seven decades; ii. these improvements have occurred despite the lack of strong

23 In fact, during the military regime Brazil ratified only two human rights treaties: the Convention on the Elimination of all Forms of Racial Discrimination in 1968 and the Convention on the Elimination of All Forms of Discrimination against Women, in 1984, i.e. in the final gasps of the military regime. After the end of the military regime Brazil has ratified all major human rights treaties: CAT (1989), CRC (1990), ICCPR (1992), ICESCR (1992), CRPD (2008) and ICPPED (2010) with the exception of the International Convention on the Protection of the Rights of All Migrant Workers and Members of their Families. https://indicators.ohchr.org.

24 In reality, it is hard to disentangle the effect of domestic and international legal norms in the field of human rights as they seem to reinforce each other. In the case of health, for instance, Brazil was actually the country that insisted, after the WWII, for health to be included in the Charter of the United Nations (arts. 57 and 62) and, together with China, the author of the joint proposal to the San Francisco Conference that an International Health Conference be called as a matter of urgency. Brazilian public health expert Geraldo Horacio Paula Souza is considered one of the leading actors in the creation of the WHO. https://apps.who.int/iris/bitstream/handle/10665/126402/1947.pdf?sequence=2.

judicial enforcement mechanisms at the international level, and in spite of often counter-productive judicial enforcement at the domestic level; iii. international human rights law works most effectively through domestic political mobilization, even when the state in question has not ratified IHRL or accepted the jurisdiction of its adjudicative bodies. If this is true, international human rights lawyers have an important role to play in supporting domestic struggles that use IHRL mostly as a political tool, i.e. to promote legislation and policy.

CHAPTER 10

Lawyers' Role in the Protection of Human Dignity of Indigenous Persons

Stefan Kirchner and Timo Koivurova

1 Introduction

In the countries which have been their home for many generations, indigenous peoples are often marginalized and subjected to systematic discrimination. This has an impact not only on indigenous societies but also on indigenous individuals. Often, human rights violations suffered by indigenous persons touch upon the dignity of the person. In this chapter, it will be investigated which role lawyers can play in the protection of the human dignity of indigenous persons.

The term 'lawyer' is used here in a wide sense, including all persons with legal training who are working in legal roles, for example as attorneys, in public administration, as judges or in similar functions. The focus will be on the work of lawyers on the local, meaning national and sub-national, level, because the realization of human rights through legal work begins on the local level.

While particular attention will be given to the potential for international human rights litigation, which has played an important role for the development and protection of the rights of indigenous peoples, the practical use of international human rights law is not limited to the international level. After all, it is in the interaction with the directly relevant public authorities that individuals experience the power of the state and its institutions. While this happens not entirely regardless of the way in which tasks are distributed between municipalities, regions or the national level, most interaction between the individual and public authorities happens on the local level. Similarly relevant is the interaction between individuals and corporations. Such interaction can be key for the protection of human rights because the power-imbalance between the individual and corporations can be similar or even more significant than that between individuals and the state. Such human rights-relevant interactions can be direct, for example, if the individual is in the role of customer or employee, in which there will often be a significant degree of dependency of the individual on the corporation, or indirect, for example if a mining company receives an exploration or exploitation permit for lands which have been

 | DOI:10.1163/9789004435650_011

traditionally used by indigenous peoples for the pursuit of their livelihoods, even if, as is often the case, these lands are not legally owned by the indigenous community. It is in such circumstances that awareness of human rights obligations is most relevant because it is in the direct interaction between authorities and individuals or groups where the state has the most direct effect on the human being. These effects can be indirect, for example in issuing a permit to a third party for an activity which can be harmful for an individual. This is a particular concern for indigenous communities who might suffer, for example, loss of traditional livelihoods if the authorities issue a mining permit for an area which has been used by the indigenous community for reindeer herding or fishing.[1]

In this chapter, we will first look at human dignity as a *legal* concept (section 2), before attempting to localize it within international human rights law, including international legal norms which are aimed at the protection of indigenous rights (section 3). In a third step, we will then look at the role of lawyers to use international human rights standards, in particular through international human rights litigation (section 4).

2 Human Dignity as a Legal Concept

From a legal perspective, human dignity is notoriously difficult to grasp as a concept because neither the nature of the concept, nor its contents are entirely clear. Indeed, it is even disputed whether dignity is a right or an inherent quality of all human beings. Some understand human dignity not only as the basis for human rights but also as a human right in itself[2] and a single permanent definition of the term 'human dignity' is thought to be impossible.[3] One widely accepted definition of human dignity is negative in nature, in so far as human dignity is thought to mean that no human being may be turned into an object[4] and always remains a subject. This notion of humans not being allowed to be turned into objects runs parallel to the development of peremptory or

1 Stefan Kirchner, 'Indigenous Rights and Livelihoods as Concerns in the Decision-Making on Extractive Industries in Finland', in Kamrul Hossain, José Miguel Roncero Martín & Anna Petrétei (eds.), *Human and Societal Security in the Circumpolar Arctic* (Brill Nijhoff 2018) 263, 271.

2 Michael Blank, Helmut Fangmann & Ulrich Hammer, *Grundgesetz, Basiskommentar, Mit der aktuellen Verfassungsreform* (Bund-Verlag 1996) 21.

3 Ibid.

4 Ibid, 22.

jus cogens norms of international law, which outlaw certain activities which would achieve exactly that without exception: genocide,[5] slavery and torture. Human dignity is both a legal and a philosophical concept.[6] This double dimension might explain why it is at times difficult to define and to grasp from a legal perspective and why the uncertainty of the meaning of human dignity has been traced back to its symbolic nature.[7] This in turn leads to questions regarding the normative value of human dignity[8] although individual human rights can be traced back to human dignity,[9] despite this not being necessarily expressed so clearly in all human rights documents.[10] Even if human dignity is not considered a human right, it is a legal principle which must be respected.[11]

The concept of human dignity as such is not dependent on a specific cultural tradition,[12] although the emphasis on the dignity of the individual may be more obviously visible in some legal traditions when compared to others. Human dignity is a philosophical term which has been discussed for about 2500 years[13] but its trans-cultural nature might explain its increasing importance as a largely indeterminate legal concept in international law in the 20th century.

Human dignity as a legal term does not have one single definition. It is rather up to those who practice law, especially lawmakers and courts, to fill the shell provided by the concept with material content which is accessible from a legal perspective. Laws follow from human rights, not the other way around,[14] and human rights serve to safeguard human dignity. Human dignity has been described by *Jarass* and *Pieroth* as the "claim to social value and respect" which every human is due by virtue of being human.[15] This definition already contains an element of equality,[16] and from the perspective of human rights law, the definition relates closely to the right to private life.[17]

5 Ibid.
6 Josef Römelt, *Menschenwürde und Freiheit* (Herder 2006) 148.
7 Bodo Pieroth, Bernhard Schlink, *Grundrechte Staatsrecht II* (18th ed., C. F. Müller Verlag 2002) 79.
8 Römelt, supra note 5, 149.
9 Ibid, 152.
10 Ibid, 153.
11 Bodo Pieroth, Bernhard Schlink, supra note 7.
12 Hans Joas, *Die Sakralität der Person – Eine neue Genealogie der Menschenrechte* (1st ed., Suhrkamp Verlag 2011) 21.
13 Bodo Pieroth, Bernhard Schlink, supra note 7.
14 Amartya Sen, *Die Idee der Gerechtigkeit* (C. H. Beck 2009) 390.
15 Hans D. Jarass, Bodo Pieroth. *Grundgesetz für die Bundesrepublik Deutschland* (C. H. Beck 2009), 41, referring to the case law of the German Federal Constitutional Court.
16 Ibid, translation by Kirchner.
17 Ibid.

Whether human dignity is a right in itself of an essential quality which is inherent to all humans by virtue of our human nature is the object of academic debate,[18] although the practical differences between these two positions are limited[19] because human dignity forms the basis for human rights norms. In practice, human dignity is protected through the effective implementation of human rights law.[20] Through human rights law, every public authority is obliged to respect human dignity and the concept of human dignity indirectly also affects relations between non-state actors because not only public law norms (here understood as including the totality of legal norms which regulate the relationship between the individual and public authorities, including criminal and procedural law) but also private law norms must be compatible with human dignity.[21] This has to be the case not only in abstract, legislative, terms but also in the practical implementation and enforcement of such norms, for example through court judgments. At the end of the day, all powers, legislature, executive and judiciary, are bound by human rights law and ultimately have to protect human dignity through the respect for and application of human rights law. Violating human dignity means violating human rights,[22] assuming that human rights laws are designed in a way that is meant to protect human dignity (which at least is the assumption underlying international human rights treaties). Human rights law is therefore the key legal tool for the protection of human dignity. Effective protection of human dignity requires effective implementation of human rights law in relation to the individual. This also applies to internationally protected human rights, the effective realization of which depends on the implementation of human rights norms on the national and sub-national levels.

As a legal concept, human dignity might be more accessible and acceptable from the perspective of international law than from the perspective of national law because the latter usually is more positivist in its approach when compared to the former. From the perspective of a positivist view of law, the concept of human dignity and the idea of international law share similarities in their vagueness. This vagueness, though, is not a bug but an inherent and relevant feature of these legal concepts. On the level of national law, human dignity becomes tangible through specific regulations, which have a direct bearing on human dignity, for example when the state regulates issues in the

18 Ibid, with further references.

19 Ibid, 40.

20 Hans D. Jarass, Bodo Pieroth, supra note 15.

21 Ibid.

22 Ibid.

field of biomedicine, such as cloning or euthanasia. Often these issues are politically contested, which can lead to situations where mere recourse to the concept of human dignity as a legal argument may be seen as taking a political statement. On the international level, human dignity has been encoded into human rights treaties, many of which were concluded more than half a century ago and remain practically relevant today. Therefore, it can be assumed that at the international level, human dignity remains more of a *legal* concept than at the national level, where it is often politicized. The following section shows how human dignity has evolved from a philosophical to a legal concept and how it has found its way into modern international human rights law.

3 Human Dignity and Human Rights

The concept of human dignity has been particularly influential in the development of international human rights standards after the end of World War II, for example in the case of the Universal Declaration of Human Rights (UDHR) and of international treaties, such as the European Convention on Human Rights (ECHR). Human dignity was not mentioned in the human rights declarations of the 18th century but since the adoption of the Universal Declaration of Human Rights (UDHR) it is considered the fundament for the understanding of human rights.[23] Despite its growing importance in national law, it was the dissemination of the idea of human dignity through international human rights treaties which shaped the international legal order after 1945. Human dignity permeates the discourse on human rights even when it is not referred to directly. For example, it was the European Union (EU) Charter of Fundamental rights which gave human dignity a positive normative role in the law of the EU.[24] Even though it may not always have been mentioned explicitly by the European Court of Justice (ECJ),[25] it can be said that human dignity influenced the jurisprudence of the ECJ already long before this codification.[26] The Charter was the first codification of human rights at the EU level,[27] although

23 Christoph Menke, Arnd Pollmann, *Philosophie der Menschenrechte, Zur Einführung* (Junius Verlag 2007) 129.

24 Frank Schorkopf, '§15 Würde des Menschen, Persönlichkeits- und Kommunikationsgrundrechte', in Dirk Ehlers (ed.), *Europäische Grundrechte und Grundfreiheiten* (2nd ed., De Gruyter Recht, 2005) 410.

25 Ibid, 411.

26 Ibid, 412.

27 Christian Callies, '§20 Die Europäische Grundrechts-Charta', in Dirk Ehlers (ed.), *Europäische Grundrechte und Grundfreiheiten* (2nd ed., De Gruyter Recht, 2005), 531.

the ECHR has long served as an inspiration also in the context of the EU. While the ECHR is based on the notion of dignity, the EU Charter emphasizes human dignity by giving it pride of place.[28]

In particular, the European Convention on Human Rights is relevant also in the everyday practice of lawyers who work at the local level. The European Convention on Human Rights is the result of a legal development which aimed to serve and protect the individual. Human dignity is the fundament for human rights treaties, such as the European Convention on Human Rights where the protection of human dignity is realized for example in the prohibition of torture (Article 3 ECHR).[29] The concept of human dignity also influences the interpretation and practical application of norms contained in the ECHR. This approach emphasizes the individual, rather than the collective and it is hardly surprising that indigenous peoples are rarely given attention in the ECHR system. But the ECHR does not exist in a vacuum. It should rather be seen in context with other international treaties, in particular the International Covenant on Civil and Political Rights (ICCPR), which has been ratified by all states parties to the ECHR. *Waldron*'s conception of law protecting dignity through human rights[30] adequately describes the relationship between human dignity and human rights law. In other words, from a legal perspective, the concept of human dignity can be understood from its function.[31] The following section illustrates this further by looking at the role of international human rights law in general, and human rights litigation in particular, in the protection of the human dignity of indigenous peoples.

4 International Human Rights Litigation and Indigenous Peoples

4.1 *Indigenous Rights in International Human Rights Law*

In an indigenous context, human dignity is realized through the enjoyment of collective human rights. Community and culture are seen as part of the identity,[32] both for the group and for the individual. Indigenous rights are both

28 Ibid, 534.

29 Robert Uerpmann-Wittzack, '§3 Höchstpersönliche Rechte und Diskriminierungsverbot', in Dirk Ehlers (ed.), *Europäische Grundrechte und Grundfreiheiten* (2nd ed., De Gruyter Recht 2005) 63, 77.

30 Jeremy Waldron, 'How Law Protects Dignity' (2012) 71 *Cambridge Law Journal* 200.

31 Adalbert Podlech 'Absatz 1', in Richard Bäumlin et al. (eds.), *Kommentar zum Grundgesetz für die Bundesrepublik Deutschland, Band 1, Art. 1–37* (Luchterhand Verlag 1989) 199, 205.

32 Alexandra Xanthaki, *Indigenous Rights and United Nations Standards – Self-Determination, Culture and Land*, (Cambridge University Press 2007) 14.

related to the individual and to the collective.[33] Especially, the level of states' recognition of collective rights, in particular land rights, is seen as an important marker for the status of indigenous rights. The recognition of collective rights has a direct effect on indigenous individuals: "Indigenous peoples view the recognition of their collective rights as a token of respect towards their identity and communities as well as the only way for their survival and development".[34] Of particular importance to indigenous peoples are environmental human rights, because indigenous communities are usually closely connected to nature for a range of purposes from livelihoods[35] and food security[36] to culture[37] and spirituality,[38] which can be protected through existing human rights mechanisms.[39]

Like everybody else, indigenous persons enjoy the full range of human rights.[40] In the places where indigenous peoples are a numerical minority, they also have rights as minorities,[41] such as language rights, even though

---

33 Ibid, 13.

34 Ibid.

35 Øyvind Ravna, 'Links between Lands, Territories, Environment and Cultural Heritage – The Recognition of Sámi Lands in Norway', in Alexandra Xanthaki, Sanna Valkonen, Leena Heinämäki (eds.), *Indigenous Peoples' Cultural Heritage: Rights, Debates, Challenges* (Brill Nijhoff 2017) 175; Lydia Heikkilä, 'Reindeer Talk – Sámi Reindeer Herding and Nature Management' (2006) *Acta Universitatis Lapponensis* 110, 269; Neil Kent, *The Sámi Peoples of the North – A Social and Cultural History* (Hurst & Company 2014), 228 et seq.

36 José Miguel Roncero Martín, 'Policies and Strategies for the Arctic: A Review of the Approaches to Human Security in the Arctic', in Kamrul Hossain, José Miguel Roncero Martín, Anna Petrétei (eds.), *Human and Societal Security in the Circumpolar Arctic, Studies in Polar Law 1* (Brill Nijhoff 2018) 19, 31.

37 Sanna Valkonen, Jarno Valkonen, Veli-Pekka Lehtola, 'An Ontological Politics of and for the Sámi Cultural Heritage – Reflections on Belonging to the Sámi Community and the Land', in Alexandra Xanthaki, Sanna Valkonen, Leena Heinämäki (eds.), *Indigenous Peoples' Cultural Heritage: Rights, Debates, Challenges* (Brill Nijhoff 2017) 149; Øyvind Ravna, 'Links between Lands, Territories, Environment and Cultural Heritage – The Recognition of Sámi Lands in Norway', in Alexandra Xanthaki, Sanna Valkonen, Leena Heinämäki (eds.), *Indigenous Peoples' Cultural Heritage: Rights, Debates, Challenges* (Brill Nijhoff 2017) 175, 176.

38 Dwight Newman, Elisa Ruozzi, Stefan Kirchner, 'Legal Protection of Sacred Natural Sites Within Human Rights Jurisprudence: Sápmi and Beyond' in Leena Heinämäki & Thora Herrman (eds.), *Experiencing and Protecting Sacred Natural Sites of Sámi and Other Indigenous Peoples: The Sacred Arctic* (Springer 2017) 11.

39 Leena Heinämäki, 'The Protection of the Environmental Integrity of Indigenous Peoples in Human Rights Law' (2006) 17 *Finnish Yearbook of International Law* 187.

40 Mary H. Durfee, Rachael Lorna Johnstone, *Arctic Governance in a Changing World* (Rowman & Littlefield 2019) 154.

41 Ibid.

international law usually distinguishes between indigenous peoples and minorities. The range of international human rights documents which are relevant for indigenous peoples is impressive.[42] At the global level, these are the 1948 Universal Declaration of Human Rights and the 2007 United Nations Declaration on the Rights of Indigenous Peoples (Durfee & Johnstone, 2019: 156). Even though these two documents are non-binding declarations by the UN General Assembly, they both have influenced the development of domestic laws and of customary international law. Customary international law has already overtaken the level of protection offered by the 1989 ILO Convention No. 169 (the Indigenous and Tribal Peoples Convention), the key specialized international treaty protecting indigenous rights. There are also a number of global human rights treaties which, in addition to numerous optional protocols to these treaties, can be utilized by indigenous litigants: the 1965 Convention on the Elimination of All Forms of Racial Discrimination (CERD),[43] the 1966 International Covenants on Civil and Political Rights (ICCPR) and on Economic, Social and Cultural Rights (ICESCR), the 1979 Convention on the Elimination of All Forms of Discrimination Against Women (CEDAW), the 1984 Convention against Torture and Other Cruel, Inhuman or Degrading Treatment or Punishment (CAT), the 1989 Convention on the Rights of the Child (CRC), the 1990 International Convention on the Rights of All Migrant Workers and Members of Their Families (MWC), the 2006 Convention on the Rights of Persons with Disabilities (CRPD) and the 2006 International Convention for the Protection of All Persons from Enforced Disappearances (CED).[44] At the regional level, the 1950 European Convention on Human Rights (ECHR), the 1948 American Declaration on the Rights and Duties of Man (ADRDM), the 1969 American Convention on Human Rights (ACHR) and the 2016 American Declaration on the Rights of Indigenous Peoples (ADRIP) need to be mentioned (Durfee & Johnstone, 2019: 156). Through the protection of a wide range of human rights, these treaties and declarations implicitly serve the protection of human dignity. Indigenous persons benefit from the effective implementation of these rights in general, and of cultural rights such as those protected under Article 27 ICCPR. In addition, the ILO 169 Convention is specifically designed to protect the rights of indigenous peoples.

---

42 Ibid, 156 et seq.

43 S. James Anaya, *International Human Rights and Indigenous Peoples* (Wolters Kluwer 2009).

44 Mary H. Durfee, Rachael Lorna Johnstone, supra note 40, 156 et seq.

4.2 *Indigenous Rights and Human Rights Litigation*

The ILO 169 Convention remains the most important international treaty for the protection of indigenous rights because the more advanced Universal Declaration of the Rights of Indigenous Peoples (UNDRIP) is not legally binding due to its nature as a resolution of the UN General Assembly. Even though it is true "that individuals are among the subjects" of the ILO 169 Convention,[45] the procedural system employed by the ILO under Article 24 of its Constitution only gives standing to representative organizations of employers or employees, thereby deviating from the common system of human rights complaints under classical human rights treaties, which either use courts or court-like bodies to deal with claims brought by individual applicants or groups of applicants against states.

Unlike many of the more general global and regional international human rights treaties, the ILO 169 Convention has not been ratified by some developed countries which are home to indigenous peoples which otherwise have a track record as leaders in international human rights law, such as Finland or Sweden. From the perspective of practicing attorneys, while still the most important international treaty for the protection of the rights of indigenous peoples, the ILO 169 Convention is of limited value in terms of litigation due to Article 24 of the ILO Constitution.[46] Not leading to a judgment, the ILO mechanism falls short of the expectations created by more modern models of human rights litigation, for example those created in the European and Inter-American human rights systems. The latter systems are crowned by international human rights courts in the proper sense of the term. The organization of these bodies and the procedural rules employed by them mirror litigants' experience of domestic legal systems. By issuing binding judgments within frameworks of larger international organizations, such as the Council of Europe in the case of the European Court of Human Rights, these international courts have set a gold standard in international human rights litigation, at least as far as the applicants are concerned. The system established under Article 24 of the ILO Constitution, while groundbreaking at the time it was initiated, no longer conforms to these expectations, especially with regard to the position of the victims of human rights violations in international proceedings, who now expect to be heard directly on the international stage as well. It is therefore not

---

45 Tanja Joona, *ILO Convention No. 169 in a Nordic Context with Comparative Analysis: An Interdisciplinary Approach* (Lapland University Press 2012) 147.

46 On the role of the ILO 169 Convention for indigenous rights litigation see Anaya, supra note 43, 133 et seq.

surprising that the regional human rights bodies have become important fora of choice for indigenous litigants.[47]

The regional and international treaties and protocols thereto provide for enforcement mechanisms. This distinguishes the treaties from mere declarations and opens the door for human rights litigation, potentially also in multiple fora.[48] (but see also Kirchner, 2018a). The possibility of indigenous human rights litigation provides a practical role for lawyers in the protection of the human dignity of indigenous persons and of the rights of indigenous peoples. From the perspective of indigenous rights litigation, the regional human rights systems in the Americas and in Europe have been particularly relevant. European human rights institutions had to deal with cases involving traditional indigenous livelihoods which are at the heart of the culture of the indigenous Sámi people of Northern Europe, in particular with reindeer herding[49] and fishing[50] but also concerning the relocation of a community of 116 people from Thule to Qaanaq in order to allow for the expansion of the US Air Base in Thule.[51]

In the Americas, "the Inter-American Commission of Human Rights and the Inter-American Court of Human Rights [...] have increasingly played a relevant role in the protection of indigenous rights".[52] This can be explained not only by the large number of indigenous peoples in Latin America but also by the specific role of the judiciary in the traditional emphasis on constitutional courts and *amparo* proceedings in the protection of human rights in many

47 Timo Koivurova, 'Jurisprudence of the European Court of Human Rights Regarding Indigenous Peoples: Retrospect and Prospects' (2011) 18 *International Journal on Minority and Group Rights* 1; Stefan Kirchner, 'Conceptions of Indigenousness in the Case Law of the European Court of Human Rights' (2016) 38 *Loyola of Los Angeles International and Comparative Law Review* 169.

48 Stefan Kirchner, 'Lis alibi pendens in International Human Rights Litigation' (2018) *Edilex*, 2 March 2018, https://www.edilex.fi/artikkelit/18545.

49 *G. & E. v. Norway* (1983) App no. 9278/81 and 9415/81 (EComHR, 3 October 1983); *Könkämä and 38 other Saami villages v. Sweden* (1996), App no. 27033/95 (EComHR, 25 November 1996); *Handölsdalen Sami Village and others v. Sweden* (2010) App no. 39013/04 (ECtHR, 30 March 2010).

50 *G. & E. v. Norway* (1983) App no. 9278/81 and 9415/81 (EComHR, 3 October 1983); *Johtti Sapmelaccat Ry and others v. Finland* (2005) App no. 41969/98 (ECtHR, 18 January 2005).

51 *Hingitaq 53 v. Denmark* (2006) App no. 18584/94 (ECtHR, 12 January 2006); Michael Byers, *International Law and the Arctic* (Cambridge University Press 2014).

52 Alexandra Tomaselli, 'Indigenous Peoples and their Right to Political Participation – International Law Standards and their Application in Latin America' (Nomos 2016) 277; see also Thomas M. Antkowiak, 'Rights, Resources, and Rhetoric: Indigenous Peoples and the Inter-American Court' (2013) 35 *University of Pennsylvania Journal of International Law*, 113; Anaya, supra note 43, 251 et seq.

states in the region. It is against this backdrop that the concept of "*vida digna*" or "dignified life" has been developed.[53] The concept of *vida digna* can be understood as the a holistic view of dignity and of what is necessary for people to live in dignity. This goes beyond human rights but goes to the core of the reality of human life, both as an individual and in community with others. The idea of such a dignified life addresses human rights from the goal of human rights protection and emphasizes the overall role of human dignity in international human rights law. Especially in Latin America, land rights and dignity are connected issues, as is evidenced by indigenous activism, for example in Bolivia[54] and Ecuador.[55]

The human rights mechanism created by the optional protocol to the ICCPR can be understood as being located half-way between the hybrid system established by Article 24 of the ILO Constitution and regional human rights courts. Indigenous litigants from different parts of the world have used that system to claim indigenous land use rights and, especially since the 1980s, through litigation have contributed to the development of the rights of indigenous peoples at the international level. While the challenges faced by indigenous peoples in the Arctic are similar to those seen by indigenous peoples elsewhere,[56] the presence of reliable court systems and solid respect for the rule of law, in particular in the Nordic countries, has facilitated the focus of Arctic indigenous peoples on human rights litigation, both under the ICCPR and the ECHR. The case law generated in this way[57] has shaped the development of customary international law.

This history of indigenous-driven human rights litigation ran parallel to the talks at the United Nations which eventually led to the UN Declaration on the Rights of Indigenous Peoples (UNDRIP). In the latter development, indigenous representatives, including indigenous lawyers, played an important role, highlighting the importance of access to education for indigenous persons and the contribution of indigenous peoples to the development of the international legal norms which protect them today. The

53 Dwight Newman, Elisa Ruozzi, Stefan Kirchner, 'Legal Protection of Sacred Natural Sites Within Human Rights Jurisprudence: Sápmi and Beyond' in Leena Heinämäki & Thora Herrman (eds.), *Experiencing and Protecting Sacred Natural Sites of Sámi and Other Indigenous Peoples: The Sacred Arctic* (Springer 2017) 434.

54 Alexandra Tomaselli, supra note 52, 286.

55 Ibid, 289.

56 Klaus Dodds, Mark Nuttall, *The Arctic – What Everyone needs to know* (Oxford University Press 2019) 156.

57 On indigenous rights litigation under the ICCPR see Anaya, supra note 46, 186 et seq.

UNDRIP was adopted in 2007 and partially reflects the customary international law concerning the rights of indigenous peoples.[58] While technically non-binding, the UNDRIP has served as an inspiration for national judges and law-makers.[59]

The International Law association (ILA), an eminent international organization of international lawyers, has worked with the UNDRIP from 2006 onwards. Its Committee on the Implementation of the Rights of Indigenous Peoples, has explored how international indigenous standards, especially the UNDRIP, have been implemented by states.[60] The Committee chose to study cases from all regions of the planet, as to how states have implemented the UNDRIP and other international conventions and standards that guarantee rights for indigenous peoples, in particular those related to their land rights. The cases demonstrate that in most regions of the world indigenous peoples' rights to their ancestral territories are not paid enough attention.[61] In many cases the difficulties with implementing their rights (land rights in particular) arise when they conflict with other values which are also important and are also protected by international law.[62] Yet, it is fair to say that when one reads the cases from around the world, not much progress is made in implementing the indigenous international standards, in particular those relating to their land rights. What is even more concerning is that many of the celebrated legal victories of indigenous peoples over their land rights face serious obstacles in becoming an implemented reality.[63]

58 Sebastiaan Johannes Rombouts, *Having a Say – Indigenous Peoples, International and Free, Prior and Informed Consent* (Wolf Legal Publishers 2014) 15; International Law Association, 'Rights of Indigenous Peoples [Sofia Report]' (2012), https://ila.vettoreweb.com/Storage/Download.aspx?DbStorageId=1243&StorageFileGuid=401ee841-8ad2-4e35-8aaf-beebd9b3aa4e, 29.

59 See Anaya, 55 et seq.

60 International Law Association, 'Implementation of the Rights of Indigenous Peoples [Sydney Report]' (2018), https://ila.vettoreweb.com/Storage/Download.aspx?DbStorageId=12120&StorageFileGuid=0b2d3262-b6a5-42ca-a878-5b76133ef818.

61 ILA, supra note 60.

62 For instance, the economic development of a country, see Federico Lenzerini, 'Implementation of the UNDRIP around the world: achievements and future perspectives. The outcome of the work of the ILA Committee on the Implementation of the Rights of Indigenous Peoples' (2019) 23 *The International Journal of Human Rights* 51.

63 Felipe Gómez Isa, 'The Decision by the Inter-American Court of Human Rights on the Awas Tigni vs. Nicaragua Case (2001): The Implementation Gap' (2016), https://ila.vettoreweb.com/Storage/Download.aspx?DbStorageId=1318&StorageFileGuid=8aa2ed22-2ede-43d0-8e65-d46d19a04006.

5 Concluding Remarks

The importance of customary international law norms for the UNDRIP and the impact of human rights litigation initiated by indigenous applicants on the development of customary international law is not to be underestimated. Indigenous rights are part of international human rights law[64] and the work of lawyers in the field of indigenous rights litigation is inseparable from general international human rights law. This work is not restricted to international fora. Human rights are realized, first and foremost, at the local level. As demonstrated by the work in the ILA Committee, lawyers need to pay attention not only to legal victories in courts, but also to how these judgments are enforced and implemented in reality. It is this work which contributes to guaranteeing human dignity through the protection of human rights. In the daily practice of law, the focus is usually on specific human rights rather than on fundamental concepts such as human dignity.[65] Human rights are the concrete, practical realization of human dignity.[66] The legal concept of human dignity cannot provide an answer for all questions.[67] For this it needs human rights and their effective realization through law. It is in the protection of human rights through the creation, application and enforcement of laws which reflect human rights, that lawyers, in their diverse professional roles, contribute to the protection of human dignity, including the human dignity of indigenous persons.

64 Marco Odello, 'Indigenous peoples' rights and cultural identity in the inter-American context' (2012) 16 *International Journal of Human Rights* 25, 31.

65 See already Adalbert Podlech (1989). 'Absatz 1', in: Richard Bäumlin, Jörg Berkemann, Michael Bothe, Hans Peter Bull, Erhard Denninger, Heiko Faber, Götz Frank, Friedhelm Hase, Wolfgang Hoffmann-Riem, Otto-Ernst Kempen, Michael Kittner, Karl-Heinz Ladeur, Adalbert Podlech, Ulrich K. Preuß, Ingo Richter, Helmut Ridder, Alfred Rinken, Hellmut Rittstieg, Gunnar Folke Schuppert, Ekkehart Stein, Rudolf Wassermann, Manfred Zuleeg, *Kommentar zum Grundgesetz für die Bundesrepublik Deutschland, Band 1, Art. 1–37* (Luchterhand Verlag 1989) 199, 205.

66 Cf. Pieroth and Schlink, supra note 7, 79.

67 Jörn Ipsen, *Staatsrecht II Grundrechte* (Luchterhand Verlag 2003), 63.

CHAPTER 11

Slaveries and New Slaveries: Which Role for Human Dignity?

Pasquale De Sena

1 Opening Remarks

No one could seriously doubt that respect for dignity is closely connected to the banning of slavery, as well as the banning of torture and human and degrading treatment. In spite of this, such a conclusion is less trivial than it may appear.

In fact, no reference to dignity is made either by the 1926 Convention on Slavery[1] (at variance with the preamble of the so-called 1956 Supplementary Convention),[2] or by the 1930 Convention on the Elimination of Forced Labour.[3]

Dignity made its appearance in the 1948 Universal Declaration of Human Rights (UDHR),[4] albeit *not* being provided with a precise definition, as a consequence of two basic circumstances. It was clearly perceived that crimes committed by Nazis amounted exactly to extreme denials of human dignity, and invoking dignity was therefore considered as the most appropriate reaction to such denials.[5] Furthermore, it was precisely the fact that dignity was *not* provided with a specific legal meaning both in the United Nations Charter

1 'Slavery Convention', signed at Geneva on 25 September 1926 <www.un.org/en/ genocideprevention/documents/atrocity-crimes/Doc.13_slavery%20conv.pdf>.

2 'Supplementary Convention on the Abolition of Slavery, the Slave Trade, and Institutions and Practices Similar to Slavery', adopted by a Conference of Plenipotentiaries convened by Economic and Social Council resolution 608(XXI) of 30 April 1956 and done at Geneva on 7 September 1956 <www.ohchr.org/Documents/ProfessionalInterest/slaverytrade.pdf>.

3 'Convention concerning Forced or Compulsory Labour' ('Forced Labour Convention', 1930 (No 29)) adopted on 28 June 1930 <www.ilo.org/dyn/normlex/ en/f?p=NORMLEXPUB:12100:0::NO::P12100_ILO_CODE:C029>.

4 References to dignity appear: a) in the Preamble of the UDHR (dignity is considered both as the '[...] foundation of freedom, justice and peace in the world [...]' and the object of a common 'faith' of the 'peoples of the United Nations', b) in art 1, according to which 'all human beings are born free and equal in dignity and rights'; c) in two other articles (art 22, right to social security; art 23, para 3, right to work).

5 J Morsink, 'World War Two and the Universal Declaration' (1993) 15 *Human Rights Quarterly* 357 ff, 362.

 | DOI:10.1163/9789004435650_012

and in the Declaration that rendered it able to reconcile different political stances.[6]

Reflecting on the role of dignity with respect to slavery and new slaveries requires, *first of all*, that a very brief reflection is carried out on the legal meaning of the notion at stake in general terms. On this basis, some remarks will be developed with specific regard to the role played by dignity concerning new slaveries. It is worth noting right now that such a role is far from being insignificant.

2 *Legal Meanings of Dignity: the Idea of Dignity as a* Minimum Standard of Treatment …

Of course, it is not even possible to sketch here a global discussion on the legal meaning and the legal status of dignity in international law.[7] A similar attempt would be manifestly pretentious and no significant result could be achieved in this way.

In spite of this, one may easily argue that both international law scholars and legal theorists display a tendency, starting from the UDHR and the UN

6 Such a circumstance is stressed by C McCrudden, 'Human Dignity and Judicial Interpretation of Human Rights' (2008) 19 *European J Intl L* 655 ff, 678.

7 To tell the truth, the above aspects are usually not dealt with by international law scholars; or rather, apart from C Le Bris *L'humanité saisie par le droit international public* (LGDJ 2012) 101 ff, JA Frowein, 'Human Dignity in International Law' in D Kretzmer, E Klein (eds), *The Concept of Human Dignity in Human Right Discourse* (Kluwer Law International 2002) 121 ff, K Dicke, 'The Founding Function of Human Dignity in the Universal Declaration of Human Rights' ibid 111 ff, O Schachter, 'Human Dignity as a Normative Concept' (1983) 77 *AJIL* 848 ff and A Verdross, 'La dignité de la personne humaine, base des Droits de l'Homme' (1980) 31 *Österreichische Zeitschrift für öffentliches Recht und Völkerrecht* 271 ff, dignity is normally investigated by constitutional law scholars (A Barak, *Human Dignity. The Constitutional Value and the Constitutional Right, Cambridge* (CUP 2015); C Dupré, *The Age of Dignity. Human Rights and Constitutionalism in Europe* (Hart 2015), S Hennette Vauchez, 'A Human dignitas? Remnants of the Ancient Legal Concept in Contemporary Dignity Jurisprudence' (2011) 9 *Intl J Constitutional L* 32 ff, S Hennette Vauchez, 'Une dignitas humaine? Vieilles outres, vin nouveau' (2008) 48 *Droits* 59 ff), human rights judges (JP Costa, 'Human Dignity in the Jurisprudence of the European Court of Human Rights' in C McCrudden (ed), *Understanding Human Dignity* (OUP 2014) 393 ff), legal theorists (J Tasioulas, 'Human Dignity and the Foundations of Human Rights', in C McCrudden (ed), *Understanding Human Dignity* (OUP 2014)) 291–313; B De Gaay Fortman, 'Equal Dignity in International Human Rights', in M Düwell, J Braarvig, R Brownsword, D Mieth (eds), *The Cambridge Handbook on Human Dignity* (CUP 2014) 355-36, J Waldron, *Dignity, Rank and Rights*, (OUP 2012), C McCrudden, 'Human Dignity in Human Rights Interpretation' (n 6).

Charter, to conclude that dignity would be a sort of empty notion under international law. According to Schachter, for example, dignity could be considered as no more than 'an ideal that has not yet been given substantial specific content', and therefore one could simply suggest some '[...] examples of conduct and ideas antithetical to or incompatible with respect for the inherent dignity of the human person'.[8]

More recently, an analogous stance is taken by McCrudden, according to whom dignity would however play *three* important 'institutional' roles in the framework of the judicial interpretation of human rights ... precisely as a consequence of it not being provided with a definite legal meaning.[9]

First of all, dignity would be able to provide a '[...] language in which courts can indicate the weighting given to particular rights and other values [...]' in the context of a proportionality test.[10] To be more precise, in Mc Crudden's opinion, '[w]hen a particular right or other value is described as engaging dignity, this indicates that the court considers that considerable (even in some cases overwhelming) weight should be attributed to it'.[11]

Secondly, having recourse to dignity would enable domestic jurisdictions – particularly during the transition to democracy of Eastern European countries – 'to develop [their] own practice of human rights', albeit on the basis of universal principles of international law.[12]

Lastly, dignity would also function 'as a source from which new rights may be derived, and existing rights extended' within the case law concerning human rights.[13]

Be that as it may, concluding that dignity is devoid of a definite legal meaning is somewhat misleading. In other words, it seems to me that such a conclusion simply reflects the difficulty of conceptualising the different *meanings* that dignity is likely to take on in the relevant practice. Among these different meanings, which cannot be dealt with in depth here,[14] the idea according to which respect for dignity implies a *minimum* standard to be observed for the treatment of individuals (who find themselves) placed under the power of public authorities comes to the fore.

---

8 Schachter, 'Human Dignity as a Normative Concept' (n 7) 852.

9 McCrudden, 'Human Dignity and Judicial Interpretation of Human Rights' (n 6) 713.

10 Ibid 716.

11 Ibid.

12 Ibid 720.

13 ibid 721.

14 A tentative, comprehensive legal analysis of these meanings is carried out in P De Sena, 'Dignité humaine et droit international' forthcoming in *Recueil des Cours de l'Académie de Droit International*.

3 ... and Its Roots

Such an idea – which entails that States have to secure the effective enjoyment of this standard of treatment, also by avoiding that private individuals may infringe it – has its roots in *two* circumstances at least.

I refer, *first*, to common Article 3, para 1, of the four 1949 Geneva Conventions on humanitarian law, applicable to international and non- international armed conflict. It is well known that this provision, in addition to the bans on 'murder', 'torture' and 'cruel treatments', also prohibits 'humiliating and degrading treatment', by expressly defining the latter as 'outrages upon personal dignity'.[15] It is therefore manifestly evident that respect for dignity constitutes the rationale of all the above bans. However, what matters most is that these bans, taken as a whole, are precisely aimed at guaranteeing a *minimum* standard of treatment for individuals in enemy hands, namely under the power of (foreign) public authorities.

As to the *second* relevant circumstance, suffice it to recall the widespread tendency to consider respect for dignity as the legal ground of both the ban on torture and cruel and degrading treatment and that of slavery; ie two bans that are commonly considered as forming part of the hard core ('noyau dur') of international human rights.

Such a tendency clearly emerges from the very fact that it is precisely by having recourse to dignity that both the bans on slavery and compulsory labour, and torture or inhuman and degrading treatments, have been extended to factual hypotheses which are not expressly covered by the corresponding rules. Leaving aside torture and degrading treatment, two judgments of the European Court of Human Rights may be recalled here with respect to slavery and forced and compulsory labour: *Siliadin v France*[16] and *Rantsev v Russia and Cyprus*.[17] In both these judgments, references to respect for dignity were made by the Court in order to trace back forms of servitude or serious exploitation of labour and trafficking of human persons, respectively, to Article 4 of the Convention.

In *Siliadin*, the case of a domestic servant who worked 15 hours a day, without a day off or pay for several years, came to the fore. Although Articles 225-13

15 '[...] the following acts are and shall remain prohibited at any time and in any place whatsoever with respect to the above-mentioned persons: a) violence to life and person, in particular murder of all kinds, mutilation, cruel treatment and torture; b) taking of hostages; c) outrages upon personal dignity, in particular, humiliating and degrading treatment [...]'.

16 *Siliadin v France*, App no 73316/01 (ECtHR, 26 October 2005).

17 *Rantsev v Russia and Cyprus*, App no 25965/04 (ECtHR, 7 January 2010).

and 225-14 of the French Criminal Code 'make it an offence, respectively, to exploit an individual's labour and to submit him or her to working or living conditions that are incompatible with human dignity',[18] the Court granted the application, by arguing that respect for human dignity of Ms Siliadin would have required the adoption of *specific* (legislative) provisions dealing with treatment contrary to Article 4 of the Convention which she complained about.[19]

In *Rantsev*, the reference to human dignity made by the Strasbourg judges appears to be even clearer and more significant. In that case, the Court was called upon to rule on the extension of the scope of application of Article 4 to trafficking of human beings, and the application was granted precisely on account that '[t]here can be no doubt that trafficking threatens the human dignity and fundamental freedoms of its victims'.[20] Subsequently, positive obligations stemming from the said article – in particular the obligation to take protective measures and the procedural obligation to investigate trafficking – were held to be violated by both the respondent States.[21]

Furthermore, it is to be added that neither in *Siliadin*, nor in *Rantsev*, did the applicants complain of being property *stricto sensu* of an owner.

4 *Dignity as a General Principle of Law Concerning New Forms of Slavery:* Katanga, Kunarac and Trabajadores de la Hacienda Brazil Verde

Having established that dignity refers, *inter alia*, to a minimum standard of treatment to be guaranteed to individuals placed under the power of public

18 *Siliadin* (n 16) para 142.

19 ibid paras 143 ff; in other words, the Court held that the French criminal law which was in force at that time did not offer the applicant an effective protection against 'servitude' or, at least, against 'forced and compulsory labour', both of them being considered as violations of dignity.

20 *Rantsev* (n 17) para 282; the above conclusion was reached, regardless of whether 'the treatment about which the applicant complains constitutes 'slavery', 'servitude' or 'forced and compulsory labour'' (ibid).

21 Ibid paras 293, 298, 300 (Cyprus) and paras 303, 306, 309 (Russia). It needs scarcely be said that both the above obligations (as well as the obligation to put in place an appropriate legislative and administrative framework, which was held to be violated by Russia in *Rantsev*) differ from the traditional obligation stemming from the ban of slavery: namely the negative duty of States to prohibit slavery and compulsory labourinto their domestic legal order.

authorities or other private individuals, another question to be dealt with is the *legal function* to be recognized to such a notion.

Making use of dignity in order to extend the scope of application of the ban at stake also sheds light upon this question. In other words, having recourse to dignity for this purpose means nothing less – and nothing more – than using dignity as a *general principle of law*. In fact, the gap-filling function, performed by dignity[22] with specific respect to slavery, undoubtedly constitutes a typical function of general principles of law.

An important confirmation of the foregoing is given by the judgment rendered by a Trial Chamber of the International Criminal Court (ICC) in *Katanga*[23] (2014), as well as the well-known judgment of the International Criminal Tribunal for the Former Yugoslavia (ICTY) in *Kunarac*[24] (2001).

In both these cases, the question of enslavement came to the fore, and in both of them, enslavement – as it occurred in *Rantsev* and *Siliadin*[25] – was considered as not implying ownership in the strict sense, namely as 'acquisition' or 'disposal' of persons for monetary or other compensation.

In *Katanga*, the ICC, starting from the premise that ownership may take many forms, including 'a situation of dependence which entails [the individual's] deprivation of any form of autonomy',[26] expressly concluded that '[t]he use of threats, force or other forms of physical or mental coercion, the exaction of forced labour, the exertion of psychological pressure, the victim's vulnerability and the socioeconomic conditions in which the power is exerted may also be taken into account', given 'that the exercise of the right of *ownership over someone need not entail a commercial transaction*'.[27]

Similar conclusions had already been reached by the ICTY in *Kunarac* at the beginning of 2000s. Suffice it to consider that according to the Tribunal 'the consent or free will of the victim' are often nullified 'by, for example, the threat or use of force or other forms of coercion; the fear of violence, deception or false promises; the abuse of power; the victim's position of vulnerability,

22 Understood as a minimum standard of treatment for individuals placed under the power of public authorities or other private individuals.

23 *Situation in the Democratic Republic of the Congo in the Case of the Prosecutor v Germain Katanga* (Judgment pursuant to article 74 of the Statute) ICC-01/04-01/07 (7 March 2014).

24 *Prosecutor v Dragoljub Kunarac Radomir Kovac and Zoran Vukovic* (Judgment) IT-96-23-T& IT-96-23/1-T (22 February 2001).

25 See above, section 3.

26 *Katanga* (n 23) para 975.

27 Ibid 976 (italics added); in this affair the Court was called upon to rule on a case of sexual slavery.

detention or captivity, psychological oppression or socio-economic conditions',[28] although this way of construing the concept of enslavement ends up being broader than the traditional definitions of slavery, slave trade, etc.[29]

That being said, it has also to be pointed out that in these judgments no *explicit* references are made to dignity in order to extend the notion of enslavement. In spite of this, no one could seriously question that the need to take into account the dignity of victims of the alleged crimes[30] led the above tribunals to state that enslavement also occurs in case of 'psychological oppression', 'control of movement', 'threat or use of force', etc.

In addition, the above circumstances have also been deemed relevant for enslavement in the judgment *Trabajadores de la Hacienda Brazil Verde v Brazil*[31] rendered by the Inter-American Court of Human Rights (IACtHR) in 2016. In this case, the applicants – 85 workers in a privately-owned estate, among whom some children – claimed to be victims of slavery, on account of their working conditions, under Article 6, para 1 of the Convention.[32] Their application was granted by the Court, precisely by arguing that deception, fraud, control of movement, physical and psychological forms of coercion against vulnerable persons amounted to a 'situation of slavery' ('situación de esclavitud'),[33] notwithstanding that such a situation did not entail that victims could be considered as being property *stricto sensu* of an owner, here either.[34] It is worth noting that the Court did not fail to stress that slavery represents a major violation of dignity,[35] being able to subsume other violations equally alleged by the applicants.[36]

28 *Kunarac* (n 26) para 543.

29 Ibid para 541 (for an in-depth analysis of the legal history of enslavement under international law, see paras 515–539).

30 Understood as the guarantee of a minimum standard of treatment.

31 Inter-American Court of Human Rights (IACtHR), *Tabajadores de la Hacienda Brasil Verde v Brazil* (20 October 2016).

32 They were recruited by fraud and deceit, and subsequently subjected to debt bondage; furthermore, their working conditions were inhuman and they were not free to leave the work place.

33 *Tabajadores de la Hacienda Brasil Verde* (n 31) para 304.

34 Ibid see paras 269–272 for an in-depth analysis of the pertinent case law.

35 Ibid para 317: 'Asimismo, la prohibición a no ser sometido a esclavitud juega un papel fundamental en la Convención Americana, por representar una de las violaciones más fundamentales de la *dignidad* de la persona humana y, concomitantemente, de varios derechos de la Convención'. (italics added).

36 Ibid para 306.

5 … and Some Recent Judgments of the European Court of Human Rights

Further and even more significant confirmation of the role played by dignity as a general principle can also be found in the recent case law of the European Court concerning new forms of slaveries.

In addition to *Rantsev*,[37] a very recent judgment rendered by the Court in *S.M. v Croatia*[38] is to be pointed out here. In this judgment, a case of forced prostitution – concerning a young Croatian woman, forced to prostitute by a former police officer – came to the fore. In spite of its purely domestic character, the crime at stake has been considered as amounting to trafficking and, therefore, as being a violation of Article 4 of the Convention;[39] subsequently, Croatia was found responsible for not fulfilling procedural obligations stemming from the above provision.[40] Such a conclusion was reached precisely by deeming trafficking and sexual exploitation violations of human dignity, regardless of whether these treatments constituted 'slavery', 'servitude' or 'forced and compulsory labour',[41] and regardless of the fact that no ownership over the victim occurred in this case.

In a similar vein, one may also recall the judgment *L.E. v Greece*,[42] adopted by the European Court in 2016. Even in this judgment, recourse to dignity was made with the aim of justifying the extension of Article 4 to a case of trafficking concerning a young Nigerian woman who had been forced into prostitution after entering Greek territory.[43] Moreover, even in this case, dignity played the role of enabling the Court to extend Article 4 to factual situations which do not amount to ownership *stricto sensu*.[44]

Lastly, it is once again the need to protect the dignity of the applicants that was at stake in *Chowdury v Greece*.[45] By means of this important judgment, the

37 See above, section 3.

38 *S.M. v Croatia*, App no 60561/14 (ECtHR, 19 July 2018).

39 Ibid para 54.

40 Ibid paras 73–81.

41 Ibid para 54: 'There can be no doubt that *trafficking and exploitation of prostitution threatens the human dignity* and fundamental freedoms of its victims and cannot be considered compatible with a democratic society and the values expounded in the Convention. In view of its obligation to interpret the Convention in the light of present-day conditions, the Court considers it unnecessary to identify whether the treatment of which the applicant complained constituted "slavery", "servitude" or "forced and compulsory labour". […]' (italics added).

42 *L.E. v Greece*, App no 71545/12 (ECtHR, 21 January 2016).

43 Ibid para 58.

44 As far as trafficking does not imply ownership '*stricto sensu*' over the victim.

45 *Chowdury and others v Greece*, App no 21884/15 (ECtHR, 30 March 2017).

European Court has got to the point of stating that in some cases 'exploitation through work' amounts to trafficking, being therefore covered by Article 4 of the Convention.[46] For the sake of precision, in *Chowdury* the Court was dealing with some Bangladeshi migrants who were obliged to work without being paid in order to repay travel expenses, and also unable to move because of being irregular as well as deprived of their personal documents.[47] Not only is dignity expressly referred to in this judgment,[48] but also such a reference is all the more important, given that the above factual situation keeps repeating again and again in the relevant practice.

6 Final Remarks

Summing up, one can easily conclude that dignity – or rather, respect for dignity – plays a very important role with regard to new slaveries understood as all those factual hypotheses in which individuals cannot be considered as property *stricto sensu* of an owner. Whether it is sexual slavery (*Katanga, Kunarac*) or servitude (*Siliadin*), serious exploitation of labour (*Trabajadores de la Hacienda Brazil Verde*) or trafficking of human beings (*Rantsev, L.E.* and *Chowdury*), dignity tends sometimes to be invoked for the purpose of making these hypotheses fall within the scope of application of existing international rules dealing with slavery or enslavement;[49] other times it tends to be against the backdrop of such an interpretative activity.[50]

Insofar as recourse to dignity is intended for a similar purpose, it is worth repeating that this notion clearly plays the role of a general principle of human rights law, being also provided with the corresponding legal status. Furthermore, the case law at stake confirms that speaking of dignity is a concise way to refer to a minimum standard of treatment to be guaranteed to individuals placed under the power of public authorities or other private individuals.

The very fact that several international courts have had recourse to the principle of dignity in order to extend the above standard with respect to new forms of slavery is therefore to be commended. By means of dignity, the said

46 Ibid para 93.

47 Ibid paras 94–99.

48 Ibid para 93.

49 I refer to the judgments rendered by both the European and the Inter-American Court of Human Rights, respectively in *Rantsev* (n 17), *Siliadin* (n 16), *S.M.* (n 38), *L.E* (n 42), *Chowdury* (n 45) and *Trabajadores de la Hacienda Brazil Verde* (n 33).

50 I refer to the decisions adopted by the ICC and the ICTY, respectively in *Katanga* (n 23) and *Kunarac* (n 26).

courts tend therefore to expand the 'hard core' of human rights, taking into account that the ban of slavery is an essential part of such a core. Against this, one could hardly invoke the extreme vagueness of a similar principle, if one only considers that vagueness is a normal feature of the category of general principles of law.

CHAPTER 12

Migrant Women at Risk of Domestic Servitude: Protecting Their Human Dignity with International Law

Philippa Webb and Rosana Garciandia

> I worked eighteen hours a day, seven days a week, without any rest.* I worked like a slave and was treated like one. They beat me regularly. The son of Madame tried to rape me several times. They always kept me locked inside the flat on the 13th floor. I couldn't go out for three years![1]

In many societies, women have traditionally worked in the home, and that work has not been recognised as having value. Those women have been wives and mothers of the family, but they have also been women employed by the household to carry out domestic tasks. In the past, these women have typically come from the same community or country, but changes in transportation and communication, and the difficulties in finding a job and generating income in certain developing countries, have led to migrant women taking on this often-invisible work.

Many work without clear terms of employment, are excluded from the scope of labour legislation and are particularly at risk of becoming victims of domestic servitude, a contemporary form of slavery prohibited by international law.[2]

* We are grateful to the British Academy which funded the underlying research for this chapter as part of a broader project on State Responsibility for Modern Slavery.

1 Fasika, Ethiopian former domestic worker in Lebanon, Anti-Slavery International website (https://www.antislavery.org/slavery-today/domestic-work-and-slavery/).

2 Supplementary Convention on the Abolition of Slavery, the Slave Trade, and Institutions and Practices Similar to Slavery (1956, 124 States Parties); ILO Domestic Workers Convention C189 (2011, 28 States Parties) and Recommendation 201 of 2011 concerning Decent Work for Domestic Workers.

 | DOI:10.1163/9789004435650_013

This chapter focuses on the threat that the risk of domestic servitude poses to the dignity of these migrant women.[3]

The connection between slavery and dignity explored by historians like Rebecca J. Scott finds a landmark reference in the 1848 decree abolishing slavery in the French empire, which considered slavery as 'an assault upon human dignity'.[4] John Tasioulas has written about two understandings of dignity: (1) the inherent value of being human 'from the moment of their coming into existence as an individual human being until their death'; (2) and having the capacity to choose a conception of the good life from a range of valuable options (autonomy) and to pursue that choice free of interference (liberty).[5] Slavery attacks both concepts.

Examining the meanings given to the concept of dignity in particular times and places, the connection of dignity with the institution of slavery becomes apparent. An interesting example of this is Brazil, where specific working conditions (*trabalho escrabo* – slave labour) are currently seen as an assault on human dignity, often because they include actions that assimilate human beings to animals or prevent workers from leaving the property of the employer.[6]

This chapter proceeds in three parts. Part 1 sets out why migrant women are at risk of domestic servitude and the conditions they often face. Part 2 explores the role of international law and international lawyers in the protection of the human dignity of these women in recent litigation on domestic servitude. Part 3 concludes with recommendations on how to prevent domestic servitude and protect victims.

1 Domestic Servitude as a Threat to Human Dignity

Migrant domestic workers are at a high risk of becoming victims of domestic servitude. According to the UN Special Rapporteur on Contemporary Forms of

3 This study is part of a broader research project entitled 'State Responsibility for Modern Slavery: Uncovering and Bridging the Gap', developed in cooperation with the United Nations University under the auspices of the British Academy 'Tackling the UK's International Challenges 2017' scheme.

4 Decree of 27 April 1848, mentioned in R J Scott, 'Dignité/Dignidade: Organizing against Threats to Dignity in Societies after Slavery', in C. McCrudden (ed.), *Understanding Human Dignity* (2013), 61–77, 61.

5 J Tasioulas, 'Human Dignity and the Foundations of Human Rights', in C. McCrudden (ed.) *Understanding Human Dignity* (2013), 293–314.

6 R J Scott et al., 'How does the Law Put a Historical Analogy to Work?: Defining the Imposition of "a Condition Analogous to that of a Slave" in Modern Brazil' (2017), 13 *Duke Journal of Constitutional Law and Public Policy* 1.

Slavery, 11.5 million domestic workers are international migrants, which represent 17.2% of all domestic workers and 7.7% of all migrant workers worldwide. The domestic work sector accounted for 24% of forced labour exploitation in 2017.[7]

At the same time, domestic work is a highly feminized sector in which gender-based inequalities and discrimination increase their risk of slavery and servitude.[8] According to the UN Convention on the Elimination of All Forms of Discrimination Against Women (CEDAW), domestic work is one of the occupations in which migrant women dominate and in countries of destination such occupations may be excluded from legal definitions of work, depriving those women of a variety of legal protections.[9] To give a sense of the scale, in Hong Kong there are 370,000 domestic workers of which 98.8% are women, and women and girls made up 71.1% of the people whose human rights were violated through contemporary forms of slavery in 2016.[10]

Domestic work is 'generally undervalued and characterized by unfair recruitment practices, low pay, high levels of precarious work, outsourcing, lack of regulation and poor working conditions, including non-payment of wages and unfair deductions for food and housing, debt bondage, excessive working hours, tied visas, restrictions on place of residence, confiscation of identity documents and lack of social protection'.[11] That increases the vulnerability of those women to various forms of coercion that are often gendered in nature.[12] In addition, discrimination based on gender is linked with other forms of discrimination based on caste, origin, nationality and social and economic status.[13]

The discrimination that these domestic workers face is often enhanced by social conventions that also threat their dignity. As an example, Sondos Alqattan, an Instagram star and makeup artist with over 2.3 million followers, criticised new laws in Kuwait giving greater rights to Filipino workers.[14] Alqattan complained: "How can you have a servant at home who keeps their own passport with them? What's worse is they have one day off every week".[15]

---

7 Report of the UN Special Rapporteur on Contemporary Forms of Slavery (2018), including its causes and consequences, 27 July, UN Doc. A/HRC/39/52, para 43.

8 Report of the UN Special Rapporteur on Contemporary Forms of Slavery (2018), including its causes and consequences, 10 July, UN Doc. A/73/139, para 10.

9 CEDAW general recommendation 26, 2008.

10 ILO and Walk Free Foundation (2017), Global Estimates of Modern Slavery.

11 A/73/139, supra note 8, para 43.

12 A/73/139, supra note 8, para 8.

13 Ibid, para 51.

14 There are 180,000 Filipinos in Kuwait of which 60% are domestic workers.

15 R Michaelson, 'Kuwaiti star faces backlash over Filipino worker comments', *The Guardian*, 23 July 2018.

Victims of domestic servitude are subject to unfair and exploitative labour practices, paid below minimum wage or not at all, and forced to live with their employers in substandard or degrading living conditions. They are also frequently subject to physical, sexual and psychological abuse. Moreover, as highlighted by the UN Special Rapporteur, victims can face specific barriers to gaining access to justice and remedy, including severe restrictions on their freedom of movement, such as passport confiscation and an inability to leave their work premises, and a dependence on their employers for retaining regular migration status.[16]

Victims usually lack information about their rights and are isolated from the community. In addition, their visas are normally tied to their employer and are only valid so long as they remain in that employment, facing deportation if they resign. In certain Gulf states, the *kafala* 'sponsorship' system leaves domestic workers outside the protection of labour law and allows their 'sponsors' to evade social security and medical costs.[17] This prevents domestic workers from changing employer and having freedom of movement. Some of those states have taken steps towards the adoption of reforms in this area. Kuwait and the UAE introduced a unified standard domestic worker's contract (2006, 2007) and Oman introduced in 2011 a pilot contract for the employment of house maids. However, implementation remains a challenge and the scope of some of those reforms does not include domestic workers.[18] An example of this is a new law that will allow the majority of migrant workers to leave Qatar without permission from their employers but does not cover migrant *domestic* workers.[19]

2 The Role of International Law and Lawyers

International conventions and human rights treaties provide a legal framework to define dignity in a way that protects the rights of migrant women domestic workers. Some examples are the International Labour Organization (ILO) Domestic Workers Convention (No. 189), CEDAW, the International Convention on the Protection of the Rights of All Migrant Workers and Members of their Families, the 1956 Supplementary Convention on the Abolition of Slavery,

16 A/73/139, supra note 8.

17 R Bajracharya, B Sijapati, 'The Kafala System and Its Implications for Nepali Domestic Workers' (2012) *CESLAM Policy Brief*.

18 Ibid, at 4.

19 P Webb, R Garciandia, 'Slavery in Domestic Work: The Potential for State Responsibility?' (17 September 2018) *EJIL: Talk!, Blog of the European Journal of International Law*.

Slave Trade and Institutions and Practices Similar to Slavery and the Palermo Protocol on Trafficking.[20]

Under article 5 of the ILO Domestic Workers Convention, 'each Member shall take measures to ensure that domestic workers enjoy effective protection against all forms of abuse, harassment and violence'. States are required to ensure that before departure, migrant domestic workers have written contracts that they can understand and that are enforceable in the country of employment.[21] States parties are called upon to regulate the recruitment of domestic workers by private employment agencies and to conclude bilateral, regional or multilateral agreements to prevent abuses and fraudulent practices in the recruitment, placement and employment of migrant domestic workers.[22] Article 15.1 (e) states that fees charged by private employment agencies should not be deducted from the remuneration of domestic workers.

However, the gender and race dimensions are far from being implemented in practice. According to the CEDAW Committee, 'women migrant workers often experience intersecting forms of discrimination, suffering not only sex- and gender-based discrimination, but also xenophobia and racism. Discrimination based on race, ethnicity, cultural particularities, nationality, language, religion or other status may be expressed in sex- and gender-specific ways'.[23] It has also been noted that 'with limited job opportunities available for women in countries of origin, transit and host countries, many migrant women end up in informal employment, particularly in the care, domestic and male-driven entertainment sectors', and that the concentration of women in these sectors not only perpetuates traditional gender stereotypes about what constitutes "women's work" but also provides no or few labour protections, such as workplace inspections, complaint mechanisms and protection from violence and abuse, thereby heightening the exposure of migrant women to severe forms of human rights violations and trafficking, as victims remain unseen, unheard and unprotected'.[24] And yet, as Christian Tomuschat observes, the existing human rights mechanisms provide 'purely formal rituals' and 'nothing else than dialogue' as the main tool for enforcement and monitoring.[25]

20 Protocol to the United Nations Convention against Transnational Organized Crime.

21 Art. 8(1).

22 Art. 15.

23 CEDAW/C/2009/WP.1/R, para 14.

24 Concept note for the Committee on the Elimination of Discrimination Against Women on its elaboration of a General Recommendation on Trafficking in Women and Girls in the Context of Global Migration, 2018, para 29.

25 See C. Tomuschat, chapter XX.

International law and international lawyers play a key role in ensuring a better protection of migrant women at risk of domestic servitude. This section examines how that occurs advising states on their international obligations and shaping the way in which justice is administered at the domestic level.

2.1 *Advising States on Their International Obligations*

International lawyers who advise states in accordance with international law have two avenues for contributing to the protection of the dignity of migrant women at risk of domestic servitude: cooperation with investigations of other states' courts and enhanced control of employment agencies.

In terms of cooperation, under article 8.3 of the Supplementary Convention on the Abolition of Slavery,[26] states have the obligation to cooperate with each other and with the United Nations to give effect to the Convention. The scope of this obligation includes cooperation at the policy level as well as cooperation in the investigation and prosecution of domestic servitude. Two paradigmatic and antagonistic cases of domestic servitude in diplomatic households illustrate what cooperation may entail in this context. It is important to emphasize that the threat to dignity is even bigger when the case involves domestic servitude in diplomatic households, given that the diplomat is protected by immunity and that may hamper victims' access to justice.

In the *Soborun* case in the US, Mauritius's ambassador to the US pled guilty to charges that he had failed to pay his domestic worker minimum wage or overtime while he was serving as his country's permanent representative to the UN. The US State Department requested a waiver of diplomatic immunity and Mauritius granted it. The case was resolved with a plea to a lesser charge, payment of back wages through criminal restitution and no prison charge.[27] In this case, which reflects the general practice between states, such a critical matter was resolved quietly and diplomatically with the cooperation of Mauritius, the sending state.

However, that is not always what happens. In *Khobragade*, the Deputy Consul General of India had allegedly forced her domestic worker (an Indian woman) to work long hours for a low wage and under an illegal employment contract in New York. India denied the waiver of immunity requested by the US State Department and obstructed the proceedings against a consular agent by transferring her to India's mission to the UN to ensure she enjoyed even more extensive immunity.[28]

26 1956, 124 States Parties.

27 Plea Agreement, *United States v Soborun*, No. 2, 2:12-mj-03121 (DNJ Sept 7, 2012).

28 M Vandenberg, S Bessell, 'Diplomatic Immunity and the Abuse of Domestic Workers: Criminal and Civil Remedies in the United States' (2016) 26 *Duke Journal of Comparative and International Law* 595, 605.

Another relevant avenue relates to the abovementioned article 15 of the ILO domestic workers convention, which calls states parties to regulate the recruitment of domestic workers by private employment agencies and to conclude bilateral, regional or multilateral agreements to prevent abuses and fraudulent practices in the recruitment, placement and employment of migrant domestic workers.[29]

The role of private employment agencies in this context is key. Recruiters, their sub-agents, pre-departure training centres, transport companies, travel agencies, medical screening centres, insurance companies and visa consultancies should be carefully monitored as this network provides 'an enabling environment for abuse and human rights violations'.[30] A state could be responsible for certain practices that take place in those employment agencies or under those agreements.[31]

2.2 *Lawyers' Contribution to Protection of Victims' Dignity*

The traditional role of women in society still has a strong influence on the way justice is administered. International law and international lawyers have a role to play in uncovering those biases and protecting the human dignity of migrant women at risk of domestic servitude.

One of the avenues is the use of supranational courts to challenge law enforcement shortages at the domestic level. Two landmark cases illustrate this, one at the European Court of Human Rights and the other at the Economic Community of West African States (ECOWAS) court.

The *Siliadin* v *France* before the ECtHR, concerned a Togolese national, Siliadin, who arrived in France when she was 15. In order to pay the cost of her ticket, she worked at the employer's home. The employer promised to arrange her immigration status and secure her a place in a school. None of this happened. Her passport and salary were withheld, she worked excessive hours, and eventually was 'lend' to another family.[32]

French courts prosecuted this family but acquitted the defendants of criminal charges as domestic criminal law did not prohibit servitude at the time. The ECtHR found France responsible for failing to protect a minor subjected to servitude. The Court held that France's 'positive obligations under article 4 of the Convention must be seen as requiring the penalization and effective

29 Art. 15.
30 A/HRC/39/52, *supra* note 7, paras 58, 60.
31 See ILC Articles on Responsibility of States for Internationally Wrongful Acts.
32 V Stoyanova, *Human Trafficking and Slavery Reconsidered. Conceptual Limits and States' Positive Obligations in European Law* (2017), 245.

prosecution of any act aimed at maintaining a person' in a situation of servitude,[33] and therefore France was in violation of article 4 ECHR. Although this judgment has been criticised for its restrictive interpretation of the definition of slavery,[34] it is illustrative of how supranational courts can contribute to the protection of the dignity of migrant women victims of domestic servitude by developing the content of international obligations of states to prosecute and punish perpetrators.

The second case is *Mani v Niger* before the ECOWAS court in 2008. Hadijatou Mani was born as the daughter of a slave, inheriting her mother's servile status. At the age of 12 years, she was sold by a representative of her mother's owner for the sum equivalent to £250. She was forced to harsh labour seven days a week without remuneration or vacation, and was subjected to constant sexual harassment and abuse, insults and degradation. Whenever she tried to escape, she was severely punished.[35]

She was kept as the man's *wahaya* (purchase of one or more girls, usually of slave descent, under the guise of a wife) for nine years[36] before being liberated in 2005 with a 'liberation certificate' signed by 'the chef du village', 'the master' and the 'beneficiary'. Once she received her 'liberation certificate', Hadijatou left and refused to marry her former master. This provoked 'two parallel lines of legal cases in Niger – her attempts to secure recognition of her right to be free, and her prosecution, at her former master's instigation, for bigamy', as she had married someone else.[37]

The ECOWAS Court found that Niger had violated its international obligations in respect of the enslavement of Hadijatou Mani. It addressed the domestic judiciary's failure to condemn slavery and highlighted the obligations of national judges to ensure that slavery is subject to criminal prosecution and punishment. It was only in 2019 that the Court of Appeals, the highest judicial body in Niger, ruled that her freely chosen marriage was not a case of bigamy.

33 *Siliadin v France*, ECHR, 26 July 2005, para 12.

34 A Gallagher, *The International Law of Human Trafficking* (2010), 187: J Allain, 'The Definition of "Slavery" in General International Law and the Crime of Enslavement within the Rome Statute', Guest Lecture Series of the Office of the Prosecutor, ICC, 26 April 2007, 18.

35 H Duffy, 'Hadijatou Mani Koroua v Niger: Slavery Unveiled by the ECOWAS Court' (2009) 9 *Human Rights Law Review* 151.

36 The *wahaya* practice involves the purchase of one or more girls, usually of slave descent, under the guise of a fifth wife (Report of the Special Rapporteur on contemporary forms of slavery, including its causes and consequences, Urmila Bhoola. Addendum. Mission to the Niger, UN Doc. A/HRC/30/35/Add.1, 30 July 2015, para 48).

37 See Duffy, *supra* note 35.

This case shows how international law and supranational courts can contribute to improving the enforcement of anti-slavery legislation in countries like Niger, where domestic servitude and slavery are still a reality. Although the Niger Constitution prohibits slavery and the domestic criminal code considers slavery as a crime since 2003,[38] prosecutions are rarely pursued in practice, including the *wahaya*.[39] Despite having evolved towards better protection than other African countries,[40] from 2003 to 2008 there had only been one prosecution for slavery.[41] This decision shows the potential of supranational courts to boost change at the domestic level.

Another avenue for international law and lawyers to contribute to this endeavour is through the interpretation of domestic law in light of international law. An important case of the UK Supreme Court on domestic servitude in diplomatic households is illustrative.

In *Reyes v. Al Malki*, a domestic worker from the Philippines sued her employer, a Saudi diplomat in London, before the Employment Tribunal alleging discrimination, excessive working hours, low pay and other charges. When the case came before the UK Supreme Court, Lord Sumption (Lord Neuberger agreeing) deployed in his arguments an analogy of the domestic worker who had been a victim of domestic servitude with stolen property.

38 See Art. 12 of the Constitution, and Art. 270.1 to 5 of the Penal Code of the Republic of Niger as revised by Law No 2003–05 of 13 June 2003.

39 A/HRC/30/35/Add.1, *supra* note 36.

40 In Mauritania, law enforcement authorities have been accused of not routinely following up reported cases of slavery, and procedures and deadlines seem not to be always respected. The investigation may be limited to bringing the enslaver and the enslaved together, asking them questions in an environment that offers inadequate voice and protection to the enslaved. There also seems to be a racial and gender bias in the way justice is administered. Often cases are settled informally or reclassified as work-related issues or exploitation (Minority Rights Group International and others, *Enforcing Mauritania's antislavery legislation: the continued failure of the justice system to prevent, protect and punish*, October 2015). In December 2017, the African Union's Committee of Experts on the Rights and Welfare of the Child urged Mauritania to make a greater effort to eliminate slavery, to better protect victims and prosecute offenders. It ruled that Mauritania was in breach of its obligations under the African Charter on the Rights and Welfare of the Child (ACHPR). The case was not related to domestic servitude, but it was a landmark decision showing how international law can play a role in protecting the dignity of victims of slavery and servitude. It concerned two brothers, Said and Yarg, who had been victims of slavery since an early age. The Committee requested the national authorities to provide remedies for the two brothers, and to impose stricter sentences in accordance with the 2015 anti-slavery law, as well as to make the adequate changes to the national practice and programmes to eradicate slavery and related practices effectively.

41 See Duffy, *supra* note 35.

> By way of analogy, if I knowingly buy stolen property from a professional fence for my personal use, both of us will incur criminal liability for receiving stolen goods and civil liability to the true owner for conversion. The fence will also be engaging in a commercial activity. But it does not follow that the same is true of me.[42]

Regardless of the content of the legal argument, comparing a victim of domestic servitude with a stolen good does not fall within any of the two understandings of dignity that Tasioulas describes.[43] Dignity requires recognising inherent value and freedom and autonomy of a person. Analogies with stolen property are false and insulting, further commodifying the human being.

Despite the unfortunate and discriminatory analogy used by Lord Sumption, the UK Supreme Court provided a judgment that will hopefully be the basis for a broader interpretation of one of the exceptions to diplomatic immunity, more protective of the dignity of victims. For that reason, this chapter explores the facts and reasoning of the Supreme Court.

Ms Reyes, a Philippines national, claimed that she had entered the United Kingdom with a contract showing that she would be paid £500 per month by Mr Al-Malki, a member of the diplomatic staff of the embassy of Saudi Arabia in London.[44] She alleged that she obtained her visa at the British Embassy in Manila by producing documents supplied by Mr Al-Malki, including the contract. Ms Reyes stated that she was paid nothing by Mr Al-Malki and his wife.[45] She said she was made to work excessive hours, had her passport confiscated, did not have proper accommodation, and was prevented from leaving the house or communicating with others.[46] After two months, she managed to escape. The United Kingdom Visas and Immigration had found that there were reasonable grounds for concluding that Ms Reyes was a victim of human trafficking.

The Court of Appeal had held that Mr Al-Malki was entitled to diplomatic immunity under Article 31 of the Vienna Convention on Diplomatic Relations.[47] Mr Al-Malki left his diplomatic post before the Court of Appeal hearing, but the Court of Appeal proceeded on the assumption that he was still in post. It was only by the time the case made its way to the Supreme Court that the change in material fact was acknowledged. On that basis, the 5 Judges held

42 *Reyes* v *Al-Malki* [2017] UKSC, para 45.
43 See Tasioulas, *supra* note 5.
44 See *supra* note 42, para 1.
45 Ibid.
46 Ibid.
47 [2015] EWCA Civ 32.

that under Article 39(2) of the Vienna Convention on Diplomatic Relations, the employment and mistreatment of Ms Reyes were not acts performed by Mr Al-Malki 'in the exercise of his functions as a member of the mission' and he was therefore not immune.[48]

The Court also commented, *obiter dictum*, on whether Mr Al-Malki would have had immunity if he had been a sitting diplomat in the UK. It is on this point where three justices used international law to shape an interpretation of the existing legal framework that would be more protective of the human dignity of a victim of domestic servitude.

The test was whether the employment of Ms Reyes would have fallen under the exception to diplomatic immunity of art. 31.1.c of the Vienna Convention on Diplomatic Relations. Under that provision, a diplomatic agent shall not enjoy immunity from the receiving state's civil and administrative jurisdiction in the case of 'an action relating to any professional or commercial activity exercised by the diplomatic agent in the receiving State outside his official functions'.[49]

The Court looked at the two elements of the exception ('commercial activity' and 'outside of official functions') showing divided views on the matter. Lord Wilson (with whom Lady Hale and Lord Clarke agreed) would have found both the "commercial activity" and "outside of official functions" tests met and the exclusion of immunity even if Mr Al-Malki had still been in post. Lord Sumption (with Lord Neuberger agreeing) found that the "outside of official functions test" was satisfied but the "commercial activity test" was not met.

In the analysis of the 'outside of official functions' test, the five Justices of the Supreme Court were in agreement. Lords Sumption and Neuberger held that the domestic duties of Ms Reyes were not done for or on behalf of Saudi Arabia. Even if such domestic duties were "conductive" to the performance of his official functions, "that could be said of almost anything that made the personal life of a diplomatic agent easier".[50] Lord Wilson, Lady Hale and Lord Clarke agreed that "there is no apparent link between the duties of Ms Reyes and the official functions of Mr Al-Malki".[51] As set out in the preamble to the Vienna Convention on Diplomatic Relations, the purpose of diplomatic immunity is "not to benefit individuals but to ensure the efficient performance of the functions of the diplomatic missions as representing States".[52] The employment of

48 See *supra* note 42, para 45.
49 Art. 31(1)(c), Vienna Convention on Diplomatic Relations.
50 See *supra* note 42, para 48.
51 Ibid., para 66.
52 Ibid.

a domestic worker for personal duties in the household is therefore not within the official functions of a diplomat.

It is in the analysis of the 'commercial activity test' where the position of Lord Wilson, Lady Hale and Lord Clarke shows that international law can have a role in shaping a broader interpretation of the commercial exception to diplomatic immunity that would ensure a better protection of the human dignity of migrant women victims of domestic servitude.

For Lord Wilson (Lady Hale and Lord Clark agreeing), the words "… commercial activity exercised …" must be interpreted "tak[ing] into account any relevant rules of international law applicable in the relations between the parties".[53] In identifying the relevant rules for the case, he referred to "the universality of the international community's determination to combat human trafficking", the ratification of the Palermo Protocol 2000[54] by the UK and Saudi Arabia, the Council of Europe Convention on Action against Trafficking in Human Beings 2005 (acceded to by the UK) and the Arab Charter on Human Rights 2004 (ratified by Saudi Arabia).[55]

More specifically, Lord Wilson referred to the definition of trafficking of the Palermo Protocol, as one that "endeavours to encompass the whole sequence of actions that leads to the exploitation of the victim".[56] In the light of these relevant rules, Lord Wilson called it a "rational view" to characterise the relevant activity for the purposes of Article 31(1)(c) as "not just the so-called employment but the trafficking".[57] As Lord Wilson observed "in addition to the physical and emotional cruelty inherent in [the exploitation], the employer's conduct contains a substantial commercial element of obtaining domestic assistance without paying for it properly or at all".[58]

This interpretation of article 31(1)(c) would consider the employer of the migrant as "an integral part of the chain, who knowingly effects the "receipt" of the migrant and supplies the specified purpose, namely that of exploiting the victim, which drives the entire exercise from her recruitment onwards".[59] It would therefore include the trafficking and exploitation of a domestic worker

---

53 Ibid., para 66.

54 This refers to the 'Protocol to Prevent, Suppress and Punish Trafficking in Persons, Especially Women and Children', supplementing the United Nations Convention against Transnational Organized Crime.

55 See *supra* note 42, para 60.

56 Ibid., para 61.

57 Ibid, para 62.

58 Ibid.

59 Ibid.

under the commercial exception to diplomatic immunity, allowing victims to overcome one of the greatest barriers to redress.

Lord Wilson, Lady Hale and Lord Clarke saw Ms Reyes as a human being – and that the underlying source of her value to the Al-Malkis was her two months' of (free) labour which provided ongoing commercial benefit and brought her employment within the exception to diplomatic immunity.

3 Recommendations

International lawyers have a role to play in incorporating the gender and race dimensions of human dignity in legal practice. They participate in many ways in shaping the practice definition of human dignity – those who defend victims, those who advise states on their international obligations, or those who draft and apply international rules and decisions in this area- should contribute to guarantee a definition of human dignity that protects migrant women from the risk of being subject to domestic servitude as a contemporary form of slavery. Their actions will be crucial in the following areas:

3.1 *Enhancing Cooperation between States*

International law creates obligations for states to cooperate in tackling domestic servitude, slavery and trafficking. Cooperation is needed at the preventive level, as well as in investigation and prosecution phases. The *Soborun* and *Khobragade* cases illustrate how different approaches to cooperation with other states' courts can threaten the dignity of victims.

States should be advised to waive the immunity from jurisdiction of public officials when there are credible allegations of their involvement in modern slavery, in the territory of the State or in a foreign country. States could require diplomatic missions give a prospective waiver of immunity for employment-related disputes when there is a reasonable basis to believe that gross violations of human rights of domestic servants could have been committed. The vast majority of states will not be content to provide a blanket waiver, so, in order to be workable, the waiver should be limited to cases where there are: (i) reasonable grounds for believing that (ii) gross human rights violations have been committed (iii) against a domestic servant. This would capture the most serious cases and provide a best practice model for other jurisdictions to follow, leading to the accumulation of state practice.[60] Once waiver is provided,

60 P Webb, 'The Immunity of States, Diplomats and International Organizations in Employment Disputes: The New Human Rights Dilemma?' (2016) 27 EJIL 3, 764–5.

states should be advised to cooperate with foreign courts' investigations of such allegations by disclosing documents and making personnel available for interviews.

3.2 *Ensuring Secure Migration*

Migrant women are willing to search opportunities for a better life for them and their families despite the risks this may entail. It is therefore necessary to establish mechanisms that ensure secure and dignified avenues for migration and to guarantee the protection from domestic servitude.[61]

There is a need to create viable, accessible and non-discriminatory employment options for women to prevent exploitation.[62] This will require transparent memoranda of understanding, more resources for labour inspections, enhanced controls of recruitment processes,[63] and making the inclusion of the gender and race perspectives a strategic priority of labour inspectorates.

In order to act in accordance with international law and avoid that responsibility, states should be advised to increase transparency and monitoring mechanisms in the way government-to-government Memoranda of Understanding (MoUs) for migration of workers are negotiated and implemented. They should also be advised to prohibit recruitment fees in their domestic law and enhance controls and inspections to ensure that employment agencies do not tolerate or use abusive practices and assess the impact of any legislation on borders and passport controls in migrant domestic workers. All this should be done in accordance with the ILO General principles and operational guidelines for fair recruitment (2016), and the ILO Recommendation on decent work for domestic workers. Promising practices in this regard include a model contract of employment developed by the US TIP Office and DLA Piper.[64]

States should also be advised to revise their visa requirements for overseas domestic workers to provide them a safe way out of potentially abusive situations by guaranteeing their right to change employer and by allowing them to apply for annual extensions. States with a *kafala* system should be encouraged to revise it to protect potential victims of modern slavery, enabling them to change employer and leave the country without permission of their employer. All workers should enjoy equal protection under domestic labour law.

In addition, as the International Trade Union Confederation has stated, one important step to protect the dignity of these women would be to 'pro-actively

61 A/73/139, *supra* note 8, para 82.

62 Ibid.

63 Ibid.

64 https://www.state.gov/j/tip/c73528.htm.

promote positive public perceptions of migrant domestic workers and raise awareness of the positive social and economic contributions of domestic workers, while combating discriminatory attitudes and gaps in rights and protections -in law and in practice-'.[65]

3.3 *Using International Law to Overcome Domestic Shortcomings*

International law provides mechanisms to overcome the limitations that in some cases domestic courts may pose. International lawyers and courts are in a position to clarify the content of states' obligations and victims' rights, and to guarantee the full protection of human rights of victims of domestic servitude.

3.4 *Interpreting Domestic Law in the Light of International Law*

International law provides a legal framework to define dignity in a way that protects the rights of migrant women domestic workers. The way justice is administered at the domestic level should be influenced by that framework. The international legal framework protecting migrant domestic workers and prohibiting discrimination should be applied effectively. The legal arguments and the language used should be gender and race inclusive, and respectful of human dignity.

In addition, legal assistance and advice should be provided with a special focus on the gender and race dimensions, and reforms in the judicial system should consider measures to remove the barriers that gender and race impose to ensure access to justice and redress.

A household can be refuge to a migrant domestic worker, but it can also be a prison. Seeing these women as humans with autonomy and freedoms, not as stolen property, is fundamental to their dignity.

65 E Torres, 'What will it take to protect Filipino domestic workers from abuse and exploitation in the Middle East?', *Equal times*, 15 June 2017.

CHAPTER 13

Dignity in Diversity: Dismantling the Criminalisation of Sexual Orientation and Gender Identity using the Right to Dignity

Téa Braun

1 Introduction

Approximately 350 million people globally[1] are lesbian, gay, bisexual, transgender or gender non-conforming (LGBT+).[2] Upwards of 71 million of those live in countries where the very conduct that defines these identities – namely consensual, same-sex sexual intimacy in private or the expression of non-conforming gender identities – is not only stigmatised, it is criminalised.[3] In these jurisdictions, and even in many non-criminalising countries, LGBT+ people can be subjected to various forms of ill-treatment including verbal abuse, intimidation, physical violence, sexual violence, generalised societal stigma, and lack of equal access to basic socio-economic services such as health, education, housing and employment.

Despite LGBT+ people making up a relatively small percentage of any given population, therefore, the global scale of the issue and the importance of understanding and protecting human rights in the context of sexual orientation and gender identity cannot be overstated.

The purpose of this paper is to look at the overarching role of the right to dignity in human rights jurisprudence relating to sexual orientation and gender identity, with a particular focus on the interplay between the right to dignity and the criminal law.

---

1 Assuming 4.5% of the world population, based on reliable estimates from countries where it is safe for people to reveal their identity: <http://worldpopulationreview.com/> last accessed 31 January 2020; Frank Newport, 'In U.S., Estimate of LGBT Population Rises to 4.5%' (*Gallup*, 22 May 2018) <https://news.gallup.com/poll/234863/estimate-lgbt-population-rises.aspx>.

2 In this chapter the acronym LGBT+ is used for simplicity, however it is acknowledged that neither this nor other acronyms that are commonly used necessarily capture all relevant sexual orientations and gender identities, and that terms used across different cultures can vary widely.

3 Figure constitutes 4.5% of the total population of the 72 criminalising jurisdictions. See footnote 4.

 | DOI:10.1163/9789004435650_014

2 Indignities

The list of indignities suffered by LGBT+ people globally, merely because of their sexual orientation and/or gender identity and expression, remains tragically long.

Amongst this list of indignities is that, at the time of writing, 72 jurisdictions globally[4] criminalise consensual sexual intimacy between persons of the same sex. These laws are variously framed as 'buggery', 'sodomy', 'carnal knowledge against the order of nature', 'unnatural offences', 'gross indecency', 'sexual relations with a person of the same sex', 'lesbianism' and the like. Many of these laws sit in the same criminal provision that criminalises bestiality, thereby directly conflating consensual adult conduct in private with the sexual abuse of animals. They similarly conflate consensual and non-consensual sexual conduct, in that anal rape (whether of a male or a female), for instance, is criminalised under 'buggery' or 'unnatural offences' provisions in the identical way that consenting males are criminalised for engaging in anal intercourse, even in the privacy of their own homes.[5] The age of the parties, the location of the act, and the fact of consent are entirely irrelevant to a successful prosecution.

The criminal provisions in Uganda[6] are common and illustrative. Titled 'Unnatural offences', section 145 of the Penal Code provides that 'any person who has carnal knowledge of any person against the order of nature' or who permits such carnal knowledge commits a criminal offence and is liable to life imprisonment. Lesser offences of same-sex intimacy, i.e. short of penetrative acts, are captured in section 148 under the title 'Indedent Practices', which penalises 'gross indecency' whether in public or in private with up to seven years in prison.

Of the 72 criminalising jurisdictions, all of which criminalise male same-sex conduct, 44 also criminalise consensual sexual intimacy between females. The maximum sentence for these crimes ranges widely, from six months to

4 Human Dignity Trust, *LGBT+ & The Law*. <https://www.humandignitytrust.org/lgbt-the-law/>.

5 This is the case given that 'rape' is defined in many penal codes to only capture penile-vaginal rape, such that anal rape can only be prosecuted under a buggery, unnatural offences or similar provision which will carry a different maximum sentence, thereby not providing equal protection for all victims of rape regardless of gender. For further information see: Human Dignity Trust, *Good Practice in Human Rights Compliant Sexual Offences Laws in the Commonwealth* (August 2019) <https://www.humandignitytrust.org/wp-content/uploads/resources/Good-Practice-in-Human-Rights-Compliant-Sexual-Offences-Laws-in-the-Commonwealth_Final.pdf>.

6 Penal Code 1950, ss.145, 146 & 148. <https://ulii.org/ug/legislation/consolidated-act/120>.

life imprisonment and, in 12 countries,[7] the death penalty.[8] At least 15 jurisdictions[9] criminalise transgender people using laws that capture the physical expression of non-conforming gender identities through a person's choice of clothing (so-called 'cross-dressing' or 'impersonation' laws), and at least 26[10] use general vagrancy and other public order offences to criminalise transgender people.[11]

In all of these jurisdictions, LGBT+ people fear and are at real or potential risk of arrest and detention and they suffer and are at perpetual risk of a wide range of additional infringements against their human dignity. Disclosing their identity as LGBT+, displaying it through clothing, appearance or conduct, or merely being suspected of it can lead to anything from ostracization to violence and even death, at the hands of both state and non-state actors.

In Ghana in 2015, for instance, a group of women perceived to be lesbians were confronted by a mob and *"stoned and pelted with human faeces."*[12] In 2013, a Jamaican gender non-conforming 17-year-old attended a party presenting as a woman. When it was discovered that he was biologically male, he was beaten, stabbed, shot and run over with a car, dying from his injuries. In August 2018, 57 men whom police suspected of being 'initiated' into a 'gay club' were arrested at a hotel in Lagos, Nigeria.[13] Forty-seven of them were subsequently charged

---

7 Afghanistan, Brunei, Iran, Mauritania, Northern Nigeria, Pakistan, Qatar, Saudi Arabia, Somalia, Sudan, United Arab Emirates, Yemen.

8 Human Dignity Trust, *LGBT+ & The Law*. <https://www.humandignitytrust.org/LGBT+-the-law/> & Lucas Ramón Mendos, *State-Sponsored Homophobia* (13th edn, ILGA 2019), pp.15–16 <https://ilga.org/downloads/ILGA_State_Sponsored_Homophobia_2019.pdf>.

9 Brunei, The Gambia, Indonesia, Jordan, Kuwait, Lebanon, Malawi, Malaysia, Myanmar, Nigeria, Oman, Saudi Arabia, South Sudan, Sri Lanka, United Arab Emirates.

10 Azerbaijan, Bangladesh, Botswana, Brunei, Cambodia, The Gambia, Georgia, Guatemala, Guyana, Honduras, Indonesia, Lebanon, Lesotho, Malawi, Malaysia, Mali, Morocco, Namibia, Saudi Arabia, Sri Lanka, Tajikistan, Tunisia, Uganda, United Arab Emirates, Zambia, Zimbabwe.

11 Human Dignity Trust, *Injustice Exposed: The Criminalisation of Transgender People and its Impacts* (2019), pp.15 & 31 <https://www.humandignitytrust.org/wp-content/uploads/resources/Injustice-Exposed-the-criminsalisation-of-trans-people.pdf>.

12 Human Dignity Trust, *Breaking the Silence: Criminalisation of Lesbians and Bisexual Women and its Impacts* (2016), p.23 <https://www.humandignitytrust.org/wp-content/uploads/resources/Breaking-the-Silence-Criminalisation-of-LB-Women-and-its-Impacts-FINAL.pdf> & Sylvia Tan, "Suspected' lesbians in Ghana's capital targeted after homophobic residents put up posters' (*Gay Star News*, 8 March 2015) <https://www.gaystarnews.com/article/suspected-lesbians-ghanas-capital-targeted-after-homophobic-residents-put-posters080315/>.

13 Odita Sunday, 'Police storm hotel, arrest 57 for alleged homosexual initiation' (*The Guardian Nigeria*, 28 August 2018) <https://guardian.ng/news/police-storm-hotel-arrest-57-for-alleged-homosexual-initiation/>.

and stood trial in December 2019 for making a 'public show of same sex amorous relationship', which is criminalised under the *Same Sex Marriage (Prohibition) Act* of 2013.[14] In April 2016, the founder of Bangladesh's only LGBT+ magazine and another individual were hacked to death by suspected Islamist militants in Dhaka,[15] and in May 2017 police arrested 27 men for 'homosexuality' after storming a community centre outside of Dhaka.[16]

In 2018, police raided several hair salons in Indonesia, arresting 12 people. Among them, nine trans women were subjected to appalling mistreatment in custody, including being forced into mock military training, and having their clothing removed and hair forcibly shaved to make them "look masculine". In 2017, two gay men in Aceh were publicly caned 83 times, each after being caught engaging in same-sex sexual activity. In Iran in April 2017, at least 30 men suspected of engaging in same-sex sexual activity were arrested at a private party. They were taken to Dastgerd Prison and told, as they were led into the prison yard, that they would be executed. Following similar raids, other arrestees were subjected to forced anal exams and other degrading treatment and sexual insults.[17]

In 2012, three lesbian women were sexually assaulted in Nairobi, Kenya by men who indicated they were going to *'funza the lesbians adabu'* (teach the lesbians a lesson) for behaving like men and occupying the role of men in sex. In just a six-month period in 2011, non-governmental organisations in Uganda reported five cases of so-called 'corrective rape' – the targeted rape particularly of lesbians or trans men with the ostensible aim of forcibly 'correcting' their sexual orientation.

These and countless other grave instances of ill-treatment of LGBT+ people are often fuelled by the rhetoric of political and religious leaders, who have the power to embed systemic abuse of these marginalised communities across whole societies. President Jair Bolsonaro of Brazil reportedly stated in a 2011

---

14 Jason Burke, 'First men go on trial under Nigeria's anti-homosexuality laws' (*The Guardian*, 11 December 2019) <https://www.theguardian.com/world/2019/dec/11/first-men-go-on-trial-under-nigerias-anti-homosexuality-laws>.

15 Mohammad Jamil Khan, 'Six months on, Xulhaz and Tonoy's killers remain at large' (*Dhaka Tribune*, 26 October 2016) <https://www.dhakatribune.com/bangladesh/2016/10/26/six-months-xulhaz-tonoys-killers-remain-large>.

16 'Bangladesh authorities arrest 27 men on suspicion of being gay' (*The Independent*, 19 May 2017) <https://www.independent.co.uk/news/world/asia/bangladesh-authorities-arrest-27-men-gay-homosexuality-muslim-country-islam-police-charge-a7744366.html>.

17 US Department of State, *Iran 2017 Human Rights Report* <https://www.state.gov/wp-content/uploads/2019/01/Iran.pdf> p.42.

interview that he would rather have a dead son than a gay son.[18] Former President of The Gambia, Yahya Jammeh declared *"we will fight these vermins called homosexuals or gays the same way we are fighting malaria-causing mosquitoes, if not more aggressively."*[19] Former President of Zimbabwe, Robert Mugabe described homosexuals as *"worse than dogs and pigs"*.[20] In 2018, Catholic Cardinal Pengo of Tanzania emphatically rejected international calls to decriminalise consensual same-sex intimacy, remarking that *"it is better to die of hunger than to receive aid and be compelled to do things that are contrary to God's desire."*[21] In response to a 2019 Kenyan High Court decision upholding the constitutionality of Kenya's criminalising provisions, Catholic Bishop Rotich declared: *"It is in our hearts to thank the court for having pronounced this and Kenya should be in a frenzy mood now."*[22] He went on to liken LGBT+ identity with a proclivity for theft:

> LGBT+ is an orientation. You cannot legalise something as an orientation. If somebody has an orientation to steal money, we cannot legalise it.[23]

Religious leaders have also fuelled and perpetuated anti-LGBT+ sentiment by conflating same-sex attraction with paedophilia. Amid the growing child sex abuse scandal in the Catholic Church, Cardinal Bertone remarked to a news conference in 2010 that "there is no relationship between celibacy and

---

18 BBC News, 'Bolsonaro: Brazil must not become 'gay tourism paradise'' (26 April 2019) <https://www.bbc.co.uk/news/world-latin-america-48062075> [original source is a 2011 Playboy interview <https://web.archive.org/web/20110709235317/http://playboy.abril.com.br/entretenimento/entrevista/jair-bolsonaro/>].

19 Reuters, 'Gambia's Jammeh calls gays 'vermin', says to fight like mosquitoes' (18 February 2014) <https://www.reuters.com/article/us-gambia-homosexuality/gambias-jammeh-calls-gays-vermin-says-to-fight-like-mosquitoes-idUSBREA1H1S820140218>.

20 Wongai Zhangazha, 'Mugabe comes face-to-face with gays' (*Zimbabwe Independent*, 27 November 2015) <https://www.theindependent.co.zw/2015/11/27/mugabe-comes-face-to-face-with-gays/> / Jeffrey Moyo, 'Worse than dogs and pigs: life as a gay man in Zimbabwe' (*Reuters*, 4 September 2017) <https://www.reuters.com/article/us-zimbabwe-rights-LGBT+/worse-than-dogs-and-pigs-life-as-a-gay-man-in-zimbabwe-idUSKCN1BF03Z>.

21 Robert Shine, '"It is Better to Die of Hunger" Than to Accept Homosexuality, Says Tanzanian Cardinal' (*New Ways Ministry*, 7 December 2018) <https://www.newwaysministry.org/2018/12/07/it-is-better-to-die-of-hunger-than-to-accept-homosexuality-says-tanzanian-cardinal/>.

22 NTV Kenya (24 May 2019) <https://www.facebook.com/NTVKenya/posts/10155681178584058>. The High Court decision is under appeal.

23 Tom Batchelor, 'Kenya refuses to overturn ban on gay sex' (Independent, 24 May 2019) <https://www.independent.co.uk/news/world/africa/kenya-gay-sex-marriage-rights-court-ban-LGBT+-a8929746.html>.

paedophilia but many others have demonstrated, I was told recently, that there is a relationship between homosexuality and paedophilia".[24] Retired Pope Benedict XVI attributed clerical sexual abuse of children to the "sexual freedom" of the 1960s, including the emergence of "homosexual cliques" in seminaries.[25]

3 Dignity, Sexual Orientation and the Criminal Law

3.1 *The Central Role of Dignity in Human Rights Frameworks*

Dignity of all persons is central to the United Nations' conception of human rights, and to that in many domestic legal frameworks. The preamble to the Universal Declaration of Human Rights (UDHR) states that '*recognition of the inherent dignity and of the equal and inalienable rights of all members of the human family is the foundation of freedom, justice and peace in the* world'.[26] It is also expressly provided for in Article 1 of the UDHR,[27] and is a key principle of the UN Charter.[28] Both the International Covenant on Economic, Social and Cultural Rights (ICESCR) and the International Covenant on Civil and Political Rights (ICCPR) state that all human rights derive from the inherent dignity of the human person.[29]

24 BBC News, 'Vatican comment on paedophiles draws gay groups' anger' (13 April 2010) <http://news.bbc.co.uk/1/hi/world/europe/8618878.stm>.

25 BBC News, 'Ex-Pope Benedict XVI blames 1960s revolution for sex abuse' (11 April 2019) <https://www.bbc.co.uk/news/world-europe-47898562>. More recent Vatican comments refute this narrative, describing it as a "great injustice": https://www.newsweek.com/its-great-injustice-link-homosexuality-pedophilia-hurts-faithful-gay-priests-vatican-1477089.

26 UN General Assembly, *Universal Declaration of Human Rights*, 10 December 1948, 217 A (III).

27 Ibid., Article 1: '*All human beings are born free and equal in dignity and rights.*'

28 The Preamble of the UN Charter states '*We the peoples of the United Nations determined [...] to reaffirm faith in fundamental human rights, in the dignity and worth of the human person, in the equal rights of men and women and of nations large and small*.' United Nations, *Charter of the United Nations*, 24 October 1945, 1 UNTS XVI.

29 The preamble to the ICESCR states that '*recognition of the inherent dignity and of the equal and inalienable rights of all members of the human family is the foundation of freedom, justice and peace in the world*', and that the rights provided in the Convention '*derive from the inherent dignity of the human person*': UN General Assembly, *International Covenant on Economic, Social and Cultural Rights*, 16 December 1966, United Nations, Treaty Series, vol. 993, p. 3. The preamble to the ICCPR uses the same words: UN General Assembly, *International Covenant on Civil and Political Rights*, 16 December 1966, United Nations, Treaty Series, vol. 999, p. 171.

Multiple other general and specific human rights treaties, at both the international and regional levels, include an obligation on states to respect the right to dignity of all persons. For instance, Article 5 of the African Charter on Human and Peoples' Rights (African Charter) provides that *'Every individual shall have the right to the respect of the dignity inherent in a human being ...'*[30] Article 11 of the American Convention on Human Rights also references dignity: *'Everyone has the right to have his honour respected and his dignity recognised.'*[31] Despite its absence in express terms from the European Convention on Human Rights (ECHR), the European Court of Human Rights has acknowledged that protection of dignity and human freedom is 'the very essence of the ECHR' and that protecting dignity is a matter of civilisation.[32] Dignity is expressly incorporated into the European Union (EU) Charter of Fundamental Rights. 'Dignity' is the title of the first of the Charter's six substantive chapters, and Article 1 thereof states: *'Human dignity is inviolable. It must be respected and protected.'*[33]

Many domestic constitutions similarly contain either an express recognition of the right to dignity or a preambular recognition of its relevance to the constitutional framework that follows. In others, it has emerged as a principle of the common law.

Wherever it is located, it is clear that dignity is a fundamental precept in the protection of human rights, and that it applies to all people. The definition in law of 'human dignity' is, of course, an issue of judicial interpretation. While recognising that it is inherently susceptible to individual, cultural and temporal subjectivities,[34] it has been described variously as being a right to autonomy over one's life choices, to bodily and psychological integrity, to the necessary conditions to enable essential needs to be satisfied, and not to be marginalised purely based on personal characteristics.[35] It has been closely associated with other rights such as the rights to privacy, equality, and freedom from inhuman or degrading treatment.

30 Organization of African Unity, *African Charter on Human and Peoples' Rights ("Banjul Charter")*, 27 June 1981, CAB/LEG/67/3 rev. 5, 21 I.L.M. 58 (1982).

31 Organization of American States (OAS), *American Convention on Human Rights ("Pact of San Jose")*, 22 November 1969, OAS Treaty Series No. 36.

32 *SW v United Kingdom*: *CR v United Kingdom* (1995) 21 EHRR 363.

33 European Union, *Charter of Fundamental Rights of the European Union*, 26 October 2012, 2012/C 326/02.

34 G. Le Moli, 'The Principle of Human Dignity in International Law', in M. Andenas, M Fitzmaurice, A Tanzi & J. Wouters (eds), *General Principles and the Coherence of International Law* (Koninklijke Brill NV 2019).

35 See for instance A. Clapham, 'Human Rights Obligations of Non-State Actors' (2006) 88 International Review of the Red Cross 491.

The South African Constitutional Court decision of *Dawood v Minister of Home Affairs* described the concept thus:

> Human dignity [...] informs constitutional adjudication and interpretation at a range of levels. It is a value that informs the interpretation of many, possibly all, other rights. This court has already acknowledged the importance of the constitutional value of dignity in interpreting rights such as the right to equality, the right not to be punished in a cruel, inhuman or degrading way, and the right to life [...D]ignity is not only a value fundamental to our Constitution, it is a justiciable and enforceable right that must be respected and protected. In many cases, however, where the value of human dignity is offended, the primary constitutional breach occasioned may be of a more specific right such as the right to bodily integrity, the right to equality or the right not to be subjected to slavery, servitude or forced labour.[36]

In *Coleman v Attridge Law*, the meaning of dignity under EU law was approached from first principles around the equal worth of every individual:

> At its bare minimum, human dignity entails the recognition of the equal worth of every individual. One's life is valuable by virtue of the mere fact that one is human, and no life is more or less valuable than another. ... Therefore, individuals and political institutions must not act in a way that denies the intrinsic importance of every human life.[37]

The Court noted further:

> A relevant, but different, value is that of personal autonomy. It dictates that individuals should be able to design and conduct the course of their lives through a succession of choices among different valuable options [see Raz, The Morality of Freedom (1986)] ... When we act as autonomous agents making decisions about the way we want our life to develop our 'personal integrity and sense of dignity and self-respect are made concrete.'[38]

36 *Dawood v Minister of Home Affairs* [2000] 5 Law Reports of the Commonwealth 147, 2000 (3) SA 936 (CC), para. 35.

37 *Coleman v Attridge Law* (2008) C-303/06, para. 9.

38 Ibid.

Even where an express right to dignity is not contained within a relevant human rights instrument, concepts of dignity have been found to be infused within other rights. For example, the Inter-American Court of Human Rights has held that the right to life '*includes, not only the right of every human being not to be deprived of his life arbitrarily, but also the right that he will not be prevented from having access to the conditions that guarantee a dignified existence*'.[39]

Similarly the Indian Supreme Court has interpreted the constitutional guarantee of life and personal liberty to include 'the right to live with human dignity and all that goes along with it, namely, the bare necessities of life such as adequate nutrition, clothing and shelter over the head and facilities for reading, writing and expressing oneself in diverse forms, freely moving about and mixing and commingling with fellow human beings'.[40]

Importantly, human dignity has been recognised as protecting against unfair treatment based merely on personal characteristics. The Supreme Court of Canada put it thus:

> Human Dignity means that an individual or group feels self-respect and self-worth. It is concerned with physical and psychological integrity and empowerment. Human dignity is harmed by unfair treatment premised upon personal traits or circumstances which do not relate to individual needs, capacities, or merits. It is enhanced by laws which are sensitive to the needs, capacities, and merits of different individuals, taking into account the context underlying their differences. Human dignity is harmed when individuals and groups are marginalised, ignored, or devalued, and is enhanced when laws recognise the full place of all individuals and groups within Canadian society.[41]

The Inter-American Court on Human Rights has similarly noted the incompatibility of according people differential treatment based on notions of superiority or inferiority:

> The notion of equality springs directly from the oneness of the human family and is linked to the essential dignity of the individual. That principle cannot be reconciled with the notion that a given group has the right to privileged treatment because of its perceived superiority. It is equally

39 Inter-American Court of Human Rights, *Case of the 'Street Children* (*Villagran-Morales v Guatemala*), Judgment of Nov. 1999 (Merits), para. 144.

40 *Mullin v The Administrator, Union Territory of Delhi*, AIR 1981 SCR (2) 516, 518.

41 *Law v Canada* (*Minister of Employment and Immigration*) [1999] 1 SCR 497, para. 53.

> irreconcilable with that notion to characterize a group as inferior and treat it with hostility or otherwise subject it to discrimination in the enjoyment of rights which are accorded to others not so classified.[42]

The right to dignity, therefore, encompasses notions of self-worth, physical and psychological integrity, human diversity, personal autonomy, equality and fair treatment.

How, then, has the right to dignity been applied to LGBT+ people in the context of the criminal law?

3.2 *What Dignity in Being Criminalised?*

A series of cases over the twenty-year period from the late 1990s to the present have recognised that laws criminalising consensual same-sex sexual conduct represent a clear violation of the right to dignity. In addition to putting LGBT+ people at perpetual risk of arrest, prosecution and detention, these laws foster and enable a wide range of abuses suffered by these communities, as briefly summarised above. They signal to societies that LGBT+ people are, by definition, criminals merely by virtue of expressing their sexual orientation with a consenting partner in private. The systemic stigma and abuse that flows from that State-sanctioned message is profound.

In one of the earliest judicial decisions on the right to dignity in the context of laws criminalising consensual same-sex intimacy, the Constitutional Court of South Africa found that the common law offence of 'sodomy' violated the constitutional right to dignity, stating:

> There can be no doubt that the existence of a law which punishes a form of sexual expression for gay men degrades and devalues gay men in our broader society. As such it is a palpable invasion of their dignity and a breach of section 10 of the Constitution [...] The harm caused by the provision can, and often does, affect his ability to achieve self-identification and self-fulfilment. The harm also radiates out into society generally and gives rise to a wide variety of other discriminations, which collectively unfairly prevent a fair distribution of social goods and services and the award of social opportunities for gays.[43]

---

42 *Proposed Amendments to the Naturalization Provision of the Constitution of Costa Rica related to Naturalization*, Advisory Opinion OC-4/84, Inter-American Court of Human Rights (19 January 1984), para. 55.

43 *National Coalition for Gay and Lesbian Equality v Minister of Justice* 6 BHRC 127 (CC, 1998), 1998 (12) BCLR 1517 (CC), paras. 28 and 36. Section 10 of the South African Constitution

A few years later, the High Court of Fiji approached the question from the opposite angle, namely through a recognition of the benefits that a proper legal understanding of dignity affords to societies, and of what the proper role of the criminal law is:

> What the Constitution requires is that the Law acknowledges difference, affirms dignity and allows equal respect to every citizen as they are. The acceptance of difference celebrates diversity. The affirmation of individual dignity offers respect to the whole of society. The promotion of equality can be a source of interactive vitality. The State that embraces difference, dignity and equality does not encourage citizens without a sense of good or evil but rather creates a strong society built on tolerant relationships with a healthy regard for the rule of law. A country so founded will put sexual expression in private relationships into its proper perspective and allow citizens to define their own good moral sensibilities leaving the law to its necessary duties of keeping sexual expression in check by protecting the vulnerable and penalizing the predator.[44]

More recently, the Supreme Court of Belize, in a decision upheld by the Court of Appeal, likewise found that a law criminalising 'buggery' violated the express constitutional right to human dignity. It recognised that even where the law applies to both opposite-sex and same-sex couples, 'the impact on the dignity of a homosexual man is disproportionate given the deep stigmatisation cause by them being the primary targets.'[45] The Court further found that the breach of this right 'operates to inform the other rights from which the concept of human dignity emanates.'[46]

The Indian Supreme Court, in a major decision decriminalising consensual same-sex conduct in 2018, went a step further in holding that the very right to choose a partner is caught by the protection of human dignity, which itself is encapsulated in the constitutional rights to life and liberty.[47]

---

provides: 'Everyone has inherent dignity and the right to have their dignity respected and protected.'

44 *Nadan & McCoskar v State*, High Court of Fiji at Suva, 26 August 2005, [2005] FJHC 500.

45 *Caleb Orozco v Attorney General of Belize*, Claim No. 668 of 2010, Supreme Court of Belize, 10 August 2016, para. 65 per Benjamin, J; *Attorney General of Belize v Caleb Orozco & Ors.*, Civil Appeal No. 32 of 2016, Court of Appeal, 30 December 2019.

46 Ibid. at para. 67.

47 *Navtej Johar Singh v Union of India*, Writ Petition (Criminal) No. 76 of 2016, Supreme Court, 6 September 2018, para. 16.1 per Malhotra, J.

As noted earlier in this chapter, the criminalisation of consensual same-sex conduct leads directly to other deprivations of human rights by State actors, including actions that engage the right to dignity. Both the High Court (Constitutional Division) and the Court of Appeal of Kenya found that where LGBT+ people are denied freedom of association, the right to dignity is breached. The High Court noted that 'the principles of equality, dignity and non-discrimination run throughout the Constitution like a golden thread'[48] and that '[a]n interpretation of non-discrimination which excludes people based on their sexual orientation would be in conflict with the principles of human dignity, ...'.[49]

Similarly, the Kenyan courts have recently recognised that where people suspected of consensual same-sex sexual conduct are forced to undergo medical examinations, such as anal examinations, in an attempt to gather evidence for a prosecution of 'unnatural offences', the right to dignity is engaged. The Court of Appeal, in upholding the lower court's finding that such examinations violated the Kenyan Constitution, stated that '[i]n determining whether the examination in question was lawful and/or reasonable, we have to give regard to the centrality of human dignity in recognition and protection of fundamental freedoms and rights.' The Court referenced the right to dignity not only in the Kenyan Constitution but in the ICCPR, ICESCR and African Charter.

The engagement with the right to dignity has also extended to jurisprudence on the criminalisation of transgender people, notably in a 2018 decision from Guyana in which the country's so-called 'cross-dressing' laws were at issue. The law forbade, under criminal penalty, males from dressing in female attire and females from dressing in male attire. The Caribbean Court of Justice held that 'the expression of a person's gender identity forms a fundamental part of their right to dignity. Recognition of this gender identity must be given constitutional protection.'[50]

These examples illustrate the firm place that dignity plays in judicial analyses of the constitutional protections of people against ill-treatment based on sexual orientation and gender identity. Notably, the cases variously apply domestic constitutional law and regional or international human rights law,

48 *Eric Gitari v Non-Governmental Organisations Co-ordination Board & Attorney General*, Petition No. 440 of 2013, High Court (Constitutional Division), 24 April 2015, para. 133; *Non-Governmental Organisations Co-ordination Board v Eric Gitari & Ors.*, Civil Appeal No. 145 of 2015, Court of Appeal, 22 March 2019.

49 Ibid. at para. 137.

50 *Quincy McEwan et al. v AG of Guyana* [2018] CCJ 30 AJ, para. 71, per Justice Saunders.

and the decisions are rooted in legal instruments that both expressly contain a right to dignity and that must locate the right to dignity in other provisions.

3.3 *Role of International Lawyers*

International lawyers, working closely with local human rights defenders and local lawyers, have played an important role in advancing human rights, including the right to dignity, in the context of sexual orientation, gender identity and the criminal law. In many of the cases cited in this chapter, the legal strategy was developed and implemented through a collaboration involving international legal support.

As part of these collaborations, legal boundaries have been pushed successfully. Over the course of 40 years, since the first decriminalisation case was decided at the European Court of Human Rights in 1981[51] focusing exclusively on the right to privacy, local and international lawyers have successfully expanded the judicial discourse on this issue to include broader notions of dignity, equality, non-discrimination on grounds of sex[52] and freedom of expression.[53]

Notably, for example, it is only very recently that any domestic jurisprudence has recognised that discrimination on grounds of sexual orientation, such as by criminalising LGBT+ people, inherently constitutes 'sex' discrimination. In Belize,[54] this came about because of the explicit strategy of international lawyers at the Human Dignity Trust to expand the pre-existing global jurisprudence. The objective was not only to succeed in Belize but to properly situate biases in respect of sexual orientation within their gender discriminatory roots and to expand the legal arguments that can be run in other jurisdictions, where there is likely a protection against sex discrimination but there may not be provisions guaranteeing the right to privacy or other applicable rights. Given that most national constitutions prohibit sex discrimination but do not explicitly mention sexual orientation discrimination, it was seen as key to embed into case law an understanding that sexual orientation discrimination is by definition a form of gender steroetyping. Likewise, given that most domestic constitutions contain a right to freedom of expression, the Belize and India decriminalisation judgments[55] – which recognised for the first time

51 *Dudgeon v UK* [1981] ECHR 5.

52 *Navtej Johar Singh v Union of India*; *Caleb Orozco v Attorney General of Belize*.

53 Ibid.

54 Ibid. A major subsequent decision of the U.S. Supreme Court in June 2020 similarly found that 'sex' includes 'sexual orientation' for purposes of discrimination law: Bostock v. Clayton County 590 U.S. 1.

55 Ibid.

that criminalising LGBT+ sexual expression is a violation of this right – have pushed boundaries which will open up new arguments in many of the remaining criminalising jurisdictions.

The contextual focus of legal cases has also begun to expand through strategic international-local collaborations. Whereas in all of the decided cases to date the experiences of gay men under the criminal law have predominated, more recent cases are engaging in a deeper analysis of and seeking redress for the rights violations experienced by diverse members of the LGBT+ community, including lesbians and trans people. As an illustrative example of these international-local collaborations, in a communication filed in 2018 with the help of international lawyers, under the Optional Protocol to the UN Convention on the Elimination of all forms of Discrimination against Women (CEDAW), it has been argued that the criminalisation of lesbians in Sri Lanka violates CEDAW, rooted as the Convention expressly is in the underlying principles of dignity and equality. The CEDAW Committee has recognised that discrimination against women manifests in many forms and can be exacerbated by virtue of women's intersecting identities along gender, race, age, sexual orientation and other lines. Women who identify as lesbian or as otherwise gender non-conforming (possibly in addition to other marginalised identities) can experience multiple layers of discrimination. This case, if successful, will be the first of its kind to recognise the impact of anti-LGBT+ criminal laws specifically on women[56] and to engage CEDAW in the global struggle against criminalisation. Likewise, in the first of its kind case on the issue of decriminalisation at the Inter-American Commission on Human Rights,[57] it has been argued that the criminal law – even where it technically only captures male same-sex conduct – impacts the entire LGBT+ community by fomenting violence and other indignities against all gender

56 As mentioned in the 'Indignities' section of this Chapter, 44 jurisdictions globally criminalise consensual sexual intimacy between females, capturing about 15 to 50 million women globally. Gebhard, P.H. and Johnson, A.B Re-analysis of Kinsey Data (1979): indicates 3.7% of women <https://kinseyinstitute.org/research/publications/historical-report-diversity-of-sexual-orientation.php> & Mosher, W.D., Chandra, A., Jones, J., 'Sexual Behavior and Selected Health Measures: Men and Women 15–44 Years of Age' (2002) Advance Data from Vital and Health Statistics (362): 1–55, 2: indicates 11% of women. <http://www.cdc.gov/nchs/data/ad/ad362.pdf> – cited in HDT, *Criminalising Homosexuality: Irreconcilable with Good Governance* (2015), p.6 <https://www.humandignitytrust.org/wp-content/uploads/resources/Criminalisation-of-Homosexuality-and-Good-Governance.pdf>.

57 Inter-American Commission on Human Rights, *Gareth Henry, Simone Carline Edwards, and Families v Jamaica*, Petition 1850-11, Report No. 80/18 on Admissibility (OEA/Ser.L/V/II, Doc. 92, 2 July 2018).

non-conforming people. A decision in this case is likely to be made public in 2020.

The role of international lawyers will, however, only be successful if a key challenge is taken into consideration. It is critical that local human rights defenders are in control of their legal and advocacy strategies, particularly on highly sensitive matters such as sexual orientation and gender identity. A major additional indignity is foisted upon local LGBT+ communities when foreign lawyers presume to launch a case in the absence of local civil society involvement and ownership. Sadly, this has been done in some (albeit rare) cases, and it has resulted in local LGBT+ people becoming significantly more vulnerable to personal security risks. In one recent instance, where local LGBT+ civil society were neither consulted, involved nor even informed of a case instigated by foreign lawyers, there was a spike in fear, vulnerability and complete unpreparedness of the local LGBT+ community once the case became public. The community was left entirely unsupported and unable to prepare security or communications plans around the litigation. Major anti-LGBT+ demonstrations were promptly organised by local faith groups,[58] and there was no preparedness for managing the backlash. This is international lawyering at its worst, demonstrating grave disrespect for the dignity of local LGBT+ communities.

In the LGBT+ decriminalisation context, as with many other contexts, it is critical therefore that international lawyers work not only with local input but with local ownership. As one academic has noted, collaborative partnerships between international lawyers and local LGBT+ human rights defenders stand *in 'positive contrast to interventions from Global North organizations that are made without local input.'*[59]

Linked to this, proper international lawyering also requires a real investment of time and patience. Simply finding a litigant and filing a case is rarely appropriate, and often dangerous. Building up the knowledge, capacity and comfort-level of local stakeholders is vital, as is providing ancillary support for media and communications strategies, security strategies and the building of support networks. In some cases, nascent or under-resourced local civil society groups, particularly in smaller countries, may also need time and support to build up their organisational infrastructure and capacity to support the litigation and the affected local LGBT+ community.

---

58 Lyf Compton, 'Christians march in protest of anti-buggery laws challenge' (*Searchlight*, 15 November 2019) < https://searchlight.vc/searchlight/front-page/2019/11/15/christians-march-in-protest-of-anti-buggery-laws-challenge/ >.

59 A. Novak, *Transnational Human Rights Litigation: Challenging the Death Penalty and Criminalization of Homosexuality in the Commonwealth* (1st ed, Springer 2020), at p. 131.

Strategic change is never about one person; it is about an entire community of people whose interests and vulnerabilities must be factored into the planning and execution of legal interventions.

Finally, consideration should always be given to the risks and benefits of international lawyers being visible in any highly sensitive strategic litigation. In some cases, local actors will consider international visibility to be helpful and strategic, particularly for the sway it will have with the relevant judiciary. Where, however, litigation is seen simply as advancing a 'foreign agenda', it can harm not only the litigation but also the interests and security of the local stakeholders, who will have to live in their communities both during a court case and long after it has concluded. Advice and direction should always be taken from the affected groups and local lawyers on the ground in any given country, as to whether international visibility would be helpful or harmful. There is almost always an option for international lawyers to work behind the scenes, with local lawyers and activists being the only visible protagonists, where that is in the best interest of the case and the local narrative that develops around it.

4 Conclusion

Strategic human rights litigation, often involving collaborations between local and international lawyers and human rights defenders, has provided a strong foothold for the right to dignity in human rights jurisprudence as it relates to sexual orientation and gender identity. The right to dignity has played a central role in the jurisprudential dismantling of laws that criminalise and persecute highly marginalised LGBT+ people globally.

The tens of millions of people globally who are still affected by these criminal laws likewise have a right to dignity, but they will need to continue to seek access to it through the courts.

CHAPTER 14

Criminalizing Holocaust Denial: from International Standards to Domestic Implementation. The Case of Italy

Giorgio Sacerdoti

1 Introduction[1]

Most European countries have enacted, and with greater momentum since the end of the twentieth century, general provisions prohibiting crimes motivated by racist, religious and ethnic hatred ('hate crimes') and incitement to hatred, racism and discrimination ('hate speech'). Antisemitic motivation is usually not specifically mentioned but is generally considered to be subsumed within the categories of religion, race or ethnicity. The persistence of antisemitism, including acts of violence, in Europe, together with the revival of ultra-nationalist xenophobic parties speculating on fears of 'illegal immigrants' invasion' of Europe justify such enactments. Not singling out antisemitism is an understandable legal perspective, since the law aims towards universality as opposed to particularity. On the other hand, many have argued that antisemitism cannot be squarely fit into one of the above-mentioned categories because it stems from a unique combination of religious, racial, economic and politically-based hatred against the Jewish people, which consist in itself of a rare combination of religion and ethnicity. The motivations of antisemitism are often different from those of racism in general and xenophobia, but the aim is similarly to exclude the addressees or victims from equal rights and participation in the civil and national society resulting in discrimination.

Few national penal codes, if any, include a specific description or mention of antisemitism, which is therefore not a crime in itself. Expressing anti-Jewish opinions, so to say, is a despicable prejudice, one that an inclusive society intends to reject and contrast. Such opinions are, however, up to a certain point, protected by the right to free speech and to express one's opinion in a democratic society. The same is true for the peaceful opposition to these views through

1 Emeritus Professor of international law, Bocconi University, Milan; President of the Jewish Contemporary Documentation Centre –Fondazione CDEC, Milan.

 | DOI:10.1163/9789004435650_015

arguments and denunciations.[2] However, campaigning to discriminate against Jews because of their being allegedly 'dangerous' to society for any reason is, may be, or should be a form of prosecutable racism. In the distinction between the one and the other attitude and conduct lies the difficulty of protecting society from the evil of antisemitism by legal means while respecting the basic liberties of a democratic society.[3]

In fact, antisemitism is not mentioned in any legally binding international or regional treaty or convention, but is clearly covered in its more virulent forms in the most recent instruments. The drafting process of the European Union Framework Decision on Combating Racism and Xenophobia of 2008 (the 'Framework Decision') exemplifies this: due to some Member States' objection, antisemitism was not mentioned in the final Framework text (except in the preamble),[4] even though it had appeared prominently in earlier drafts.[5] In any case, the Decision clearly includes Holocaust denial in its core obligation of criminalization certain conduct by EU Member States, as is evident from the text of Art. (1).[6]

---

2 In two recent (unpublished) cases in Italy, the Jewish Contemporary Documentation Centre (CDEC) was challenged in court by known holocaust deniers and 'antizionists' who complained having been victims of defamation because CDEC had listed them among publicly active antisemites in its public bulletins. Both complaints were dismissed, considering that CDEC had used its own freedom of expression in labelling correctly as antisemitic the opinions publicly expressed by the complainants, Tribunale Roma, I° sez.civile, Judge E.Serrao, sentenza (civil) No12545, 6–10 June 2013 (Moffa c. CDEC); Tribunale Roma (criminal), Decreto di archiviazione, Judge (GIP) A.M.Gavoni, No 26570/14 R.G.N.R, No33067/14 R.G.GIP, 15 May 2014.

3 See N. Lerner, 'From 'Defamation of Religions' to Incitement Based on Religion or Belief' (2013) 52 *Justice (IAJLJ)* 15 ff.

4 See paragraph 2: 'In the Hague Programme of 4 and 5 November 2004, the Council recalls its firm commitment to oppose any form of racism, anti-Semitism and xenophobia as already expressed by the European Council in December 2003."

5 EU Council Framework Decision 2008/913/JHA of 28 November 2008 on combating certain forms and expressions of racism and xenophobia by means of criminal law. Framework Decisions were the equivalent of Directives in the 'Second Pillar' under the Maastrich Treaty (1992), relating to Police and Judicial Cooperation in criminal matters (Justice and Home Affairs). With the Treaty of Lisbon (2007) the 'pillars' have been abolished. Framework Decisions of the former Second Pillar have been replaced by Directives adopted through 'ordinary legislative procedure'(Arts.288, 298, 294 TFEU).

6 *Article 1 reads as follows*:

1. Each Member State shall take the measures necessary to ensure that the following intentional conduct is punishable:
   (a) publicly inciting to violence or hatred directed against a group of persons or a member of such a group defined by reference to race, colour, religion, descent or national or ethnic origin; (b) the commission of an act referred to in point (a) by public dissemination or distribution of tracts, pictures or other material; (c) publicly

The Framework Decision called upon the Member States to enact minimal standards for the criminal prohibition of denial, justification and gross trivialization of genocide and other international crimes against humanity. The minimal standard set in Art.1(2) is the obligation to criminalize the denial of internationally-sanctioned genocides (including the Nazi-perpetrated Holocaust against the Jewish people) at least when it is 'carried out in a manner likely to incite to violence or hatred against such a group or a member of such a group', or 'which is either carried out in a manner likely to disturb public order or which is threatening, abusive or insulting.'

In view of the peculiarity of Judaism and the traditional religious base of the Jewish people, Art.1(3) is of special significance. It states that 'For the purpose of paragraph 1, the reference to religion is intended to cover, at least, conduct which is a pretext for directing acts against a group of persons or a member of such a group defined by reference to race, colour, descent, or national or ethnic origin.'

2 Holocaust Denial

Holocaust denial constitutes a modern (post-World War II) manifestation of antisemitism. As highlighted below, it is not a legitimate opinion on past events that may be subject to historical, academic research, discussion and debates. It is put forward as an ideological statement aimed at denying the genocide's perpetrators responsibility by putting in doubt the factual veracity of their criminal actions, although they have been historically and judicially established in an incontrovertible way, beyond any reasonable doubt. By doing so, as Primo Levi famously stated, what has happened may happen again.[7] The

condoning, denying or grossly trivialising crimes of genocide, crimes against humanity and war crimes as defined in Articles 6, 7 and 8 of the Statute of the International Criminal Court, directed against a group of persons or a member of such a group defined by reference to race, colour, religion, descent or national or ethnic origin when the conduct is carried out in a manner likely to incite to violence or hatred against such a group or a member of such a group; (d) publicly condoning, denying or grossly trivialising the crimes defined in Article 6 of the Charter of the International Military Tribunal appended to the London Agreement of 8 August 1945, directed against a group of persons or a member of such a group defined by reference to race, colour, religion, descent or national or ethnic origin when the conduct is carried out in a manner likely to incite to violence or hatred against such a group or a member of such a group.

7 The EU Framework Decision of 2008 acknowledges the tension between racism and xenophobia on the one hand (see para 1 of the Preamble), and the protection of fundamental freedoms on the other hand (para 11 of the Preamble).

moral inhibitory brakes against the hideous crime may be set loose again. Not necessarily another time against the Jews. The bell could ring for other groups or minorities and their members, as it indeed happened in recent decades, from Yugoslavia to Myanmar.[8]

An important contribution to squarely addressing Holocaust denial in connection with antisemitism – the first being an especially vicious form of the second, which deserves criminalization – came in 2013 and then in 2016 from the 'International Holocaust Remembrance Alliance' (IHRA). This is an 'informal' international organization comprising 34 member countries, initially established in 1998, in order to strengthen, advance and promote Holocaust education, research and remembrance.[9]

According to the IHRA 2016 'non-legally binding working definition of antisemitism', which has in the meantime been 'adopted' in different forms (by parliament or government) in a number of member states, 'Antisemitism is a certain perception of Jews,[10] which may be expressed as hatred toward Jews. Rhetorical and physical manifestations of antisemitism are directed toward Jewish or non-Jewish individuals and/or their property, toward Jewish community institutions and religious facilities'.

The IHRA text includes a number of 'explanations' and examples to guide its application, such as

> Calling for, aiding, or justifying the killing or harming of Jews in the name of a radical ideology or an extremist view of religion ... Making mendacious, dehumanizing, demonizing, or stereotypical allegations about Jews as such or the power of Jews as collective – such as, especially but not exclusively, the myth about a world Jewish conspiracy or of Jews controlling the media, economy, government or other societal institutions ...

8 See C. Vercelli, *Il negazionismo. Storia di una menzogna* (Laterza 2013).

9 The HIRA *'unites governments and experts to strengthen, advance and promote Holocaust education, research and remembrance and to uphold the commitments to the 2000 Stockholm Declaration'. It was initiated in 1998 by former Swedish Prime Minister Göran Persson and is currently integrated by 34 member countries, 'each of whom recognizes that international political coordination is imperative to strengthen the moral commitment of societies and to combat growing Holocaust denial and antisemitism. The IHRA's network of trusted experts share their knowledge on early warning signs of present-day genocide and education on the Holocaust. This knowledge supports policymakers and educational multipliers in their efforts to develop effective curricula, and it informs government officials and NGOs active in global initiatives for genocide prevention'* (https://www.holocaustremembrance.com/).

10 If the term 'negative' (perception) had been added, the text would have been clearer and closer to its intent and the explanations that follow.

> Denying the fact, scope, mechanisms (e.g. gas chambers) or intentionality of the genocide of the Jewish people at the hands of National Socialist Germany and its supporters and accomplices during World War II (the Holocaust) ... Accusing the Jews as a people, or Israel as a state, of inventing or exaggerating the Holocaust.[11]

3 Legal Reactions to Antisemitism and Holocaust Denial: Is There a Limit in Freedom of Speech?

All the above efforts to react to antisemitism and Holocaust denial, especially those aimed at addressing them legally (and the second one, also through criminalization), have raised the issue of the difference between the inadmissible advocation of discrimination, hate and violence on the one hand, and the exercise of the internationally and constitutionally-protected right of free speech (freedom of opinion) on the other hand. The question is not new. It dates back at least to when the 1948 Convention on the Prevention and Punishment of the Crime of Genocide and the 1965 International Convention on the Elimination of All Forms of Racial Discrimination (CERD) were adopted, and to whichever domestic legislation has been enacted in relation to their provisions which prohibit advocating and publicly praising genocide[12] and racial hate, respectively.[13]

Genocide has been recognized as a crime of such gravity that the punishment of incitement prevails on the otherwise fundamental right to freedom of

11 The HIRA explanations include derogatory statements on Israel such as: 'Manifestations might include the targeting of the state of Israel, conceived as a Jewish collectivity. However, criticism of Israel similar to that leveled against any other country cannot be regarded as antisemitic ... Denying the Jewish people their right to self-determination, e.g., by claiming that the existence of a State of Israel is a racist endeavor ... Using the symbols and images associated with classic antisemitism (e.g., claims of Jews killing Jesus or blood libel) to characterize Israel or Israelis.'

12 See Art. III of the 1948 Convention on the Prevention and Punishment of the Crime of Genocide, which includes within the punishable acts '(c) Direct and public incitement to commit genocide'. According to Art. IV, 'Persons committing genocide or any of the other acts enumerated in article III shall be punished, whether they are constitutionally responsible rulers, public officials or private individuals.'

13 See Art. IV (c) of the UN International Convention on the Elimination of All Forms of Racial Discrimination of 1965, according to which State Parties '(a) Shall declare an offence punishable by law all dissemination of ideas based on racial superiority or hatred, incitement to racial discrimination, as well as all acts of violence or incitement to such acts against any race or group of persons of another colour or ethnic origin, and also the provision of any assistance to racist activities, including the financing thereof.'

opinion and expression. In other conflicting cases, the latter protects even the apology of crime, except when expressed in such forms that may amount to incitement to commit a crime.[14]

As is well known, the conflict between domestic statutes that prohibit and punish Holocaust denial and freedom of expression under Article 10 the European Convention on Human Rights has been raised more than once before the Strasburg Court. The Court has consistently held that these laws, which focus on the Nazi genocide of the Jews, (notably the German legislation and the French Law Gayssot of 1990) are in compliance with the Convention, relying predominantly on Article17 ECHR on the prohibition of abuse of rights.[15]

In its seminal decision on *Garaudy* in 2003 the Court stated:[16]

> Having analyzed the book concerned, the Court found that, as the domestic courts had shown, the applicant had adopted revisionist theories and systematically disputed the existence of the crimes against humanity which the Nazis had committed against the Jewish community. There could be no doubt that disputing the existence of clearly established historical events, such as the Holocaust, did not constitute historical research akin to a quest for the truth. The real purpose of such a work was to rehabilitate the National-Socialist regime and, as a consequence, to accuse the victims of the Holocaust of falsifying history. Disputing the existence of crimes against humanity was, therefore, one of the most severe forms of racial defamation and of incitement to hatred of Jews. The denial or rewriting of this type of historical fact undermined the values on which the fight against racism and anti-Semitism was based and

14 The exceptional nature of Art. III (c) was recognized by the Italian Supreme Court (Cassazione 29.3.1985 n.507, published in *Giurisprudenza Costituzionale*, 1986, II-1, 76ff with a comment by S.Lariccia) in the only known case of application of this provision in Italy. The Court held that the punishment of apology of genocide under Art.III (c) of the Genocide Convention (implemented in Italy by Art. 8 of Law No.962 of 1967) is lawful *'because of the unbearable inhumanity of genocide also in view of the horror that the memory of Nazi exterminations arouses, irrespective of any unlikely contagion by such ideas'.*

15 For a complete overview of the Court's jurisprudence on the issue focusing on the 'exceptionalism' of the case law on the Jewish Nazi genocide, see M. Castellaneta, *La repression del negazionismo e la giurisprudenza della Corte europea dei diritti dell'uomo,* Diritti umani e Diritto internazionale, 5/2017, 65 ff.

16 *Roger GARAUDY v. France*, App no. 65831/01 (ECtHR, inadmissibility decision of 24 June 2003), Press Release of 7 July 2003, with references to the petitioner's condemnation in France in respect to his holocaust denying book. See also *Perinçek v. Suisse*, App no 27510/08 (ECtHR, 17 December 2013), holding that a light condemnation for denial of the Armenian genocide was not in breach of Art. 10.

constituted a serious threat to public order. It was incompatible with democracy and human rights and its proponents indisputably had designs that fell into the category of prohibited aims under Article 17.

4 The Italian Case

The Italian implementation of the 2008 Framework Decision has been laborious, leading to the triggering by the EU Commission of an infraction procedure, first because of the lack of any implementing legislation within the prescribed deadline (2013), and later for incomplete implementation. The reason of this delay has been the opposition to criminalization of this 'reato d'opinione' ('crime of expression') by a group of respected historians that held forcefully the view that Holocaust denial should be fought through historians' debates, not by criminal provisions, thus in the Universities not in the courts of justice.[17] In our view this is a purely academic approach that ignores the blatant bad faith of the deniers and the danger that outrageous Holocaust denial, especially through the internet, represents.

It was only by law No. 115 of 16 June 2016 that Italy finally enacted as law the crime of denying the Shoah or *negazionismo*. This law concludes a legislative process that has lasted more than three years, with the Senate and the House of Deputies almost playing ping pong with a bill that was alternatively amended by one or the other Chamber which were each time unhappy with the text tentatively approved by the other. Indeed, the passing of the law, which was finally approved by a large majority with several abstentions but with almost no negative vote by the Chamber in the text finalized by the Senate, was hampered by perplexities from members of different parties as to the alleged limitations to freedom of expression that the prohibition of Holocaust denial would create under threat of criminal penalties.

The delay in passing the legislation was even more striking if one considers that introducing criminal penalties for Holocaust denial had been made mandatory for Member States of the European Union years before, as recalled above, by the 2008 EU Framework Decision No. 913 against racism and xenophobia, including the 'apology, denial and gross trivialization' of the Nuremberg crimes and of those listed in the Statute of the International Criminal

17 This opposition has led to a rare instance of hearing in the competent Parliament commissions in 2014, where some historians testified against, while the present writer intervened with others in favor of the bill that had been presented by a group of legislators of different parties but was opposed by others.

Court. In turn the EU text was the outcome of a political compromise that had required years to be reached in the EU Council.

The implementation of the Framework Decision in Italy was effected by adding an aggravating circumstance to the crimes listed and punished by the existing statute No. 654 of 1975 as amended in 1993 (new art. 3-bis). This law had been originally enacted in order to enforce in Italy the CERD and had already been reinforced subsequently by law No. 295 of 1993.[18] The importance of the new provision is twofold. On the one hand, denial of the Holocaust, as well as of the crime of genocide, crimes against humanity and war crimes, is punished more severely than other forms of racist propaganda, hate and violence. On the other hand, through an explicit mention, the new provision clarifies once for all that indeed Holocaust denial is a form of racism (and a serious and worrying one), thus closing an interpretative loophole exploited by deniers to escape prosecution.

In any case, the new provision subjects incrimination to the requirement that denial be committed in such a way that 'an actual danger of spreading' (of violence, hate or discrimination) ensues. This ambiguous requirement was added in the last phase of the parliamentary discussions in order to overcome the conflict between those who asked that denial be made 'publicly' as a condition to be punishable, and those who opposed this qualification considering the difficulty of applying it when the use of the web is involved. This additional requirement, which is implicitly included in the 2008 EU Framework Decision, is meant to distinguish between legitimate expressions of opinions and punishable hate speech or incitement to violence. The singling out of the Holocaust and the use of the very term *Shoah* in the new provision are by themselves quite remarkable.

Before the 2016 amendment the statute punished by a fine or imprisonment whomever makes propaganda of ideas based on racial or ethnically superiority or hate, or instigates the commission or commits acts of discrimination or violence or provocation to violence on racial, ethnically, national or religious grounds.

The new 2016 provision (Article 3-bis of Law No. 654) increased the penalties up to two to six years of prison 'if the propaganda, instigation or incitement, committed in a way that an actual danger of spreading ensues, is based

18 So-called 'Legge Mancino' from the name of the Minister of Justice at the time (1993). In 2018 the content of the law has been transformed in Article 604 *bis* of the Italian Criminal Code " Propaganda e istigazione a delinquere per motivi di discriminazione razziale, etnica e religiosa" (propaganda and instigation to commit a crime for motives of racial, ethnic or religious discrimination).

in whole or in part on the denial of the Shoah, or of the crime of genocide, the crimes against humanity or war crimes as defined by Art.6, 7, 8 of the statute of the International Criminal Court ratified by law of 12 July 1999 No. 232.'

The 'saga' of the implementation of the Framework Decision was not thereby concluded. A loophole subsisted that the Commission duly pointed out to Italian authorities.[19] Implementation through Law No. 115 of 16 June 2016 was not fully compliant with the Framework Decision because, due to the opposition in Parliament mentioned above, the criminal law provision which was adopted was limited to 'denial' and to acts of 'propaganda, instigation and incitement'. This was remedied by the 'European Law' of 2017, Law No. 167 of 20 November 1967, which provided for the implementation by a single statute of a number of provisions of various directives and similar EU acts, as is now the practice in Italy every year. The loophole left by Law No. 115 of 2016 was remedied by Article 5 of Law No. 167. This provision contained an addition to the implementing provision of the Framework Decision adopted in 2016 by punishing at Art. 3-bis of Law No. 654 also whomever publicly condones (*apologia*) or grossly trivializes (*minimizzazione in modo grave*) the above-mentioned international crimes. It is noteworthy that while the passing of the 2016 legislation was met by the above mentioned objections, no opposition was raised against Art. 5 of Law No. 267 of 2017, although it extended the criminalization to *apologia*, exactly what can be considered closer to an objectionable 'reato d'opinione'('crime of expression'). This 'oversight' by those who had opposed the passing in 2016 of Law No. 115 was possibly due to the broad coverage of the European Law, which is routinely submitted to Parliament by the Government. Furthermore, the new provisions make applicable to the crimes listed in Article 3-bis of Law No. 654, as modified, the general regulation of Legislative Decree No. 231 of 2001 providing for liability for crimes committed by legal entities, including companies, and their managers on their behalf (thus complying with Article 2.2 of the Framework Decision).

5 Concluding Remarks

With the passing of Law No. 115 of 2016 and Art. 5 of Law No. 167 of 2017 Italy has complied fully with the EU 2008 Framework Decision and has aligned itself with the best standards of other nations in Europe.[20] Italy has succeeded

19 EU Pilot Case 8184/15/Just.

20 See A. Latino, *Il diritto alla memoria e le norme anti-negazioniste,* Genocidio. Conoscere e ricordare per prevenire (F. Lattanzi, ed.), Università Roma3, 2020, 83–93.

in attaining two valuable objectives. First of all, the new penal provision fully safeguards freedom of expression, criticism and historical research, differently from recent legislation in other states such as in Poland, meant to impose a politically correct, State-imposed unilateral 'truth' in respect of controversial historical events of the recent past.[21]

On the other hand, while the main concern behind the new legislation was that of opposing Holocaust denial, the new provisions do not single out this conduct but do so within a broader criminalization of any advocation, praise or denial of all crimes against humanity, including genocide.

21 See Act on the Institute of National Remembrance – Commission for the Prosecution of Crimes against the Polish Nation of 1998 (Art. 55 (a) (1)), as amended in February and rectified (to take care of vehement protests from abroad) in June 2018.

CHAPTER 15

State Negationism and the Rule of Law

Alessandra Pietrobon

1 Introduction

Negationism is the term commonly used to identify revisionist "theories" that oppose the prevailing historical reconstruction and the widespread collective memory of cases of genocide or other international crimes.[1] A negationist doctrine is never a neutral, scientific historical reconstruction, as it offends the memory of the victims, the survivors and their descendants, by denying or diminishing their suffering. As defined by human rights treaty bodies and by the European Court for Human Rights (ECtHR), the diffusion or propaganda of negationist theories is considered hate speech. It may encourage violence against the targeted group but – well before it – it might reduce the critical thinking of the general population and somehow anaesthetize their sensitivity towards future acts of intolerance. In the worst-case scenario, negationism could pave the way to repetition of the same criminal acts it aims at denying.

Holocaust denial is one of these theories,[2] and presently one of the most dangerous, while anti-Semitism is on the rise in many European countries.[3] In 2008,

1 This is a working definition, meant for the purposes of the present paper. It does not include cases in which the revisionist theory does not question the truth of a genocide as such, but rather the fact that a given State had contributed to its perpetration: on a case of this kind, see S. Geissbühler, 'Staring at the Past with Eyes Wide Shut: Holocaust Revisionism and Negationism in Romania' (2012) *Israel Journal of Foreign Affaires* 126 ff. This paper refers to genocides that have been acknowledged as such by an international court, but there are several more cases of alleged genocides whose actual legal definition as such is controversial: see William A. Schabas, *Genocide in International Law: The Crime of Crimes* (Cambridge 2000) 453 ff.

2 Other cases of genocide are not immune to negationism: see *Srebrenica was not genocide: Bosnian Serb leader,* 27 April 2010, http://www.france24.com/en/20100427-srebrenica-was-not-genocide-bosnian-serb-leader; J. Wizeye, 'To claim Tutsis caused Rwanda's genocide is pure revisionism', *The Guardian*, 25 July 2011, https://www.theguardian.com/commentisfree/2011/jul/25/tutsi-rwanda-genocide-hutu.

3 See European Commission against Racism and Intolerance, *Annual Report of ECRI's Activities*, 2019, https://rm.coe.int/ecri-annual-report-2019/16809ca3e1e. There are various situations of concern: for a recent case, see the Letter of 27 February 2020, by several members of the European Parliament, to the President of the European Commission, concerning a carnival parade in Aalst: "[w]hat happened in Aalst has nothing to do with entertainment. This is also

 | DOI:10.1163/9789004435650_016

a framework decision of the Council of the European Union required member States to consider negationism as a criminal offence in their domestic law.[4] Many States then enacted the so-called "memory laws", but their purpose, the contents of the criminal provisions and the related sanctions are very different.[5] The ECtHR has already dealt with several cases concerning individuals convicted under such laws, claiming that this was in contrast with the freedom of expression granted by the European Convention on Human Rights (ECHR): as will be seen, the level of defence of European legal systems against negationism is particularly high.

By contrast, the issue of negationism promoted or endorsed by a State and its possible consequences is currently unexplored, not being perceived as an actual problem. Yet, at least one State in recent years did officially support negationist theories concerning the Holocaust, so it is worth wondering whether such a conduct would violate any international law norm. Then, it will be possible to assess whether and to what extent other States could react, to restore the dignity of the targeted group, preventing the situation from evolving into more severe discrimination or into repetition of acts of genocide.

This paper will first consider the jurisprudence of the UN Human Rights Committee (UNHRC) and the European Court of Human Rights (ECtHR) concerning negationism . This will provide elements for analyzing State negationism and the actions that could be taken to address it, according to the current international legal framework.

2 The Human Rights Committee and the European Court of Human Rights Confronting Negationism: Guillotine Rule or Risk Assessment?

Both the Human Rights Committee of the United Nations (UNHRC) and the ECtHR have been dealing with a number of cases concerning negationism, following the

---

not even camouflaged antisemitism. These floats and wagons are made to diminish human beings to centuries-old prejudices and stereotypes and to reinforce these symbols in a time when conspiracy theories, racism and xenophobic attacks are on the rise. This is the dirty face of uncovered and blunt antisemitism ..." (full text available at https://ep-wgas.eu/docs/MEPs%27%20Reaction%20to%20Aalst%20Carnival.pdf). The festival had been authorized by local authorities notwithstanding the previous official letter – asking for a stricter control – sent by the Working Group on Atisemitism of the European Parliament.

4 Council Framework Decision 2008/913 HA, of 28 November 2008, *on combating certain forms and expressions of racism and xenophobia by means of criminal law*, in *OJ* L328 of 6 December 2008.

5 See Jeroen Temperman, *Religious Hatred and International Law* (Cambridge 2016) 280 ff.

application by revisionist politicians or historians, that had been prosecuted and convicted under domestic laws because of their theories and, therefore, claimed that their fundamental freedom of expression had been violated.

In *Fourisson v. France*, the UNHRC took a very strict approach: right upon consideration of the content of the applicant's statements, it found that they could "raise or strengthen anti-semitic feelings".[6] As a consequence, the restrictions imposed in France to Mr Fourisson's freedom of expression were found necessary for granting the Jewish community the right "to live free from fear of an atmosphere of anti-semitism": other circumstances of the case were not taken into account. This position was overturned some years later by the same Committee. In *Malcolm Ross v. Canada*, it took into account the actual risks that the diffusion of a negationist theory could bring about in the specific social environment concerned, to assess whether – under those specific circumstances – the application of the Canadian memory law could be justified in the light of the ICCPR.[7]

Both kinds of reasoning are mirrored in the jurisprudence of the ECtHR. In *Garaudy v. France*, the first apodictic kind of reasoning was brought to its extreme consequences, in a decision based on the so-called guillotine approach.[8] The applicant was a French philosopher and a politician, who had published in France a book whose title was indeed very clear: *Les Mythes fondateurs de la politique israelienne*. It aimed at demonstrating how the history of the Holocaust had been magnified, if not just invented by the Jews, in a well orchestrated international plot, to gain and exploit the consent of the international community to the foundation of the State of Israel. The author, having been prosecuted and convicted by French courts, applied to the ECtHR claiming that rights granted under art. 10 of the ECHR had been violated. The Court held that the true purpose of the book, far from being historical, was to rehabilitate the Nazi regime and to accuse the victims of falsifying history: "the applicant attempts to deflect Article 10 (…) from its real purpose by using his right to freedom of expression for ends which are contrary to the text and spirit of the Convention. Such ends, if admitted, would contribute to the destruction of the rights and freedoms guaranteed by the Convention".[9] The ECtHR concluded that, by reason of Article 17 ECHR, the applicant could not benefit from the

---

6 *Fourrisson v. France*, Communication n. 550/1993 (UNHRC, 1993).

7 *Malcolm Ross v. Canada*, Communication n. 736/1997 (UNHRC, 1997).

8 The term is borrowed from Joeren Temperman, supra note 5, 149; see *Garaudy v. France*, App no 65831/01 (ECtHR, Admissibility Decision of 24 June 2003); see also *Pavel Ivanov v. Russia*, App no 35222/04 (ECtHR, Admissibility Decision of 20 February 2007); *Williamson v. Germany*, App no 64496/17 (ECtHR, Admissibility Decision of 8 January 2019).

9 *Garaudy v. France*, Ibid, 23.

protection afforded by the Convention and declared the application inadmissible, without any exam on the merits.

Yet, the ECtHR follows a radically different approach in dealing with cases of negationism other than Holocaust denial, as in *Perinçek v. Switzerland*.[10] In this case, the applicant was a Turkish politician and doctor of law, living in Switzerland where, in several public meetings, he argued that the Armenian genocide was an "international lie". Mr Perinçek did not deny that mass atrocities had been perpetrated against the Armenians but disputed the legal qualification of such acts as genocide. According to his view, the facts occurred in 1915 were actually provoked by the Great Powers that – interfering in the internal affairs of the Ottoman Empire – had fomented the Armenian uprising, with the purpose of weakening the old Empire.[11] Having been convicted under Swiss criminal law, Mr Perinçek applied to the ECtHR, for violation of his freedom of expression.

After a Chamber had declared that such a violation had actually occurred, the case was brought before the Grand Chamber by the Swiss Government, arguing that the atrocities committed against Armenians could in any case amount to crimes against humanity – if not to genocide – and that negationism in both cases was a criminal offence under Swiss law.

The Grand Chamber did not consider its task to solve the historical issue, in order to qualify the events. Its reasoning could rather proceed by assessing the circumstances of the specific case, in the light of art. 8 and art. 10 of the Convention. To strike the balance between the two, the Grand Chamber recalled the criteria already consolidated by its previous jurisprudence.[12]

10 *Perinçek v. Switzerland*, App no 27510/08 (ECtHR, Grand Chamber, Decision of 15 October 2015).

11 According to his reconstruction, "Great Powers, which wanted to divide the Ottoman Empire, provoked a section of the Armenians, with whom we had lived in peace for centuries, and incited them to violence. The Turks and Kurds defended their homeland from these attacks": Ibid, para. 13.

12 The Court took into account "the concrete aspects of the two rights that were at stake, the need to restrict, or to protect, each of them, and the proportionality between the means used and the aim sought to be achieved (…) by looking at the nature of the applicant's statements; the context in which the interference occurred; the extent to which they affected the Armenians' rights; the existence or lack of consensus among the High Contracting Parties on the need to resort to criminal-law sanctions in respect of such statements; the existence of any international-law rules bearing on this issue; the method employed by the Swiss courts to justify the applicant's conviction; and the severity of the interference": Ibid, para. 228. For an overview on international law instruments balancing freedom of expression with the need to fight hate speech, N. Wenzel, 'Opinion and Expression, Freedom of, International Protection' (2014) *MPEPIL*; E. Fronza, *Memory and Punishment. Historical Denialism, Free Speech and the Limits of Crimilal Law* (Springer 2018) 73 ff.

So, art. 8 came into consideration, as the diminishing of the suffering of the ancestors amounts to a violation of the right to private life and individual dignity of today's Armenians. However, the Grand Chamber fully considered all the circumstances of the case, to conclude that the doctrine endorsed by the Turkish politician was not conceived as a direct accusation to Armenians, but rather as a criticism to the imperialist politics of the Great Powers of the time.[13] The risk assessment approach did involve consideration of geographical and time factors, leading the ECtHR to conclude that the dissemination of Mr Perinçek's theories could not be considered as hate speech, nor as an incitement to it, and the measures taken by the Swiss authorities were not justified.[14]

The Grand Chamber assumed that a full knowledge of the events that struck the Armenians is still to be achieved: the crucial element – on which full evidence is still to be provided – would be the specific intent of the Turkish authorities to commit genocide. Although striking, the radical difference between the approach in Perinçek and the guillotine rule applied in *Garaudy* is quite understandable, being grounded on the fact that Holocaust denial was acknowledged as such by an international Court, while a trial on the events concerning the Armenians was never held.

3 State Negationism and International Law

State negationism refers to situations in which the State itself officially develops or supports some negationist theory, or tolerates it, without taking any measure to contrast its diffusion among the population.

It was rather striking for the public opinion in the West to hear that the President of Iran in official speeches used to describe the Holocaust as a myth, an international lie, arguing that the State of Israel had to be "wiped off the

13 *Perinçek v. Switzerland*, supra note 10, para. 156.

14 The ECtHR concluded that "the lapse of time between the applicant's statements and the tragic events to which he was referring was (…) about ninety years, and at the time when he made the statements there were surely very few, if any, survivors of these events (…) The Court is aware of the immense importance attached by the Armenian community to the question whether the tragic events of 1915 and the following years are to be regarded as genocide, and of that community's acute sensitivity to any statements bearing on that point. However, it cannot accept that the applicant's statements in issue in this case were so wounding to the dignity of the Armenians who suffered and perished in these events and to the dignity and identity of their descendants as to require criminal law measures in Switzerland" (Ibid, para 250–252).

map".[15] Several States reacted when in the Iranian Minister of Foreign Affaires convened an international conference, in Teheran, aimed at reconsidering the "global vision" on the Holocaust: a conference to which all the most famous western negationist thinkers were welcomed guests.[16] Under the following Presidency, the Iranian Government took a softer attitude and those declarations, as seen today from distance, might even be considered – some argue – as due to mistranslation.[17] Be that as it may, the lesson learnt is the need to be ready to address any future similar events. It is therefore worth wondering whether such a State conduct would violate any norm of international law and what could be done to address the problem, in addition to issuing diplomatic statements.

In the resolution designating the 27th of January as Holocaust memorial day, the UN General Assembly calls to *reject* "any denial of the Holocaust as an historical event, either in full or in part".[18] The resolution was adopted by *consensus*, revealing a shared, general opinion but this is not enough to assume that a general customary rule exists, prohibiting State negationism. A perusal of international practice shows that, while a number of States criminalize diffusion of such a theory, many others prefer a different approach to counteract the phenomenon. Indeed, action needed to *reject* negationism (as the resolution requires) does not necessarily entail that it should be considered as a criminal offence, and many States consider that education, rather than punishment, is the right way to address the problem. A general customary rule could eventually be established, if most States (not just Western ones) had a similar norm in their domestic law, showing a consistent practice and a corresponding *opinio iuris*: but this is far from being the case.

As for conventional law, the Additional Protocol to the European Convention on cyber-crime, requires State parties to criminalize, when committed

---

15 Al Jazeera, 26 October 2005, *Ahmadinejad: Wipe Israel off map*, https://www.aljazeera.com/archive/2005/10/200849132648612154.html.

16 See R. Tait, 'Holocaust deniers gather in Iran for 'scientific' conference' *The Guardian*, 12 December 2006; for reference to reactions of Western States, see *International Conference to Review the Global Vision of the Holocaust*, in https://en.wikipedia.org/wiki/International_Conference_to_Review_the_Global_Vision_of_the_Holocaust.

17 See G. Kessler, 'Did Ahmadinejad really say Israel should be 'wiped off the map'?' *The Washington Post*, 5 October 2013, at https://www.washingtonpost.com/blogs/fact-checker/post/did-ahmadinejad-really-say-israel-should-be-wiped-off-the-map/2011/10/04/gIQABJIKML_blog.html. Actually, Holocaust denial in Iran still remains an issue: B. Sharafedin, 'Why Iran takes issue with the Holocaust', *BBC News*, 9 October 2013, at https://www.bbc.com/news/world-middle-east-24442723.

18 UNGA Resolution of 1 November 2005, *Holocaust remembrance*, A/RES/60/7.

intentionally, the conduct consisting in "distributing or otherwise making available, through a computer system to the public, material which denies, grossly minimises, approves or justifies acts constituting genocide or crimes against humanity, as defined by international law and recognised as such by final and binding decisions of the International Military Tribunal, established by the London Agreement of 8 August 1945, or of any other international court established by relevant international instruments and whose jurisdiction is recognised by that Party".[19] The Protocol is presently in force (only) between 32 States and some of them made a reservation, to exclude full application of this article.

Failing specific rules, the norms to which reference shall be made for fighting State negationism can be found in human rights law, in particular in the ICCPR and in the CERD. These conventions do not address negationism as such, but a State endorsing it would almost unavoidably violate the rights guaranteed by these conventions.[20] First of all, because negationism is a form of hate speech: in its General Recommendation n 35, the CERD Committee condemns "the role of racist hate speech in processes leading to mass violations of human rights and genocide", underlining that hate speech by public authorities or public institutions is to be considered "of particular concern".[21] Negationism by a State would be far more dangerous depending on the presence in that State of individuals belonging to the ethnic, religious or national group of the victims of the contested genocide. It is hard to believe that the fact of being officially described as deceitful persons, gaining political and financial

19 See Art. 6 of the *Additional Protocol to the Convention on Cybercrime, concerning the criminalisation of acts of a racist and xenophobic nature committed through computer systems* (28 January 2003, ETS n. 189), available at https://www.coe.int/it/web/conventions/full-list.

20 In other words, neither the ICCPR nor the CERD or the ECHR provide for a specific "human right to be free from negationism". Art. 4 of CERD provides that "States Parties condemn all propaganda and all organizations which are based on ideas or theories of superiority of one race or group of persons of one colour or ethnic origin, or which attempt to justify or promote racial hatred and discrimination in any form, and undertake to adopt immediate and positive measures designed to eradicate all incitement to, or acts of, such discrimination". However, the mandatory nature of art 4 is still debated: see Jeroen Temperman, supra note 5.

21 See Committee on the Elimination of Racial Discrimination, *General Recommendation* No. 35, CERD/C/GC/35, of 26 September 2013, *Combating racist hate speech*, para. 3 and 22. About hate speech as symptom of a looming genocide, see, W.A. Schabas, 'Hate Speech in Rwanda: The Road to Genocide' (2000) 46 *McGill Law Journal* 147 ff.; Z. Barany, 'Where Myanmar Went Wrong. From Democratic Awakening to Ethnic Cleansing' (2018) 97(3) *Foreign Affairs* 141 ff.

advantages from a false condition of victims – or the like – would go without painful consequences. The misrepresentation could severely harm the dignity of the targeted people and undermine their living condition, exposing them to social discrimination and careless violation of human rights, both by authorities and by other groups in the same country.[22]

4 Negationism under the Genocide Convention

Could State negationism amount to a violation of the Genocide Convention? The issue would emerge when consequences were particularly serious, provoking new actual or attempted genocidal acts. As held by the ICJ in *Bosnia v. Serbia*, State parties to this Convention undertake not only to prevent and punish genocide but also not to commit genocide themselves, nor to commit any of the acts indicated by art. III.[23] The norms that could come into consideration here are those concerning complicity in genocide, the obligation to prevent genocide and the obligation to prohibit any form of incitement to it.[24]

As for the first, a negationist State could be held responsible of complicity, in case of a genocide committed by other States, if the negationist activity of the first State was aimed at justifying and protecting the perpetrators, or at diminishing the consequences of the crime, in order to limit or avoid reactions by the international community.[25] The responsibility of the negationist State – as complicity by aiding and abetting – would be held upon demonstration of the *dolus specialis*, i.e. that the accomplice State be aware

22 See Christian Tomuschat, 'Prosecuting Denials of Past Alleged Genocides' in P. Gaeta (ed.), *The UN Genocide Convention, A Commentary* (Oxford 2009) 520.

23 See *Application of the Convention on the Prevention and Punishment of the Crime of Genocide, Bosnia and Herzegovina v. Serbia and Montenegro*, Judgement of 26 February 2007, in *ICJ Reports*, 2007, para. 166–168.

24 The judgement in *Bosnia v. Serbia* opens to the "dual" reading of the Genocide Convention, as a treaty not only establishing the character of the (individual) crime that State parties undertake to prevent and punish, bur also setting a *lex specialis* concerning State responsibility for genocide. For many purposes, each perspective would involve different concepts (as State responsibility is not meant as a criminal one). For brevity needs, the issue cannot be addressed here, but see Anja Seibert-Fohr, 'State Responsibility for Genocide under the Genocide Convention', in P. Gaeta (ed.), *The UN Genocide Convention*, supra note 22, 365 ss.

25 By denying the crime within an international organization, the accomplice State might prevent the adoption of any measures aimed at condemning genocide and, in case of a permanent member of the UNSC, it could prevent every action by the UN.

of the genocidal intent of the perpetrators.[26] Since the Convention prevails – as *lex specialis* – over general rules on State responsibility, the negationist State could be considered as breaching art. 3, even in case the complicity was meant at aiding or assisting non-State actors, groups or entities (whose conduct would not be otherwise attributable to a State, according to general rules).[27]

The obligation to prevent genocide is at the core of the Convention. In *Bosnia v. Serbia*, the ICJ specified that every State party is required "to employ all means reasonably available to them, so as to prevent genocide so far as possible" and that "responsibility is incurred if the State manifestly failed to take all measures to prevent genocide which were within its power, and which might have contributed to preventing the genocide".[28] Proper compliance with this obligation should necessarily include the duty of every State (not only to prevent and prohibit but also) to refrain itself from practicing or endorsing any official negationist propaganda, knowing that this could lay down the conditions in which any of the acts listed in art. II might occur. In other words, a State sponsoring negationism could not claim to be employing all means reasonably available to prevent a genocide, as it would rather be moving in the opposite direction. Negationism as hate speech brings about a poisonous situation, in which risk assessment should be crucial: and not only where people belonging to the targeted minority were all living in that same State.[29] Then, the obligation to prevent would apply with reference to any situation in which a State had the capacity "to influence effectively the action of persons likely to commit, or already committing genocide".[30]

In *Bosnia v. Serbia*, the ICJ held that a breach of the obligation to prevent genocide occurs (only) when genocide *is* committed.[31] Therefore – just as

26 Although the subject matter is not the same (supra note 24), reference can be made to the jurisprudence of international criminal courts, see International Criminal Tribunal for Rwanda, Decision of 2 September 1998, *Prosecutor v. J.P. Akayesu*, (case ICTR-96-4-T), para. 538 ff.

27 See Paolo Palchetti, State Responsibility for Complicity in Genocide, in *The UN Genocide Convention*, supra note 22, 385.

28 See *Bosnia v. Serbia* cit., para. 430.

29 The groups who were victims of genocide in the past could now be living in several different countries, for many previous historical reasons but, more than that, just because of the genocide, as it is for the Jews and the Armenians.

30 See *Bosnia v. Serbia* cit., para. 430; Serena Forlati, *The Legal Obligation to Prevent Genocide: Bosnia v. Serbia and Beyond*, in G. Arangio-Ruiz, F. Salerno, C. Fioravanti (eds.), *Scritti giuridici in ricordo di Giovanni Battaglini*, Napoli, 2013, p. 134.

31 The conclusion reflects the general rule of 14.3 of the Project of Articles on Responsibility of States for Internationally Wrongful Acts.

seen above for complicity – the responsibility of a negationist State could be assessed only *ex post*, after a genocide actually occurred: but, before that moment negationism as such – no matter how dangerous – would not amount to a violation of the Convention. Would this be appropriate? In *Bosnia c. Serbia,* the reasoning developed taking into account just the "ordinary" situation: namely, a case in which – after mass atrocities were committed – the ICJ had to ascertain whether (where, when and by whom) a genocide had actually taken place, to eventually assess possible responsibilities for the failure to prevent it.

The case of the hypothetical negationist State could be legally distinguished: the issue would be whether that State could be held responsible for the conduct of its organs, consisting – here – not in a failure to act for prevention, but – to the opposite – in positive actions (i.e. the negationist propaganda) practically and logically at variance with a proper compliance with the obligation to prevent genocide. If people who were victims of a previous genocide were living in the negationist State, the same fact of knowingly exposing them to the risk of repetition of genocidal acts could be considered as a breach of the obligation to prevent genocide. Indeed, the tremendous power of hate speech among the factors leading to genocide is well known.[32]

This interpretation would allow to hold the negationist State responsible for breach of the obligation to prevent genocide, even if it were eventually averted (i.e. for the intervention of other States or international organizations) but a situation of real danger had actually occurred.[33] Such a "pre-emptive defence" against genocide would be in line with the object and purpose of the Convention, as its Preamble underlines the unique magnitude of the crime of genocide and the absolute necessity to prevent it from occurring ever again, so to "liberate mankind" from an "odious scourge". Moreover, the Declaration on the Prevention of Genocide assumes the principles of early warning and urgent action as essential in the fight against genocide.[34] The interpretation proposed here would be in line with the need to consider human rights conventions as "living instruments" and should apply – at least – to negationism

32 See F. *Shannon, Tracking Hate Speech Acts as Incitement to Genocide in International Criminal Law*, in 30 *Leiden Journal of International Law*, 2017, p. 523; W. K. Timmermann, 'The Relationship between Hate Propaganda and Incitement to Genocide: A New Trend in International Law Towards Criminalization of Hate Propaganda?', in 18 *Leiden Journal of International Law*, 2005, p. 257.

33 In this sense, see Andrea Gattini, *Breach of the Obligation to Prevent and Reparation Thereof in the ICJ's Genocide Judgment*, in 18 *European Journal of Int. Law*, 2007, p. 702.

34 See CERD Committee, *Declaration on the Prevention of Genocide*, of 17 October 2005, CERD/C/66/1, p. 3.

concerning cases of genocide that have been recognized as such by an international court.[35]

The official endorsement or propaganda of negationist theories might breach the prohibition of "direct and public" incitement to genocide. The "upgrading" of the negationist propaganda from hate speech to incitement to genocide would depend on the circumstances of the case and on the specific intent of the responsible State. In the first case, the mental element could go far as to anticipate and accept the risk that a genocide might follow, but the will of the State promoting hate speech would not be focused on causing that consequence. This conduct might be considered a violation of the obligation to prevent genocide, as seen above.

By contrast, for the crime of incitement to occur, the purpose of the negationist State should be precisely that of fomenting the public to commit new acts of genocide, with the clear purpose of destroying a group.[36] Even to assess the responsibility of a negationist State for incitement to genocide, the need might arise to understand whether, in case a genocide were eventually *not* committed, a violation of the Genocide Convention might equally occur. The first draft of the Convention was more precise, considering the crime as perpetrated "whether the incitement be successful or not". However, this last part of the sentence was removed from the final text.[37] The amendment is read by some commentators as evidence of the proper meaning of the text, limiting the wrongfulness of acts of incitement to the case in which they should prove ... "successful".[38] Nevertheless, the remark is far from being pivotal since – according to the general international law rules on treaty interpretation, as

35 Not only to Holocaust denial but also to negationism of the genocide in Rwanda or in Srebrenica: sadly, none of them is immune from negationism (supra note 2).

36 For a deeper analysis of the different possible attitudes of the mental element in the crime of incitement, see F. Shannon, *Tracking Hate Speech Acts as Incitement to Genocide* cit., p.

37 See previous drafts in W.A. Schabas, *Genocide in International Law* cit., p. 553 ff. Even the need for a specific provision on incitement was strongly debated and the United States eventually insisted on having the entire provision deleted, arguing that incitement would have been punishable as complicity, if a genocide were committed. To the contrary – according to the same US – as long as a genocide were *not* committed, freedom of expression would have to prevail, to the same extent granted by the US Constitution: see W.A. Schabas, *Hate Speech in Rwanda* cit., p. 149 ss.; on today's US perspective, see A. Clooney – P. Webb, *The Right to Insult in International Law*, in *Columbia Human Rights Law Review*, 2017/2, p. 15 ss.

38 The mental element in genocide involves a *dolus specialis*, consisting in the "intent to destroy, in whole or in part, a national, ethnical, racial or religious group, as such": art. I of the Convention.

codified by the Vienna Convention[39] – preparatory works can only be referred to as subsidiary means of interpretation, in case the resort to primary means would leave a question ambiguous. Indeed, for the same reasons above indicated, reference to the object and the purpose of the Convention could clearly support the stricter interpretation here proposed, excluding the need to consider the subsidiary means, not even the history of the negotiations.

5 The Possible Means to Address State Negationism by Promoting the Rule of Law

The 2005 *Declaration on the prevention of genocide* by the CERD Committee underlines how the international community had failed to prevent the genocides in Rwanda and Srebrenica *because of lack of will.*[40] The *Declaration* contends that military intervention should be a measure of last resort, to stop genocide in extreme cases, inviting all States to strengthen cooperation at the international level, by involving competent international bodies.

The Committee established by the CERD can examine inter-state communications by any State party assuming that another State party "is not giving effect" to the provisions of the Convention.[41] After inquires on the facts, the conciliatory procedure leads to a non-binding report. For decades, however, no State made resort to this option: presently, the very first three cases are pending.[42] A similar inter-State procedure is provided for by the International Covenant on Civil and Political Rights (ICCPR), but can operate only between States having recognized the competence of the Committee by acceptance of an optional clause.[43]

The Genocide Convention expressly provides that every State party "may call upon the competent organs of the United Nations to take such action

39 On the point, the Vienna Convention on the Law of Treaties corresponds to general rules of international law (as the ICJ reminds even in *Bosnia v. Serbia* cit., para. 160).

40 *Declaration on the Prevention of Genocide* cit., p. 1.

41 See Arts 11–13 CERD.

42 At the end of 2019: see CERD Committee, *Information Note on Inter-state communications (13 December 2019)*, available at https://www.ohchr.org/EN/HRBodies/CERD/Pages/InterstateCommunications.aspx. The rule on exhaustion of domestic remedies applies: but, according to general international law rules, it could be overcome where no domestic remedies are actually available or if they are supposed to remain ineffective (although art. 11.3 CERD only admits derogation to the rule "where the application of the remedies is unreasonably prolonged".

43 Art. 41 CCRP.

under the Charter of the United Nations as they consider appropriate for the prevention and suppression of acts of genocide or any of the other acts enumerated in art. III".[44] The provision could even appear pleonastic, as the faculty it provides for is just inherent in the *status* of every UN member State.[45] Yet, even without setting legal obligation, art. VIII underlines how all States parties should consider as their duty to keep close attention to detect every situation of possible concern and to report it to the UN. In other words, all parties should not remain passive bystanders when a risk of genocide is arising.

More importantly, both the Genocide Convention (art. IX) and the CERD (art. 22) provide for the jurisdiction of the ICJ, upon unilateral request, in case of disputes concerning the interpretation or the application of the same conventions. In case of violation by a State party, any other State party willing to react could actually bring the issue to the Court: a specifically qualified interest is not required, as the ICJ underlined in its recent decision concerning provisional measures against Myanmar, for the alleged genocide perpetrated against the Rohinya minority.[46]

The possibility of obtaining the Court's assessment on such dramatic events is due to the remarkable initiative of one single State, the Gambia, whose application is based on art. IX of the Genocide Convention. Indeed, this is a good example of how violation of an *erga omnes* obligation can be faced not (or not only) by an armed intervention or by economic sanctions, but by enacting the rule of law, when the possibility to do so is provided. As the ICJ points out, the same initiative could have been taken by every other State party to the same Convention.[47]

Then, the interpretation issues drafted above could well be brought to the ICJ, to get an assessment that would in any case contribute to legal certainty. As for the existence of a dispute, it could emerge after one good-willing State

---

44 Art. VIII.

45 However, the history of the negotiations clearly explains the relevance of art. VIII at the time in which the Convention was drafted: see William A. Schabas, *Genocide in International Law* cit., p. 448 ff.

46 ICJ, *Application of the Convention on the Prevention and Punishment of the Crime of Genocide,* (The Gambia v. Myanmar), Order of 23 January 2020, *Provisional measures*, para. 41: "any State party to the Genocide Convention, and not only a specially affected State, may invoke the responsibility of another State party with a view to ascertaining the alleged failure to comply with its obligations *erga omnes partes*, and to bring that failure to an end".

47 *Ibidem*. The Court needs to underline the *erga omnes partes* character of the obligation to prevent genocide, so to declare its jurisdiction under art. IX. In fact, if rooted just in customary law, the same *erga omnes* nature of the obligation would not have been *per se* sufficient as a ground to establish the jurisdiction of the ICJ.

had invoked the responsibility of the State sponsoring negationism, presenting its conduct as a violation of the pertinent Convention – according to a given interpretation – and asking for immediate cessation of the alleged wrongful act. After the very likely possible dismissal of the request, a dispute between the parties would be established, probably opening the way for submitting the interpretation issue to the ICJ.[48] Some obstacles might actually arise from reservations since several States, including some that could be particularly concerned by negationism, did not accept those articles, often to both of them.[49] These States, then, cannot be brought before the ICJ without their specific consent.[50] Nevertheless, it would still be possible for good-willing States to promote the request for an advisory opinion by the UNGA, as done in the case of the wall in Palestine.[51]

6 Conclusions

International law is often described as an anarchic system, in which the rule of law plays little role.[52] However, some mechanisms or procedures are available that could enhance respect for the rule of law, but they are not properly taken into account by States. Much more attention is paid to other means of reaction, not consisting in judicial (or quasi-judicial) remedies. In particular, the debate on the the responsibility to protect focuses on the issue of the possibility of States taking action when massive violation of fundamental human

48 "A dispute between States exists where they hold clearly opposite views concerning the question of the performance or non-performance of certain international obligations": see *The Gambia v. Myanmar* case cit., para 20 ff.

49 Including, probably for opposite reasons, Israel (that could react to negationist policies of other States, but is also accused of genocide and war crimes against the Palestinians) and Turkey (that some consider responsible for violation of the Genocide Convention in Northern Cyprus or against the Kurds populations (more in William A. Schabas, *Genocide in Interantional Law* cit., p. 433 ff.)). Probably, the issue of the Armenian genocide would be in any case excluded, because of the non retroactive character of the Genocide Convention: see Simona Pinton, *The Armenian massacres in International Law*, in M. L. Picchio Forlati (ed.), *Rassicurazione e memoria. Per dare un futuro alla pace*, Padova, 2012, p. 45 ff.

50 See Robert Kolb, Sandra Kräehenmann, *The Scope Ratione Personae of the Compulsory Jurisdiction of the ICJ*, in *The UN Genocide Convention* cit., p. 425 ff.

51 Infra., note 58.

52 For long, International law has been pictured as not being actually "law": see Sir Hersch Lauterpacht, *The Function of Law in the International Community*, Oxford, 2011, p. 407 ff.; R. Jennings, A. Watts, *Oppenheim's International Law*, I, 9th ed., Longman, 1992, p. 8 and the critical remarks of Jan Brownlie, *Principles of International Law*, 7th ed., 2008, p. 640.

rights are perpetrated, to the point that – according to many scholars[53] – even armed humanitarian intervention would be admissible, in cases in which the UNSC were prevented from acting.[54] By contrast, it strikes how poor attention is paid to the option of enacting the existing peaceful legal means, aimed at provoking an assessment by competent treaty bodies, a decision or an advisory opinion by the ICJ.[55]

In all respects, it is evident how States are reluctant to trigger inter-state procedures where they can avoid it. …[56] When violations of *erga omnes* obligations are at stake, any reluctance is inappropriate, at the very least, considering that the right of any State to invoke the responsibility of the wrongdoing State at the international level is clearly granted by the general rules on State responsibility.[57] Then, to activate possible judicial means for addressing the situation should be not an option, but rather a duty: according to the ICJ, every State – while respecting the United Nations Charter and international law – should act to seek that violations of *erga omnes* obligations are "brought to an end".[58] The ICJ does not specify what kind of action may be expected, but it is clear that States, although non directly affected, should not remain passive.[59]

For the reasons seen above, this applies to cases of State-negationism. Negationism might trigger an extremely dangerous situation, that might collapse

53 Literature on the matter is huge: suffice it here to mention, even for further references, C. Focarelli, *Responsibility to Protect and Humanitarian Intervention: Too Many Ambiguities for a Working Doctrine*, in 13 *Journal of Conflict & Security Law*, 2008, p. 191 ff.

54 "The Security Council should take into account in all its deliberations that, if it fails to discharge its responsibility to protect in conscience-shocking situations crying out for action, concerned states may not rule out other means to meet the gravity and urgency of that situation – and that the stature and credibility of the United Nations may suffer thereby": see *The Responsibility to Protect. Report of the International Commission on State Sovereignty and Humanitarian Intervention*, p. 29, available at http://responsibilitytoprotect.org/ICISS%20Report.pdf.

55 Or other international courts chosen by the parties, as both art. IX and 22 admit.

56 The same happens not only before the UN treaty bodies or the ICJ – as seen above – but also before the ECtHR, to whom inter-state applications, from 1956 to present, were about 30: data available at https://www.echr.coe.int/Pages/home.aspx?p=caselaw&c=#n14600328386149446327969_pointer.

57 As for the meaning of the expression "invoking the responsibility" and the steps that may be taken to the purpose, see J. Crawford, *State responsibility* cit., p. 68.

58 ICJ, *Legal Consequences of the Construction of a Wall in the Occupied Palestinian Territory*, Advisory Opinion of 9 July 2004, in *ICJ Reports* 2004, p. 136 ff., para. 159.

59 In this perspective, violation of *erga omnes* norms triggers a positive obligation for States, in addition to the negative ones usually associated with the situation (such as the duty not to recognize the illegal situation and not to give aid or assistance in the maintaining of it).

giving way to genocide or other massive violation of human rights. Needless to say, the danger is magnified if negationism is supported by a Government. Therefore – following a (sort of) precautionary principle – other States should act to prevent the worst evolution and, when possible, resort to the ICJ (or to the competent treaty-bodies) should be considered and sought for. As seen above, coming to the Genocide Convention some delicate interpretation issues might arise, but art. IX expressly provides for the jurisdiction of the ICJ, even on disputes concerning interpretation. The good willing States could provoke the Court's assessment even before the situation evolves into dramatic breach of *erga omnes* obligations. The Court's intervention would be in any case a powerful reminder to any State that, even at the international level … *there is a judge*.

Nevertheless, considering Holocaust denial, most interpretation problems would probably be confronted with a major issue: that is, the very meaning of anti-Semitism, as expression of a racist thinking. According to the definition adopted in 2016 by the International Holocaust Remembrance Alliance (IHRA), anti-Semitism "is a certain perceptive on Jews, which may be expressed as hatred toward Jews. Rhetorical and physical manifestations of anti-Semitism are directed toward Jewish or non-Jewish individuals and/or their property, toward Jewish community institutions and religious facilities".[60] In its first part, this definition seems tautological, but further indications are provided, one of them adding that anti-Semitism includes the "denying the Jewish people their right to self-determination, e.g., by claiming that the existence of a State of Israel is a racist endeavour". In other words, the definition does include anti-Zionism into the same notion of anti-Semitism.

According to a different opinion, anti-Semitism – as racism against Jews – is to be considered as different from an anti-Zionistic attitude, the latter opposing not the Jewish people as such, but rather the foundation of the State of Israel, besides its on-going politics, especially in the occupied Territories.[61] In turn, to Israel and like-minded States the assuming of such a distinction is *per se* an admission of anti-Semitism, being perhaps its most insidious form.[62]

---

60 HIRA is an intergovernmental organization to whom 34 States are parties, plus 7 observer Countries: more information at the Organization website: at https://www.holocaustremembrance.com.

61 Even Mr Garaudy argued that his book was aimed at condemning Zionism and Israel as a State but was not against Jews and thus it was neither racist nor anti-Semitic. As seen above (para. 3) his case was just dismissed by the ECTHR following the guillotine approach!.

62 The definition of anti-Semitism by the HIRA includes further examples of how consideration of Israel as a State and of the Jewish people as such are not seen as

The conundrum is clearly mirrored by some reservations to the Genocide Convention and the objection raised to them by Israel: for instance, Bahrain's reservation reads: "the accession by the State of Bahrain to the said Convention shall in no way constitute recognition of Israel or be a cause for the establishment of any relations of any kind therewith". And the objection is: "[i]n the view of the Government of the State of Israel, such declaration (…) is incompatible with the purpose and objectives of this Convention".

The issue involves major problems, the solution of which is far beyond the purposes of the present paper and far beyond the possibilities of its author. However, this same difficulty is just a further element to advocate for greater attention by every State in evaluating the opportunity to resort to means at its disposal to get a judicial assessment by an international court.

---

separate issues: for a critical analysis see P. Beinart, *Debulking the Myth that Anti-Zionism is Antisemitic*, in *The Guardian*, 7 March 2019, available at https://www.theguardian.com/news/2019/mar/07/debunking-myth-that-anti-zionism-is-antisemitsm; but see also L. Harcov, *French parliament decides anti-Zionism is antisemitism*, in *The Gerusalem Post*, 4 December 2019, available at https://www.jpost.com/Diaspora/Antisemitism/French-parliament-decides-anti-Zionism-is-antisemitism-609764.

CHAPTER 16

Hospitality and Integration of Migrants and Refugees

Christian Walter

I Introduction

The treatment of refugees and migrants is one of the most obvious current topics which need to be discussed in the historical perspective of the overall subject of this book, which follows a conference on "International Lawyers and Human Dignity". For that purpose, I would like, in a first step, to briefly recall the different functions which human dignity assumes at the international level (II). From there I will draw certain consequences regarding the treatment of migrants and refugees in their countries of arrival (III). In doing so, I replace the term "asylum seekers", which was originally used as a title for my contribution to the conference, by the terminology currently used in the UN, i.e. "migrants and refugees". The broadening of the scope, which goes along with this change in terminology, is a consequence of the human dignity perspective which is assumed in this chapter. In a third step, I want to broaden the subject and look at the current debate on the "Global Compact for Safe, Orderly and Regular Migration"[1] from the perspective of human dignity (IV). The paper concludes by highlighting the role of human dignity as a regulatory idea shared by the international community (V).

II The development of Human Dignity in International Law and Its Functions as a Legal Concept

While human dignity has a long-standing tradition in moral philosophy, its tradition as a legal norm of constitutional law and international law is rather short. The concept of human dignity only entered the legal sphere after the end of the Second World War. In fact, before 1945 only five national constitutions

1 The text is available at: https://refugeesmigrants.un.org/sites/default/files/180713_agreed_outcome_global_compact_for_migration.pdf.

 DOI:10.1163/9789004435650_017

contained provisions explicitly referring to human dignity. After the end of World War II, the number increased exponentially, Germany, Italy and Japan being among the first countries to introduce such a provision.[2] In the international context, a similar development took place. Human dignity is mentioned in the Preamble of the UN Charter and the preamble provisions of a number of Human Rights instruments (e.g. the 1966 Human Rights Covenants, the 1966 Convention against Racial Discrimination, the 1979 Convention against all Forms of Discrimination of Women). However, the most prominent expression of human dignity is still found in Art. 1 of the Universal Declaration of Human Rights of 10 December 1948, which reads: "All human beings are born free and equal in dignity and rights."

By contrast, there is no explicit mentioning of human dignity in either the 1951 Geneva Convention on the Status of Refugees or its 1967 Protocol, even though there can be little doubt that human dignity also constitutes at least one underlying rationale of these instruments.[3] A similar argument may also be made regarding the European Convention on Human Rights of 1950 which does not contain an explicit reference to human dignity, but where Art. 3 with its prohibition of inhuman or degrading treatment or punishment undoubtedly protects important elements of human dignity. In fact, after having mentioned human dignity for the first time in the Tyrer-case,[4] the European Court of Human Rights repeatedly confirmed the human dignity aspect of Art.3 ECHR regarding detention and punishment,[5] but more recently also in the context of refugee protection.[6]

What then, is the normative value of human dignity? While most instruments do not spell out human dignity as a separate human right, nevertheless

2 Doron Shulztiner, Guy E. Carmi, 'Human Dignity in National Constitutions: Functions, Promises and Dangers' (2014) 62 *AJCL* 461, 465.

3 As to the tension between the humanitarian purpose of refugee protection on the one side and the preservation of a state's sovereignty concerning entry into its territory, see Christian Walter, 'Zwischen individuellem Menschenrechtsschutz und legitimer Migrationssteuerung: Der völkerrechtliche Rahmen der Flüchtlingspolitik', in Christian Walter, Martin Burgi (eds.), *Die Flüchtlingspolitik, der Staat und das Recht* (Mohr 2017), 7, 8 et seq.

4 *Tyrer v. UK* App no 5856/72 (ECtHR, 15 March 1978), para. 33; see Jochen A. Frowein, 'Human Dignity in International law', in David Kretzmer, Eckart Klein (eds.), *The Concept of Human Dignity in Human Rights Discourse* (Kluwer 2002), 121, 124.

5 See the comprehensive analysis of the existing case-law in Lennart von Schwichow, *Die Menschenwürde in der EMRK* (Mohr 2016), 42 et seq. (punishment) and 54 et seq. (detention).

6 See prominently *Khlaifia v. Italy* App no 16483/12 (ECtHR GC, 15 December 2016), para. 158: "The Court would reiterate at the outset that the prohibition of inhuman or degrading treatment is a fundamental value in democratic societies [...] closely bound up with respect for human dignity, part of the very essence of the Convention [...]."

three normative functions may be derived which are fulfilled by human dignity: Human dignity serves a foundational function with regard to other human rights (1), it is of great importance as a normative guidance when interpreting other human rights (2), and, finally, it serves the purpose of defining a community value which is shared by all members of the international community (3). These three functions do not operate in an independent manner, but are mutually interdependent and reinforce each other (4).

1 *Foundational Function*

Human dignity serves a foundational function. This has been pointed out in manifold ways regarding the basis of all human rights in considerations of human dignity. As *Aharon Barak*, former President of the Supreme Court of Israel, put it, human dignity is a "mother-right" from which a number of daughter-rights can be derived by way of interpretation.[7] This mother-daughter relationship is especially important for a legal order, which, like the Israeli constitution, does not spell out a detailed catalogue of human rights. Under such conditions, courts will tend to derive concrete legal positions from the mother right.[8] Human dignity also serves a foundational function within instruments with a detailed list of human rights, like the European Convention of Human Rights or the International Covenant on Civil and Political Rights or national constitutions. In fact, many classical rights and freedoms, like freedom of religion, freedom of expression or the right to private life are built around a human dignity core. It is precisely because of this relationship that courts make reference to human dignity when interpreting these rights.[9]

Beyond that, the foundational function of human dignity is of an even more fundamental nature and touches upon the very idea of human rights. "Human dignity is the central argument for the existence of human rights. It is the rationale for them all."[10] This fundamental form of the founding function of human dignity for the idea of human rights as such is clearly expressed in the first paragraph of the Preamble of the Universal Declaration of Human Rights:

---

7 Aharon Barak, *Human Dignity – The Constitutional Value and the Constitutional Right* (CUP 2015), 156 et seq.

8 See, regarding Israel, the impressive list of „daughter-rights" mentioned in Barak (n 7), 288 et seq.

9 See II.2.

10 Barak (n 7), 104 quotation without footnotes; *Juan José López v. Argentina*, Report no. 73/11 (Inter-American Court of Human Rights 20 July 2011), para. 34; *Jehovah's Witnesses of Moscow and others v. Russia* App No 3012/02 (ECtHR, 10 June 2010), para. 135.

> Whereas recognition of *the inherent dignity and of the equal and inalienable rights of all members of the human family is the foundation of freedom, justice and peace in the world,*

It has been convincingly argued that the foundational function in this elementary sense serves the purpose of legitimizing human rights in general.[11] It may be said that, given the extremely diverging positions on possible contents of human dignity, it was precisely its vagueness and openness which allowed the international community of the time to reunite behind that norm:

> Based upon political experience, [the Universal Declaration of Human Rights] spells out a political program to establish conditions under which human beings can equally enact their responsibilities as citizens of the world. It thus gives place to the experience that behind cultural and religious pluralism and behind conflict of interests, an ethical unity of mankind exists.[12]

In sum, the foundational function of human dignity is twofold: in its first dimension, it describes core elements of classical rights and freedoms. And in a second, more fundamental dimension, it serves as a catalyst for an ethical minimum that is shared by the entire community standing behind a given instrument.

2 *Interpretive Guidance*

A second important function, which is of utmost practical importance and closely linked to the foundational function just described, is the function of human dignity as instrument of interpretative guidance. Notably the jurisprudence of the European Court of Human Rights helps in setting out in more detail what is meant by interpretive guidance. In the absence of a concrete provision on human dignity in the Convention, the Court could have easily operated without mentioning human dignity at all. One might even have presumed that it was not necessary to take recourse to the concept, given that there is no express mentioning of human dignity in the text of the Convention. And yet, notably in important cases (the Tyrer-case concerning corporal

---

11 Klaus Dicke, 'The Founding Function of Human Dignity in the Universal Declaration of Human Rights', in Kretzmer, Klein (n 4), 111 et seq.; see also Haim H. Cohn, 'On the Meaning of Human Dignity', (1983) 13 *Israel Yearbook on Human Rights* 227, 232: "It is that human dignity provides the causa, as well as the ratio, for all human rights legislation."

12 Dicke (n 11), 120.

punishment being the first one, has already been mentioned above), the Court took great care in setting out why its decision was also a consequence of considerations of human dignity.[13] A closer look at the relevant cases reveals that the Court makes reference to human dignity either where this appears helpful in justifying its decision against possible criticism or where it is necessary in order to underline the gravity of the violation.[14] It is also used as instrument of justification when new, fundamental questions need answers.[15] This function of human dignity as an interpretative guidance can also be observed at the international level of human rights jurisprudence where the concept of dignity is invoked in relation to conditions in detention[16] and the right to a dignified life.[17]

When used as a means of interpretive guidance, human dignity is not applied directly and as a human right of its own, but rather as a regulatory idea, which must be kept in mind when interpreting and applying the law in general and human rights more specifically. In that sense, human dignity fulfils an inventive function in that the different cases specify and actualize different features of human dignity which, in turn, when viewed together give a more complete and coherent view of the normative substance of human rights in general.[18]

3 *Human Dignity as a Value Shared by the International Community as a Whole*

A third aspect, which is again closely related to the two functions just described, is the role played by human dignity as a common value shared by the

13 Rather scarcely in *Tyrer* (n 4), paras. 33 and 35; more elaborate for example in *Khlaifia* (n 6), para 158, 160, 169, 175, 184 (regarding Art. 3 in situations of detention); *Pretty v. UK* App No 2346/02 (ECtHR, 29 April 2002), paras. 65 ff. (regarding the relevance of Art. 8 in situations of end of life).

14 See particularly *M.S.S. v. Belgium and Greece* App no 30696/09 (ECtHR GC, 21 January 2011), paras. 221, 233, 253, 263 concerning both, detention and living conditions; and *Cyprus v. Turkey* App no 25781/94 (ECtHR GC 10 May 2001), para. 304, 306, 309 concerning living conditions and discrimination based on race.

15 *Pretty* (note 13).

16 *Prashanta Kumar Pandey v. Nepal*, communication no. 2413/2014 (Human Rights Committee, 30 October 2018), para. 8.7; *Mr. X v. Argentina* communication no. 8/2012 (Committee on the Rights of Persons with Disabilities, 11 April 2014), para. 8.4.

17 *Ioane Teitiota v. New Zealand* communication no. 2728/2016 (Human Rights Committee, 15 September 2015), paras. 9.4, 9.11.

18 Jürgen Habermas, 'The concept of human dignity and the realistic utopia of human rights', in Amos Nascimento, Matthias Lutz-Bachmann (eds.), *Human Dignity – Perspectives from a Critical Theory of Human Rights* (Routledge 2018) 52, 55.

international community as a whole. There can be little doubt that the express or indirect reference to human dignity in the human rights documents of the immediate post-World War II period served the purpose of underlining a common value as a reaction to the atrocities of World War II and the holocaust. At the same time, the open and neutral formulation of Art. 1 UDHR ("All human beings are born free and equal in dignity and rights.") avoids allusion to any specific philosophical or religious tradition. In this regard, a closer look at the travaux préparatoires is telling. The original proposal would have read: "all human beings are by nature free and equal". This was rejected by China as being too closely related to a single philosophical tradition (French enlightenment and natural law).[19] Furthermore, any reference to religion as a source of defining human dignity was avoided.

The result is a broad consensus regarding the concept of human dignity as such, which may thus be labelled a community value of the international community as a whole. However, and this limitation is of utmost importance, there is no consensus regarding any concrete content of that value. The sole concrete element is the requirement of equal respect for each human being, which is expressed in the terms "equal in dignity". It is tempting to conclude that a "value" without content is of little practical relevance. However, such a conclusion would be premature. As the multiple references to the concept show, for instance in the jurisprudence of the European Court of Human Rights mentioned above, a jurisprudential invention[20] is going on in which the concept is clarified and developed. Sometimes decisions will be challenged and different contents of dignity will be proposed, or there will be disagreement on whether certain aspects (like the notion of "living conditions") are to be covered by human dignity.[21] However, in serving as a kind of vanishing point for the debate, human dignity channels arguments and, over time, the notion itself is clarified and receives additional substance.

4 *Mutual Interdependence of the Functions*

It is obvious that these functions of human dignity are intertwined and mutually reinforcing. The character as a fundamental value is due to the foundational

19 Dicke (n 11), 117; and in more detail Klaus Dicke, 'Die der Person innewohnende Würde und die Frage der Universalität der Menschenrechte', in Heiner Bielefeldt, Winfried Brugger, Klaus Dicke (eds.), *Würde und Recht des Menschen, Festschrift für Johannes Schwartländer* (Königshausen & Neumann 1992) 161. 170.

20 In the sense of the term "inventive function" used by Habermas (n 16).

21 See, for example, the criticism voiced by Judge Sajó in his dissenting opinion in *M.S.S. v. Belgium and Greece* (n 14).

nature of human dignity, its guiding force in interpreting other norms has its roots both in its foundational character and its function as a fundamental value of the community. And, finally, the character as a fundamental value of the international community largely rests on the foundational function of human dignity and on its role in guiding interpretation of existing norms when new and fundamental questions arise. In their interaction, the three functions and characteristics may be summarized as characterizing human dignity as a regulatory idea which is both at the same time: an aim to be achieved and a foundation on which the interpretation and application of existing human rights rests.

III Consequences for the Treatment of Migrants and Refugees

What are, then, possible consequences of the overall analysis of the role and function of human dignity in general when it comes to the specific situation of migrants and refugees in their host country? At least three points deserve further comment: First of all, it is a necessary consequence of the equality element inherent in human dignity that there is no specific human dignity which applies for migrants and refugees (1). However, as migrants and refugees are a specifically vulnerable group, both when in transit and when arriving in a new host state, certain fundamental guarantees based on human dignity can be spelled out in more detail. These guarantees relate to what has been called "deterrence policies" (2) and to the notion of integration which becomes important when it comes to a long-term perspective in the host state (3).

1 *No Specific Human Dignity of Migrants and Refugees, but Situations of Specific Vulnerability*

The very idea of human dignity is based on the idea of the equal dignity of all human beings, which is why the UDHR stresses that all human beings are born "equal in dignity" and the preamble of both UN covenants emphasizes the inherent dignity of all members of the human family. This perception of human dignity necessarily means that there is no specific human dignity of migrants and refugees. They are "equal in dignity" when compared with the resident population. Thus, there is no difference in the applicable law when it comes to human dignity. However, there is a difference in the factual situation. Migrants and refugees are a specifically vulnerable group, notably when in transit and after arrival in their new host country. In this situation, they are particularly vulnerable and dependent and therefore the risk of their human rights being violated is imminent, which means that their human dignity is at stake.[22] Any particular reference to human dignity of "vulnerable groups" in the human rights jurisprudence does therefore not aim to ascertain a specific dignity of persons belonging to these groups, but rather to address the unequal factual situations and the resulting increased dangers of violations of human dignity.[23] This vulnerable situation of migrants and refugees is the reason why human dignity deserves special attention when it comes to hospitality and integration.

2 *Human Dignity Stands against Deterrence Policies*

In recent years, a number of possible host countries have adopted what has been called in the refugee law literature "deterrence policies".[24] While these policies initially specifically aimed at preventing refugees from entering the country, they increasingly also affect the situation of refugees (and migrants) once they have arrived in their country of destiny. Examples are new and enhanced restrictions on freedom of movement,[25] reduction of social welfare subsidies[26] or the change from financial support to noncash subsidies.[27] Restrictions on freedom of movement can, especially if increased to the level of systematic detention, place the persons concerned in a state of particular vulnerability and open the way to inhuman and degrading treatment.[28] The

22 This is stressed by the ECJ: "(…) such a 'national treatment' may be insufficient to respect the dignity of persons who have been granted international protection, given that they are typically vulnerable and uprooted (…)" (ECJ, Abubacarr Jawo v. Federal Republic of Germany, C-163/17, para. 46).

23 See also Lourdes Peroni, Alexandra Timmer, 'Vulnerable groups: The promise of an emerging concept in European Human Rights Convention Law' (2013) 11 *International Journal of Constitutional Law* 1056, 1074.

24 See e.g. Thomas Gammeltoft-Hansen, 'International Refugee Law and Refugee Policy: The Case of Deterrence Policies' (2014) 27 *Journal of Refugee Studies* 574 et seq.

25 For the use of detention in response to global migration in e.g. Greece, Bulgaria, Italy and Hungary see "The Detention of Asylum Seekers in the Mediterranean Region" by the Global Detention Project (available at https://www.refworld.org/pdfid/556736e24.pdf, last accessed 17 April 2020, 3 pm). The grounds on which asylum-seekers can be detained have also been increased in Denmark (Amendment to the Danish Aliens Act, Law No. 1273, 20 November 2015).

26 E.g. in Denmark the social benefits for refugees have been cut by 50% (Amendment to the Danish Aliens Act, Law No. 1000, 30 August 2015). For the deterrence policy in Denmark in general see also Gammeltoft-Hansen, Danish Foreign Policy Yearbook 2017, 99.

27 See for example the 2015 revised §1a of the Asylbewerberleistungsgesetz (AsylbLG, "Asylum Seekers Benefits Act") under which benefits are now to be provided primarily in noncash subsidies. § 1a AsylbLG was amended "to eliminate possible disincentives that may lead to unjustified asylum applications" (BT-Drs. 18/2592).

28 As seen in *M.S.S v. Belgium and Greece* App No 30696/09 (ECtHR, 21 January 2011).

reduction of social welfare subsidies endangers dignity in respect to the subsistence level required in order to lead a dignified life.[29] Granting vouchers or allowances in kind instead of cash benefits limits refugees and migrants in their right to self-determination, which is closely linked to human dignity.[30] The effect is enhanced when the voucher solution is limited to migrants and refugees only, while nationals remain entitled to direct financial support.

Obviously, it is not always easy to distinguish a clear motive of deterrence when such policies are adopted. They are often based on a bundle of reasons, some of which are perfectly legitimate. To take just one example: When migrants, and especially refugees, arrive in a country of destiny, questions of legal status have to be clarified, a place to stay has to be found, etc. In order to settle these issues, restrictions of movement are sometimes inevitable. However, these aims only justify restrictions for a limited period of time and the conditions under which refugees and migrants are placed must respect the limits established by the prohibition of inhuman or degrading treatment, as set out for example for European States in Art. 3 ECHR.

Conversely, when there are no legitimate aims justifying restrictive measures, or if a state adopts measures which are more intrusive or more restrictive than what can be justified under the criteria of proportionality solely for the purpose of deterring further migrants or refugees, such a policy would violate the idea of "equal dignity" since it uses ill-treatment as a political instrument. The persons concerned are thus objectified and treated less favorably than other residents for the purpose of deterring other refugees.

3 *The Right to Private Life as a Nucleus for a Right to Integration*

With regard to integration (which comes into play only at a later point in time, when it has been established that a person has a right to remain in the country of refuge) another aspect of the jurisprudence of the European Court of Human Rights may be taken into consideration. In the context of expulsion, the European Court of Human Rights established an important jurisprudence on

29 In this respect, § 1a AsylbLG, which regulates limits to benefit claims, is continuously being criticized for being unconstitutional, as reductions of the financial support resulting in benefits below the subsistence level are considered a violation of the human dignity guaranteed in Art. 1 of the German Constitution. (see e.g. Ibrahim Kanalen, Neue Zeitschrift für Sozialrecht 2018, 641). The Federal Social Court, however, deemed the provision to be lawful (BSG, Judgement of 12 May 2017, B 7 AY 1/16 R).

30 *Jehovah's Witnesses of Moscow and others v. Russia* App No 3012/02 (ECtHR, 10 June 2010), para. 135.

the right to private life, guaranteed under Art. 8 ECHR. The most important passage of the judgement in that regard reads as follows:

> The Court also recalls that, as Article 8 also protects the right to establish and develop relationships with other human beings and the outside world and can sometimes embrace aspects of an individual's social identity, it must be accepted that the totality of social ties between settled migrants such as the applicants and the community in which they are living constitutes part of the concept of "private life" within the meaning of Article 8.[31]

It is highly plausible to argue that the notion of "an individual's social identity" has its foundation in the concept of human dignity. In another judgement, the Court speaks of "the network of personal, social and economic relations that make up the private life of every human being."[32] Again, I would suggest that – without that having been expressly said so by the Court – the foundation of that jurisprudence in the notion of human dignity suggests itself when the Court speaks of "every human being". These judgments stem from cases in which the negative dimension of Art. 8 ECHR came into play. The defendant states (the UK and Latvia) had attempted to remove long-term foreign residents from their territory. However, it is also clearly established that Art. 8 ECHR is not limited to that negative dimension but entails positive obligations on the part of the member states.[33] It may thus be argued that the jurisprudence of the European Court of Human Rights just cited contains a nucleus of a right to integration into the society of the receiving state.

In order to avoid misunderstandings, one clarification is necessary. The idea just sketched does not imply a right to immigration derived directly from human dignity. Nor does it exclude limitations based on legitimate grounds of immigration policies and restrictions. There will always be a necessity to balance the individual interests of immigrants and refugees with public interests of the receiving states. Also, the notion of margin of appreciation will certainly play an important role in such cases. However, what can be claimed is that the notion of "private life" in Art. 8, founded on the concept of human dignity and interpreted in the light of the regulatory idea established by

31 *A.H. Khan v. UK* App No 6222/10 (ECtHR, 20 December 2011), para. 32.

32 *Slivenko v. Latvia* App no 48321/99 (ECtHR GC, 9 October 2003), para. 96.

33 Karin de Vries, 'Respect to Private and Family Life', in Pieter van Dijk, Fried van Hoof, Arjen van Rijn, Leo Zwaak (eds.), *Theory and Practice of the European Convention on Human Rights* (5th ed. Intersentia 2018) 667, 669.

human dignity, serves as a legal tool paving the way towards social integration of migrants.[34]

IV The "Global Compact for Safe, Orderly and Regular Migration" from the Perspective of Human Dignity

The current debate on the "Global Compact for Safe, Orderly and Regular Migration"[35] raises many, mainly political, issues, most of which are not related to the subject of hospitality and integration of migrants and refugees. It also raises serious question on the role of soft law in regulating highly politicized issues such as the treatment of refugees.[36] These issues, interesting and important as they may be, are not of relevance here. Given the focus of this chapter, I will concentrate on the role which the Global Compact assigns to human dignity when it comes to the treatment of migrants and refugees. From that perspective, it is noteworthy that the Compact mentions human dignity expressly only with regard to the situation in the home countries (1). However, human dignity is not mentioned expressly at all when it comes to the treatment of migrants and refugees in countries of destination (2).

1 *Human Dignity and the Situation in Countries of Origin or Transit*

Interestingly, human dignity is only expressly referred to in a very limited way in the text of the Global Compact. The areas addressed are telling in their own way. The first mentioning of human dignity concerns the situation in the home countries and occurs in the context of a general policy aiming at conditions which allow people to live in their countries of origin in human

34 See with regard to long-term foreign residents, Daniel Thym, 'Residence as De Facto Citizenship? Protection of Long-Term Residence under Article 8 ECHR', in: Ruth Rubio-Marin (ed.), *Human Rights and Immigration* (OUP 2014), 130 and 144.

35 The text is available at https://www.un.org/pga/72/wp-content/uploads/sites/51/2018/07/migration.pdf.

36 See generally Thomas Gammeltoft Hansen et al., *What is a Compact? Migrants' Rights and State Responsibilities Regarding the Design of the UN Global Compact for Safe, Orderly and Regular Migration*, available at https://rwi.lu.se/app/uploads/2017/10/RWI_What-is-a-compact-test_101017.pdf; from the perspective of German constitutional law, Frank Schorkopf, ‚Der Deutsche Bundestag und der Migrationspakt – Anlass zur Stärkung parlamentarischer Beteiligung an völkerrechtlichen Soft Law-Prozessen?' (2019) *Zeitschrift für Ausländerrecht* 90 et seq.; Daniel Thym, 'Viel Lärm um Nichts? – Das Potential des UN-Migrationsrechts zur dynamischen Fortentwicklung der Menschenrechte' (2019) *Zeitschrift für Ausländerrecht* 131 et seq.

dignity.[37] The other two passages referring to human dignity concern conditions of return.[38]

2 *Human Dignity and the Situation in Countries of Destination*

While there is no express mentioning of human dignity concerning countries of destination, a number of situations are addressed where human dignity might play a role in the background (e.g. workplace-related vulnerabilities). In any case, in the overall perspective of human dignity, the details of the various goals set out and commitments entered into do not seem to be of decisive importance. These details are either already covered by specific treaty provisions, notably those contained in international human rights instruments, or the commitments are spelled out in vague and broad terms which leave possibilities for various solutions.

What really seems important from the perspective of human dignity is the holistic perspective with which the compact deals with migration. It covers all forms of migration (including but not limited to migration triggered by persecution as defined in the 1951 Geneva Convention on Refugees); it includes a variety of situations ranging from the countries of origin over countries of transit to countries of arrival; it highlights that a number of specific vulnerabilities need to be addressed and taken care of irrespective of the legal status of a person or the geographical area where he or she finds herself, etc. In doing so, the Compact does not blur, let alone destroy, existing legal distinctions. To the contrary, these distinctions are consistently and expressly referred to. However, in offering that holistic and comprehensive perspective on migration as such, the Global Compact looks at migration from the perspective of the individuals concerned rather than from that of the states involved. Refugees and migrants are presented and treated as actors or agents and not as pure objects of regulation.[39] It is this human-centered perspective of the Global Compact, which deserves to be praised. In taking this perspective, the Global Compact, without explicitly saying so, renews the basic promise of human dignity contained in Art. 1 UDHR for the specific context of migration.

37 "We must work together to create conditions that allow communities and individuals to live in safety and dignity in their own countries". Global Compact (note 25), para. 13.

38 Global Compact (note 25), paras. 37 e) and 37 f).

39 Benedikt Behlert, 'The Global Compact for Safe, Orderly and Regular Migration – Hope for our Constitutive Commitments?' *VerfBlog* 2018/11/30, https://verfassungsblog.de/the-global-compact-for-safe-orderly-and-regular-migration-hope-for-our-constitutive-commitments/.

V Conclusion: Human Dignity as a Regulatory Idea of the Law on Migration and Refugees

The brief analysis of the Global Compact confirms the overall concept of human dignity as a regulatory idea. Here, as in many other areas where human rights become particularly relevant, the importance of the concept of human dignity must be seen less in concrete legal positions that could be directly derived from its codification in a norm like Art. 1 UDHR. Also, with regard to the protection of migrants and refugees, human dignity draws its attraction from its foundational function and its role as interpretive guidance with regard to other human rights. In setting an ambitious aim for the integration of migrants and refugees and by providing for a normative background also in the area of migration, human dignity once again proves to be a regulatory idea which is fundamental to the international community.

CHAPTER 17

Adjudicating Human Dignity of Irregular Migrants

Francesca Ippolito

1 Introduction: Human Dignity as Context Specific in Irregular Migration and the Proxy Approach with Vulnerability

Human dignity is mentioned in several international instruments ranging from the Preamble of the founding charter of the United Nations[1] and the Universal Declaration of Human Rights (UDHR),[2] to international human rights treaties[3]

1 It affirms that 'the peoples of the United Nations' have 'faith in fundamental human rights' that include, among others, 'the dignity and worth of the human person'.

2 Universal Declaration of Human Rights (adopted 10 December 1948) UNGA Res 217 A(III) (UDHR) preamble; art 9 to 11; art 22 and art 23(3).

3 International Covenant on Civil and Political Rights (adopted 16 December 1966, entered into force 23 March 1976) 999 UNTS 171 (ICCPR) preamble and art 10(1); International Covenant on Economic, Social and Cultural Rights (adopted 16 December 1966, entered into force 3 January 1976) 993 UNTS 3 (ICESCR) art 13; Convention on the Rights of Persons with Disabilities (adopted 13 December 2006, entered into force 3 May 2008) 2515 UNTS 3 preamble at (h); Convention against Torture and Other Cruel, Inhuman or Degrading Treatment or Punishment (adopted 10 December 1984, entered into force 26 June1987) preamble; Convention on the Elimination of all Forms of Racial Discrimination (adopted 7 March 1966, entered into force 4 January 1969) 660 UNTS 195 preamble; Convention on the Rights of the Child (adopted 20 November 1989, entered into force 2 September 1990) 1577 UNTS 3 art 23(1), art 28 par.2, art 37(c), art 39, art 40(1); Rome Statute of the International Criminal Court (adopted 17 July 1998, entered into force 1 July 2002) 2187 UNTS 3 art 8; Geneva Convention Relative to the Treatment of Prisoners of War (adopted 12 August 1949, entered into force 21 October 1950) 75 UNTS 135 art 3; Convention for the Suppression of the Traffic in Persons and of the Exploitation of the Prostitution of Others (adopted 21 March 1950, entered into force 25 July 1951) 96 UNTS 271; Supplementary Convention on the Abolition of Slavery, the Slave Trade, and Institutions and Practices Similar to Slavery (adopted 7 September 1956, entered into force 30 April 1957) 266 UNTS 3; Declaration on the Protection of All Persons from Being Subjected to Torture and Other Cruel, Inhuman or Degrading Treatment or Punishment, UNGA Res 3452 (XXX) (9 Dec 1975) art 2; Council of Europe Convention on Action against Trafficking in Human Beings (adopted 16 May 2005, entered into force 1 February 2008) CETS No.197 preamble and Convention for the protection of Human Rights and Dignity of the Human Being with regard to the Application of Biology and Medicine (Convention on Human Rights and Biomedicine) (adopted 4 April 1997, entered into force 1 December 1999) ETS No.164 preamble; UNESCO, Universal Declaration on the Human Genome and Human Rights (11 November 1997) art 1.

 | DOI:10.1163/9789004435650_018

and regional agreements,[4] exception made for the European Convention on Human Rights (ECHR), which does not actually mention human dignity (contrary to the Revised European Social Charter), though in its interpretation the European Court of Human Rights (ECtHR) and the European Commission of Human Rights have called upon the right to dignity numerous times.[5]

It can be derived from those instruments that human dignity "serves as the single most widely recognized and invoked basis for grounding the idea of human rights generally".[6] As Christopher McCrudden has suggested,[7] human dignity should be seen in terms of a 'context specific notion', varying from

4 American Declaration of the Rights and Duties of Man, O.A.S Res XXX, adopted by the Ninth Int'l Conf. of American States (1948), reprinted in Basic Documents Pertaining to Human Rights in the Inter-American System, OEA/Ser.L.V./II.82 Doc 6 Rev 1 at 17 (1992) preamble. The Inter-American Court of Human Rights has interpreted the right to life as incorporating a right to dignity by noting that the right to life 'includes, not only the right of every human being not to be deprived of his life arbitrarily, but also the right that he will not be prevented from having access to the conditions that guarantee a dignified existence'. Case of the 'Street Children' (Villagrán-Morales et al.) v. Guatemala, Merits, Inter-Am. Ct.H.R.S. C No 63 (19 November 1999) para 144. But also, African Charter on Human and Peoples' Rights (adopted 27 June 1981, entered into force 21 October 1986) 1520 UNTS 217 and the League of Arab States, Arab Charter on Human Rights, (adopted 22 May 2004, entered into force 15 March 2008,) (2005) 12 Int'l Hum.Rts. Rep.893. See also, TEU art 2 and art 21 par. 1 and Charter of Fundamental Rights of the European Union (18 December 2000),in OJ 2000/C serie 364/01,preamble, arts. 1, 25, 31.

5 In *East African Asians v. United Kingdom* (1973) 3 EHRR 76 (Commission Decision), 86; *Moldovan v Romania* (No. 2) (2007) 44 EHRR16 (Commission Decision) the European Commission held that 'publicly to single out a group of persons for differential treatment on the basis of race' would 'constitute a special form of affront to human dignity', and was therefore impermissible under Article 3 of the European Convention, which prohibits degrading treatment. Similarly, the ECtHR – *Tyrer v UK*, (1978) 2 EHRR 1, para 33 – has interpreted Article 3's main purpose as: 'to protect (…) a person's dignity', meaning that it is intended primarily to prevent behavior that is 'seriously humiliating [and] lowering as to human dignity' (See *Pretty v. United Kingdom* (2002) 35 EHRR.1,34). But the ECtHR has gone even further beyond Article 3 ECHR admitting that the notion is not exclusively pertinent to Article 3 but throughout the European Convention underpinning human dignity in the entirety of the document as a general principle of law. See, e.g., *Bock v Germany* (1989) 12 EHRR 247, 263 as to due process right to a fair hearing; *SW v UK* and *CR v UK*, (1995) 21 EHRR.363,374 referring dignity to criminal procedure protection against being charged for something not unlawful; and *Goodwin v UK*, (2002) 35 EHRR 447, 476–477 relatively to the right to privacy; while see *Pretty v UK*, above, 38 noting that according to the ECtHR 'the very essence of the Convention is respect for human dignity and human freedom'.

6 P. G. Carozza, 'Human Rights, Human Dignity and Human Experience', in C. McCrudden (ed.), *Understanding Human Dignity* (The British Academy 2013), 932.

7 C. McCrudden, 'Human Dignity and Judicial Interpretation of Human Rights' (2008) 19(4) European Journal of International Law 655 ff.

jurisdiction to jurisdiction and (often) over time within particular jurisdictions, and even varying in the interpretation of particular substantive areas, resulting in widely divergent opinions.[8]

Using the migratory context as spectrum of analysis of case law of the two main human rights regional systems of jurisdictional protection – the European Court of Human Rights and the Inter-American Court and Commission of Human Rights (hereinafter respectively IACtHR and IAcommHR), this Chapter aims to answer the question of whether (human) dignity adds anything to promoting human rights of irregular migrants, putting special emphasis on what the effects are when irregular migrants are approached as a group and individually, in particular through the interpretative tool of the notion of vulnerability. This tool appears to increasingly be used in a proxy approach within the practice of both IACtHR and ECtHR – although to different extents. Methodologically, the two notions find their place within an hortatory language, thus under an expressive approach, which captures an "added dimension" of the problem being discussed, in terms of human dignity and/or vulnerability that might not exist in other cases and that possibly could be underappreciated should the hortatory language be omitted. In this way, the reference to human dignity and vulnerability helps judges provide context in cases that might present significant interpretative or semantic difficulties.

Another approach is also discernible looking at the two human rights courts considered in this chapter, namely, a method to integrate dignitary rights within a legal framework, because of the link between dignity and another given element or other rights within the context of a specific factual scenario of vulnerability. Such an heuristic-proxy approach has the merit of overcoming the theoretical problematic consequences of reducing human dignity to autonomy according to which, on one hand, "everything it means is already captured more clearly and precisely by the principle of autonomy itself", in a sort of unconvincing reductionism that has brought to consider that there are good reasons why "dignity and autonomy ought to be regarded as separate values".[9]

8 ibid. According to A. Clapham, *Human Rights Obligations of Non-State Actors* (Oxford University Press 2006), 545–546 instead the concern for human dignity appears to have at least 4 core common aspects: '(1) the prohibition of all types of inhuman treatment, humiliation, or degradation by one person over another; (2) the assurance of the possibility for individual choice and the conditions for 'each individual's self-fulfilment', autonomy, or self-realization; (3) the recognition that the protection of group identity and culture may be essential for the protection of personal dignity; and (4) the creation of the necessary conditions for each individual to have their essential needs satisfied'.

9 M. Neal, 'Respect for human dignity as "substantive basic norm"' (2014) 10(1) International Journal of Law in Context 26.

On the other hand, by equating autonomy with dignity, only autonomous individuals could be said to possess dignity; while this conduces to the unacceptable consequence of making it impossible to discuss 'dignity' precisely in the contexts where it is most affected such as in cases regarding very young children, elderly people, people with mental impairments, victims of abuse, or those who lack legal capacity. The fact that human dignity can become most urgent in cases where autonomy is lacking, since it is often when dealing with incapacitated persons that the risk of dignity-violation can become most acute, makes it more rational to see autonomy (often but not always) as a part of dignity,[10] or flowing from it.[11]

Furthermore, according to our understanding, using the combination of the notions of human dignity and vulnerability leads to a 'concretisation'/contextualisation of the vague notion of human dignity, promoting a sense of *mutual responsibility* for each other's welfare, going beyond the negative duties implied by the Kantian version of human dignity – simply requiring that individuals act in a way that does not violate the dignity of others. Instead, it also conduces to the 'relational' quality of dignity,[12] so that the scope of duties is broadened to also firmly engage with positive duties, such as the provision of a minimum standard of living or for the protection of cultural values.[13] As such, human dignity brings rights and duties together and creates a stronger relationship between humans' basic worth and their proper obligations to society.[14]

2 Vulnerability of Irregular Migrants

The vulnerability of irregular migrants has been differently apprehended by the two regional human rights Courts. Since its *Advisory Opinion 18/03*, the IACtHR

---

10 See White's view of autonomy as an 'aspect' of dignity in E.K. White, 'There is no such thing as a right to human dignity: A reply to Conor O'Mahony' (2012) 10(2) International Journal of Constitutional Law 575.

11 As to C. O'Mahony's view of autonomy as a right flowing from dignity, see C. O'Mahony, 'There is no such thing as a right to dignity' (2012) 10(2) International Journal of Constitutional Law 551.

12 E. Foster, *Human Dignity in Bioethics and Law* (OUP 2011) 14. J. Waldron, 'The Dignity of Groups, Acta Juridica' (2008) NYU School of Law, Public Law Research Paper No. 08-53 considers the possibility that dignity might attach to communities or groups. As suggested by Crépeau and Samaddar to maintain one's dignity is to stand up for the rights of others: 'our own dignity is at stake if we do nothing'.

13 C. McCrudden, (n 7).

14 D. Shultziner, 'Human dignity: functions and meanings' (2004) 3(3) Global Jurist Topics, 1–21.

linked undocumented migrant's vulnerability to (i) their individual situation of difference of power with regard to non-migrants (nationals or residents) pertaining to *de jure* (in the laws) and *de facto* (structural) inequalities in the access to basic rights;[15] to (ii) a lack of protection of their human rights with impunity;[16] or to being in a 'legal limbo', separated from their families and at risk of deportation or even stateless;[17] and (iii) to 'prevailing detention, criminalization'.[18]

Conversely, the ECtHR has not recognized irregular migrants as a vulnerable group *per se*, nor as vulnerable individuals. Neither has it employed the universal acceptance of vulnerability as *'a universal, inevitable, enduring aspect of the human condition'.*[19] Rather than considering irregularity as an autonomous element to render an individual or a group vulnerable, when the ECtHR has stressed the vulnerability of irregular migrants it has done so emphasizing that being deprived of a legal status is only one of those relevant factors. Therefore, the undocumented status generally stands out in addition to personal emotional circumstances,[20] abuses and exploitation, particularly in the case of victims of trafficking,

15 *Juridical Condition and Rights of the Undocumented Migrants,* Advisory Opinion OC-18, IACtHR Series A No 17 (17 September 2003), paras 112, 152 [Juridical Condition]. This also applies if those migrants are considered as migrant workers: undocumented workers 'are frequently employed under less favorable conditions of work than other workers and (…) certain employers find this an inducement to seek such labor in order to reap the benefits of unfair competition', para 131.

16 ibid, para. 113. In this respect, vulnerability was also referred to in the UNGA resolution on the 'Protection of migrants' (24 February 2000) UN Doc A/RES/54/166,para. 114. It linked vulnerability to *inter alia,* the absence from the State of origin and to the difficulties they encounter because of differences of language, custom and culture in the host State where they are exposed to racism and violence, which adds to the economic and social difficulties and obstacles for the return to States of origin. See also *Undocumented Workers v United States of America,* IACommHR, Report No. 50/16 Case 12834 (30 November 2016), para 98 <https://www.escr-net.org/caselaw/2017/undocumented-workers-v-united-states-america-iachr-report-no-5016-case-12834-merits> accessed 18 May 2020.

17 *Girls Yean and Bosico v Dominican Republic,* (Preliminary Objections, Merits, Reparations and Costs Judgment), IACtHR Series C No 130 (8 September 2005) para. 3;, *Dilcia Yean and Violeta Bosico v Dominican,* (Admissibility) IAComHR Report No. 28/01, Case 12.819 (22 February 2001).

18 *Juridical Condition and Human Rights of the Child,* Advisory Opinion OC-17/02, IACtHR Series A No 17 (28 August 2002) para. 2.

19 M. Albertson Fineman, 'Equality, Autonomy, and the Vulnerable Subject in Law and Politics', in M. Fineman, A. Grear (eds.), *Vulnerability: Reflections on a New Ethical Foundation for Law and Politics* (Ashgate 2013) relying on 'constructionist' books. See also A Masferrer, E. García-Sánchez, *Human Dignity of the Vulnerable in the Age of Rights. Interdisciplinary Perspectives* (Springer 2016) 2: '[V]ulnerable human beings. That's what we are. Precariousness and frailty are constitutive features of human life'.

20 As to uncertainty and precariousness, see in the context of Article 8 ECHR the analysis by D. Thym, 'Respect for Private and Family Life under Article 8 ECHR in Immigration

including exploitative work,[21] age,[22] health,[23] and a history of prejudice and stigmatization,[24] structural limitation of rights in the national systems; institutional omissions/inactions or an actively discriminatory or criminalising attitude.

When children are involved, associating their vulnerability with human dignity in the context of Article 5 ECHR has led the ECtHR to ascertain that "the extreme vulnerable situation takes precedence over the consideration of [their] status of an illegal immigrant".[25] Moreover, when trafficking victims have been considered under the spectrum of vulnerability, their human dignity has either been considered as evidently threatened in a manner contrasting with a democratic society and with the values expounded in the Convention.[26] Most interestingly, according to the ECtHR case law, within the context of Article 3 ECHR, the ECtHR has opened up to the possibility of recognizing some embryonic forms of social rights for irregular migrants.

3 Vulnerability in a Proxy Approach with Human Dignity

3.1 *The IACtHR Progressive Approach Albeit with Methodological Criticism*

As noted above, the sensitivity of IACtHR to the vulnerability of irregular migrants has been strengthened through an interpretative link of this situational

---

Cases: A Human Right to Regularize Illegal Stay?' (2008) 57(1) International and Comparative Law Quarterly 87.

21 In *Chowdury and others v Greece* App no 21884/15 (ECtHR, 30 March 2017) the ECtHR insisted on the vulnerability 'caused by a precarious administrative situation being emphasized as source of applicants' vulnerability, exacerbated by their lack of financial means and the risk of detention or deportation should they contact the authorities, increasing the risk of labour exploitation' (para 97). In the case of those deprived of any legal status who have been victims of trafficking as stated in *Rantsev v Cyprus and Russia*, App no 25965/04 (ECtHR, 10 October 2010) 'there can be no doubt that trafficking threatens the human dignity and fundamental freedoms of its victims and cannot be considered compatible with a democratic society and the values expounded in the Convention'.

22 *Rahimi v Greece* App no 8687/08 (ECtHR, 5 April 2011), where the ECtHR has referred to the fact that they were 'of very young age, illegal immigrant[s] in a foreign land and unaccompanied by their families'. Also *Khan v France*, App no 12267/16 (ECtHR, 28 February 2019); *Ponomaryovi v Bulgaria* App no 5335/05 (ECtHR, 21 June 2011).

23 *Ahmed v Malta* App no 55352/12 (ECtHR,23 July 2013); *Paposhvili v Belgium* [GC] App no 41738/10 (ECtHR, 13 December 2016).

24 *Uner v Netherlands* App no 46410709 (ECtHR, 18 October 2006). See also *Gaygusuz v Austria*, 39/1995/545/631 (ECtHR, 23 May 1996), para 42.

25 *Rahimi v Greece* (n 22).

26 *Rantsev v Cyprus and Russia*(n 21).

notion with the concept of human dignity since the *Advisory Opinion on the Juridical Status and Rights of Undocumented Migrants*. On that occasion, the Court underlined not only the role of dignity as a limit to and as a shaper of national immigration controls,[27] but also of the right to life, endorsing the entitlement of those migrants to certain economic, social and cultural rights, as well as a due process right.[28] For that purpose, the IACtHR anchored human dignity to the general principle of equality before the law,[29] but not without some pitfalls. A first criticism stems from the fact that non-discrimination has been considered by the IACtHR as entered into the domain of *jus cogens*,[30] resting the whole legal structure of national and international public order on such a fundamental principle.[31] In particular, this consideration of the IACtHR led to consider that States are not being allowed to discriminate, or tolerate discriminatory situations, to the detriment of migrants, and are under the duty to guarantee the due process of law to any person, irrespective of their migratory status. According to Judge Cançado Trindade "the State is bound by the *corpus juris* of the international protection of human rights, which protects every human person *erga omnes*, independently of her statute of citizenship (sic), or of migration, or any other condition or circumstance' being binding to 'the public power and likewise to the private persons or individuals (e.g. employers), in the inter-individual relations".[32]

On the other hand, no less criticism is conferred to the consideration of the general obligation to respect and ensure the exercise of rights (all the rights included in the ACHR and the ICCPR) as having an *erga omnes* character with imposition of horizontal effects.[33] The outputs are the recognition of due process rights, child friendly justice and the obligations upon States of a diversified

27 *Juridical Condition* (n 15), para 119. The IACtHR's emphasis on the rights of undocumented migrants was reiterated in the case of *Velez Loor v Panama* (Preliminary Objections, Merits, Reparations and Costs) IACtHR, Series C No 218 (23 November 2010).

28 This is reiterated in *Rights and Guarantees of Children in the Context of Migration and/or in Need of International Protection,* Advisory Opinion OC-21/14, IACtHR,Series A No 21 (19 August 2014) [*Rights and Guaranteed of Children*].

29 ibid, paras 45, 47.

30 ibid, paras 97–101. Also A. Cançado Trinidade, 'The Case-Law of the Inter-American Court of Human Rights: An Overview' in *Studi di Diritto Internazionale in Onore di Gaetano Arangio-Ruiz*, vol. III (Ed. Scientifica 2004) 1873.

31 *Juridical Condition* (n 16), para 100.

32 ibid [paras. 1–89] (A. Cançado Trinidade) and [paras. 44, 46 and 72] where he underlined that doctrinal evolution points 'to the direction of the crystallization of the obligations *erga omnes* of protection (…). Without the consolidation of such obligations one will advance very little in the struggle against the violations of human rights'.

33 *Juridical Condition* (n 15), para 109.

range of reparations as well as the obligation to put in place measures capable of remedying irregular migrants' situation and of recognising labour human rights. Bianchi in particular has pointed to them, warning of the risks of this "somewhat axiomatic reasoning of the Court, linked with fairly vague notions of natural law (…) unlikely to foster the cause of *jus cogens*, particularly among the sceptics".[34]

Such criticisms positively conditioned the Court's reasoning when considering the Advisory Opinion of the IACtHR in 2014[35] which, more broadly, indicated that States are obliged to provide children with real access to procedures. This should include "not impeding the child's entry into the country", giving individuals access to the entities that can determine their status, priority processing for children, health evaluations, examinations conducted in a manner that does not re-traumatise the child (in order to define the child's age, nationality, whether the child is unaccompanied or separated from its family, the reasons for the child's departure, and if the child needs international protection or special measures for protection), providing accommodation, issuing an identity document to avoid return, and assigning an independent and trained guardian to the case.[36] The motive, cause or reason why the person is in the State's territory has no relevance as regards the State's obligation to respect and to ensure that her or his human rights are respected. In particular, it has no significance whatsoever in this regard whether or not the entry of that person into the State's territory was in keeping with the provisions of its laws. The respective State must, in all circumstances, respect these rights, because they are based precisely on the attributes of the human personality; in other words, regardless of whether the person is a national or resident of its territory or whether the person is there temporarily, in transit, legally, or in an irregular migratory situation.[37]

Here the approach to *jus cogens* has been more cautious, referring to it only when mentioning two central principles for the protection of migrants' rights: the 'peremptory prohibition contained in customary international law of torture and cruel, inhuman or degrading treatment or punishment'[38] and the principle of 'non-return or non-refoulement'.[39]

34 A. Bianchi, 'Human Rights and the Magic of Jus Cogens' (2008) 19(3) European Journal of International Law 491, 506.

35 *Rights and Guarantees of Children* (n 28) para 39.

36 ibid, paras 82–6; 114, 116, 154, 180–82 and 261.

37 ibid, para 62.

38 ibid para 224.

39 ibid para 225.

3.2 *The Use of Dignity and Vulnerability by the ECtHR: the* **extreme case** *Approach*

The ECtHR approach to human dignity of irregular migrants and to their aggravated vulnerability (as conceived in the precedent paragraphs) shows a certain social protection through the lens of the provisions of absolute rights, mainly Article 3 ECHR, given to the obvious *indignity* that is entailed in what we can qualify as 'extreme cases'.

3.2.1 Extreme Poverty

One of those 'extreme cases' relates to States' obligation to take action in cases of 'extreme poverty', so that the indifference of a national legal order as to providing minimum decent social assistance should possibly be seen as punishable and amount to a breach of Article 3 ECHR.[40] *Hunde v. Netherlands* is paradigmatic in this regard. In this case, the ECtHR differentiates the status of a 'failed asylum seeker' under a legal obligation to leave the territory of the host State from that of an asylum seeker whose application is pending (as was the case in *M.S.S*) as to the correlative positive obligations of States under Article 3 to provide emergency social assistance.[41] In particular, according to the Court the differences with the situation of *M.S.S.* stem from the fact that in the latter case, the relevant facts which had culminated in a finding of violation of Article 3 were the long duration in which the applicant had lived in a state of the most extreme poverty (lack of food, hygiene and a place to live), and of fear of being attacked and robbed together with the fact that there had been no prospect of improvement. Additionally, that situation was linked to his status as an asylum-seeker and, consequently, the applicant's suffering could have been alleviated if the Greek authorities had promptly assessed his asylum application. By failing to do so the applicant was left in uncertainty.

On the contrary, the applicant's uncertainty in *Hunde v. Netherlands* was underlined as inherently different from that of M.S.S. in that it was not linked to the national authorities' assessment of his asylum request; nor to their inaction: his asylum statement had already been examined and his asylum application refused, and the applicant had not complained about this decision

40 *Hunde v Netherlands* App no 17931/16 (ECtHR, 5 July 2016).

41 *M.S.S. v Belgium and Greece* App no 30696/09 (ECtHR, 21 January 2011) has been considered an example of the interrelation between human rights and of the protection of social rights through rights that are 'classically' understood as civil and political: B. Ryan, V. Mantouvalou, 'The Labour and Social Rights of Migrants in International Law' in R. Rubio-Marín (ed), *Human Rights and Immigration* (OUP 2014), 205–206.

before the Court. Furthermore, after the applicant's asylum proceedings had come to an end, the applicant was afforded a four-week grace period to organize his voluntary return to his country of origin during which period he retained his entitlement to State-sponsored care and accommodation. Besides, after he had overstayed this grace period, the applicant had the possibility of applying for reception facilities at a center where his liberty would be restricted, subject to the condition that he would cooperate in organizing his departure to his country of origin or prove that it had been impossible to return to his country of origin – either voluntarily or involuntarily – for reasons which cannot be attributed to him; he had the possibility of applying for a residence permit for persons who, through no fault of their own, are unable to leave. But nothing in the case file showed, however, that he had ever applied for such a residence permit, nor that he had ever contended at any stage during the domestic proceedings that he could not leave the host State.[42]

However, even if the ECtHR in the case at hand "reiterates that there is no right to social assistance as such under the Convention",[43] at the same time it underlines that such a right to social assistance is lacking "to the extent that Article 3 requires States to take action in situations of the most extreme poverty – also when it concerns irregular migrants".[44] The Court linked the inadmissibility of the claim to the fact that "it cannot be said that the Netherlands authorities have fallen short of their obligations under Article 3 by having remained inactive or indifferent". Therefore, any indifference of national legal order also as to a minimum decent social assistance should *a contrario* possibly be seen as punishable, amounting to a breach of Article 3 ECHR. In particular, the Court gives some guidance in orientating national practices in this regard when it underlined that "the Netherlands authorities have already addressed this in practical terms", for instance granting applicants who have failed to obtain asylum the possibility of applying for a "no-fault residence permit" and/or to seek admission to a center where their liberty would be restricted; as well as allowing undocumented migrants to seek a deferral of removal for medical reasons and to receive free medical treatment in case of emergency; or setting up a special scheme providing basic needs for undocumented migrants living in their territory in an irregular manner.[45]

42 See for these considerations *Hunde v. Netherlands* (n 40), paras 55–58.
43 ibid, para 59.
44 ibid.
45 ibid.

3.2.2 The "very exceptional circumstances" of the Threshold of Article 3 ECHR in the Health Deportation Context

Though Article 3 ECHR has proven a popular choice for those seeking to resist deportation on health grounds, the ECtHR has affirmed that only in certain circumstances the denial of health care to undocumented migrants may amount to an infringement of the right to be free from degrading and inhuman treatment contained in the conventional provision. Undocumented migrants who are ill may invoke Article 3 of the ECHR to prevent their expulsion to countries of origin or third countries with inadequate health care facilities,[46] but this principle will only apply *exceptionally*.[47] In 1997, the Court introduced in the *N. v. the United Kingdom* case a test of "very exceptional circumstances",[48] which relies on the gravity and stage of illness – physical illness – particularly on physical chronic illnesses such as AIDS/HIV,[49] chronic lymphocytic leukemia and tuberculosis,[50] chronic kidney failure;[51] the availability of medical treatment/care and the availability of social and familial support in the receiving country.[52] States' assumption conceiving basic social rights for migrants as a pull factor and as 'too great a burden' on national resources has been endorsed by the ECtHR since then. Accordingly, finding the respondent state in breach of Article 3 ECHR would amount to requiring states 'to alleviate [unavoidable social and economic disparities between countries] disparities through the provision of free and unlimited health care to all aliens without a right to stay within its jurisdiction'.[53] The rationale is that in contrast with short-term and undocumented migrants, the applicant who was in possession of a lawful residence and work permit 'did not belong to the category of persons who, as a rule, do not contribute to the funding of public services and in

46 *D. v United Kingdom* App no 30240/96 (ECtHR, 2 May 1997).

47 See cases *Karara v Finland* App no. 40900/98 (ECtHR, 29 May 1998); *S.C.C. v Sweden* App no 46553/99 (ECtHR, 15 February 2000); *Bensaid v the United Kingdom* App no 44599/98 (ECtHR, 6 February 2001); *Arcila Henao v the Netherlands* App no 13669/03 (ECtHR, 24 June 2003); *Ndangoya v Sweden* App no 17868/03 (ECtHR, 22 June 2004); *Amegnigan v the Netherlands* App no 25629/04 (ECtHR, 25 November 2004); *N v the UK* App No 26565/05 (ECtHR, 27 May 2008) and *Yoh-Ekale Mwanje v Belgium* App no 10486/1020 (ECtHR, 20 December 2011).

48 *N v the United Kingdom* (n 47) paras 50, 51, 47 and 48.

49 *D. v the United Kingdom* (n 46); *N. v the United Kingdom* (n 48); *Yoh-Ekale Mwanje v Belgium* (n 47) and *S.J. v Belgium* App no 70055/10 (ECtHR, 19 March 2015).

50 *Paposhvili v Belgium* (n 23), paras 124–133.

51 *M.T. v Sweden* App no 1412/13 (ECtHR, 26 February 2015).

52 *Bensaid v the United Kingdom,* (n 47); *Tatar v Switzerland* App no 65692/12 (ECtHR, 14 April 2015), and *Kochieva and Others v Sweden* App no 75203/12 (ECtHR, 30 April 2013).

53 *N v. the United Kingdom* (n 47), para 44.

relation to whom a State may have legitimate reasons for curtailing the use of resource-hungry public services such as social insurance schemes, public benefits and health care'.[54]

However, such an attitude disregards an attentive look at national immigration policies which for instance might be responsible of making regularized migrants fall back into an irregular situation as a result of changes in the law,[55] or of the "gap between [foreign nationals] liable to deportation, "deportable", and 'those actually deported' ".[56] Moreover, it no less disregards previous lines of jurisprudence according to which the scarcity of resources has not so easily deterred the ECtHR from finding a breach of the ECHR, particularly where Article 3 is concerned.[57] It is true that in these cases the social impact is of less significance considering that the cases where the ECtHR was prepared to enforce an Article 3 obligation irrespective of the respondent State's financial position concerned the substandard conditions of Ukrainian prisons.[58] *Poposhvili*[59] partially advanced the Court's position clarifying that where the applicant would face a real risk of ill-treatment (including a decline in their state of health, severe suffering and a decline in life expectancy)[60] due to the lack of appropriate health care, national authorities of the host State should conceive these forms of care as '[un]available in reality, not merely in theory' in the country of origin in order to lead to the exceptional circumstances necessary to attain the threshold of Article 3 of the Convention.[61] Furthermore, the Grand Chamber seems to dismiss the third condition of the very exceptional

54 *Dhahbi v Italy* App. no 17120/09 (ECtHR, 8 April 2014), para 84; *Fawsie v Greece* App no 40080/07 (ECtHR, 16 April 2010).

55 R. Cholewinski, 'Identifying and Clarifying Concepts on "irregular Migration" ' (10th IOM Regional Conference on Migration, Singapore, 2006).

56 E. Paoletti, 'Deportation, non-deportability and ideas of membership' (2010) Refugee Studies Centre Working Papers Series No 65, 14 <https://www.rsc.ox.ac.uk/files/files-1/wp65-deportation-non-deportability-ideas-membership-2010.pdf> accessed 18 May 2020.

57 D. Hand, C. Davis, and R. Healey, 'The Right to Healthcare: A Critical Examination of the Human Right of Irregular Migrants to Access State-Funded HIV/AIDS treatment in the UK' in A. Diver and J. Miller (eds), *Justiciability of Human Rights Law in Domestic Jurisdictions* (Springer, 2016) 64.

58 *Aliev v Ukraine* App no 41220/98, (ECtHR, 29 April 2003) where the Court remarked that a 'lack of resources cannot in principle justify prison conditions which are so poor as to reach the threshold of treatment contrary to article 3 of the Convention'.

59 *Paposhvili v Belgium*, (n 23), 182.

60 The impact of removal on an applicant must now be assessed by considering how the applicant's condition 'would evolve after transfer to the receiving State' (ibid, para 188) so re-aligning with the 'preventive purpose' of Article 3. But the temporal horizon is circumscribed to situations involving an applicant's 'rapid decline'.

61 ibid, para183.

circumstances test, ergo, the lack of family and social assistance. In any case, the threshold of severity for preventing the deportation of an alien suffering from an illness remains high. However, the work of assessment is primarily for the national authorities, who must put in place adequate procedures in order to evaluate the risks run in the event of deportation. The assessment must take account of both the general situation in the receiving State (obtaining assurances that medical treatment will be available and accessible to the person concerned) and of the alien's particular case and their vulnerability. Vulnerability therefore becomes determinant for such a more protective outcome; not without its combination with the human dignity narrative discourse discernible in several dissenting opinions expressing the need for the Court to reconsider its approach as not easily reconcilable with the letter and spirit of Article 3, which guaranteed an absolute right *inherent in human dignity,* so calling for focusing more on the specific vulnerability.

Since *N v. the United Kingdom, in fact,* the ECtHR was invited to focus on preventing further *vulnerabilisation* through an assessment of how societal structures could dynamically build resilience to overcoming different sources of vulnerabilities. In their Joint Dissenting Opinion, Judges Tulkens, Bonello and Spielmann emphasized that "the very nature of the rights guaranteed by the Convention (that) would be completely negated if their enjoyment were to be restricted on the basis of *policy considerations* such as budgetary constraints".[62] Also in *Yoh-Ekale Mwanje v. Belgium,* it was the argument of human dignity that brought six out of seven judges to express the need for the Court to reconsider its approach of 'this extreme severity threshold – to be close to dying' as not easily reconcilable with the letter and spirit of Article 3, which guaranteed an absolute right inherent to human integrity and *dignity*.[63] More explicitly, finally, in his partly dissenting opinion in the recent case of *Tatar v. Switzerland,* Judge Lemmens proposed a more humane approach to the expulsion of persons with a severe long-term illness. He urged to move away from the requirement of very exceptional circumstances to apply to the high threshold of Article 3 of the Convention. He called explicitly the Court to focus "more on the specific vulnerability of these persons".[64]

62 ibid para. 8.

63 *Yoh-Ekale Mwanje v Belgium* (n 47), para. 6 referring to the partly Concurring Opinion of Judges Tulkens, Jočienė, Popović, Karakaş, Raimondi and Pinto De Albuquerque.

64 *Tatar v Switzerland* (n 52), [paras 4–5] (Judge Lemmens). He argued that the mere possibility of medical treatment in other regions of Turkey was solely based on theoretical assumptions. Instead, he proposed a similar approach as in the case of *Tarakhel v Switzerland* App no 29217/12 (ECtHR, 4 November 2014). In *Tarakhel,* the Court requested

3.2.3 The Hardcore Hypothesis of a Right to Education

If we turn our attention to the case of children faced with their parents' expulsion, or their own expulsion due to an irregular entry and/or stay in the contracting State, there are some exceptions to the general assumption that aliens can't derive from the right to education the right to enter or remain in the territory of the contracting State,[65] and that the child's obligation to accompany the parents will not amount *per se* to a violation of Protocol 1, Article 2.[66] These exceptions have been recognized when the timing of the child's return is likely to have a negative effect on the culmination of a concrete phase of the migrant child's education and there is no imperative need for this expulsion to take place.[67] They have also been recognised when the child would not be able to obtain secondary education in the country to which he/she and his/her parents were being expelled. The idea of extreme impact on the education of irregular migrant's children has been more strongly built up through a reasoning based on human dignity in *Ponomaryovi v. Bulgaria.*[68] While the ECtHR premised that a State could have legitimate reasons for curtailing the use of resource-hungry public services (such as welfare programmes, public benefits and health care) by short-term and irregular immigrants who, as a rule, did not contribute to their funding, it emphasized that, although similar arguments applied to a certain extent in the field of education, they could not be transposed there without qualification. According to the Court's reasoning, the State's margin of appreciation increases with the level of education, in inverse

---

that the Swiss authorities first obtain sufficient assurances on the appropriate accommodation of this family before they could send them back to Turkey. In this case, the Swiss authorities settled with *prima facie* assurances, not taking into account the real circumstances the applicant would endure upon his return to Turkey. In other words, regarding medical expulsion cases, a State should always obtain sufficient assurances by the receiving country. See E. Brems, 'Moving away from N v UK – Interesting tracks in a dissenting opinion (Tatar v Switzerland)' (*Strasbourg Observers*, 4 May 2015) <https://strasbourgobservers.com/2015/05/04/moving-away-from-n-v-uk- interesting-tracks-in-a-dissenting-opinion-tatar-v-switzerland/> accessed 1 November 2018.

65 *15 Foreign students v. UK* App no 7671/76 (ECtHR, 19 May 1977), where the ECtHR found inadmissible an application founded in the lack of education in the countries of education of the applicants.

66 *Sorabjee v UK* App no 23938/94 (ECtHR, 23 October 1995); *Jaramillo v UK* App no 24865/94 (ECtHR, 23 October 1995); *Dabhi v United Kingdom* App no 28627/95 (ECtHR, 17 January 1997); *Ajayi and others v UK* App no 27663/95 (ECtHR, 22 June 1999).

67 In *Vikulov and others v Latvia* App no 16870/03 (ECtHR, 29 April 2013), the removal of the family, a Russian couple and their son, was postponed until the completion of the child's school year. For this reason, the ECtHR concluded that there had not been a violation of Protocol 1, Article 2.

68 *Ponomaryovi v Bulgaria* (n 22).

proportion to the importance of that education for those concerned and for society at large. Thus, at the university level, which thus far had remained optional for many people, higher fees for aliens – and indeed fees in general – seemed to be commonplace and could, in the present circumstances, be considered fully justified. The opposite applied to primary schooling, which provided basic literacy and numeracy – as well as integration into and first experiences of society – and was compulsory in most countries. Secondary education, which was at issue in the applicants' case, fell between those two extremes.

According to the ECtHR, with more and more countries moving towards what has been described as a "knowledge based" society, "*secondary education* played an ever-increasing role in *successful personal development* and in the social and professional integration of the individuals concerned. Indeed, in a modern society, having no more than basic knowledge and skills constituted a barrier to successful personal and professional development and *prevented those concerned from adjusting to their environment, with far reaching consequences for their social and economic well-being*".[69] In the ECtHR's view, the concept of 'human development' incorporates the notion of human dignity applied, in this case, to the peculiarly vulnerable category of children. So, a more sophisticated and advanced notion of 'human dignity', which refers to 'successful personal development' and 'social and economic well-being' is defended by the Court. As a consequence of this, when the applicants are not in the position of individuals arriving to the country unlawfully and then claiming for the use of its public services, including free schooling, but they fell, somewhat inadvertently, into the situation of being aliens lacking permanent residence permits and the authorities had not had any substantive objection to their remaining in the host State, or any serious intention of deporting them, and the ECtHR considered that the requirement for the applicants to pay fees for their secondary education on account of their nationality and immigration status was not justified.[70] Such a progressive approach taken by the Court did not however suggest that it might not have reached the same conclusion if the applicants had been illegal immigrants seeking to take advantage of free public services.

4 Concluding Remarks

Because of greater responsiveness to only 'extreme fact patterns' by the European system, it could be argued that Europe so far is still not the strongest

69 ibid, para 57 (emphasis added).

70 ibid, para 60.

mainstreaming actor for the progress of international standards when it comes to the treatment of irregular migrants, though it has generated significant achievements. However, despite the theoretically more protective approach of the Inter-American system, which has pushed the boundaries of *its pro-homine* response to the realm of international migration, this approach also presents some pitfalls. From the methodological perspective the Inter-American system's use of *jus cogens* and *erga omnes* categories could be partially reversed by a more fruitful and conscious reliance on the Vienna Convention methods of interpretation as implemented in the 2014 Advisory Opinion. Other legal and institutional limitations are also worth noting, such as the restricted membership of the ACHR; the inadequacy of compliance with the IACtHR's decisions; and circumscribed effectiveness of human rights in the Americas – which may still restrain the full application of the Inter-American jurisprudence in this field.

In sum, despite the numerous challenges remaining in the protection of irregular migrants, there are signs of international courts working to close the existing gaps between the different categories of human rights. Recourse to the interpretative argument of vulnerability has contributed to the definition of a shared global understanding of the importance of human dignity in the quest to protect fundamental rights of irregular migrants. This has resulted in an integrated approach to a minimum core of economic and social rights for this vulnerable sub-population of migrants. An integrated approach anchored in a 'concretisation' of the vague notion of human dignity promoting a sense of mutual responsibility for each other's welfare, goes beyond the negative duties implied by the Kantian version of human dignity, which simply require that individuals act in a way that does not violate the dignity of others. Instead, this integrated approach aims to create a stronger relationship between the basic worth of individuals and their proper obligations to society.[71]

71 D. Shultziner, 'Human dignity: functions and meanings' (n. 14).

Index

www.ingramcontent.com/pod-product-compliance
Lightning Source LLC
LaVergne TN
LVHW021725021026
849161LV00004BA/721
* 9 7 8 9 0 0 4 4 3 5 6 4 3 *